Scotland: Global Cinema

For my mum and dad

Scotland: Global Cinema

Genres, Modes and Identities

David Martin-Jones

Edinburgh University Press

© David Martin-Jones, 2009

Edinburgh University Press Ltd
22 George Square, Edinburgh

www.euppublishing.com

Typeset in Monotype Ehrhardt by
Servis Filmsetting Ltd, Stockport, Cheshire, and
printed and bound in Great Britain by
CPI Antony Rowe, Chippenham and Eastbourne

A CIP record for this book is available from the British Library

ISBN 978 0 7486 3391 3 (hardback)

The right of David Martin-Jones
to be identified as author of this work
has been asserted in accordance with
the Copyright, Designs and Patents Act 1988.

Contents

Illustrations

Acknowledgements

An earlier version of Chapter 3 appeared as 'Kabhi India, Kabhie Scotland: Bollywood Productions in Post-Devolutionary Scotland' in *South Asian Popular Culture*, 4: 1 (2006). It is reprinted with the permission of Taylor & Francis Ltd, http://www.tandf.co.uk/journals. An earlier version of Chapter 5 appeared as 'National Symbols: Scottish National Identity in *Dog Soldiers*' in *Symbolism: An International Annual of Critical Aesthetics*, 7 (2007). It is reprinted with the permission of AMS Press. I am indebted to the Carnegie Trust for the Universities of Scotland and the British Academy for grants that enabled me to visit the Scottish Screen offices and archive in Glasgow, and the British Film Institute in London.

Throughout the writing of this book I have been helped by a number of people. Firstly, those who patiently helped me find my feet when I blundered into the field of Scotland and cinema: Jonathan Murray, Duncan Petrie, John Caughie and Colin McArthur, in particular to Jonny, for being so patient and for selflessly doing me so many favours. Specific thanks to the following for considered feedback and/or for acting as readers and referees on applications related to the project: Mette Hjort, Duncan Petrie, Julian Petley, John Caughie, Steve Blandford, Jonathan Murray, Sarah Neely, Ian Goode, Jane Sillars, Belén Vidal and Sergio Casci. Thanks to colleagues in the Department of Film Studies at the University of St Andrews for their support, in particular to Belén Vidal for being such a great friend and colleague. Thanks to the St Andrews Scottish Studies Centre and the AHRC funded Window to the West Project for inviting me to speak on Scotland and cinema, and to all staff at the Scottish Screen archives and the British Film Institute.

My gratitude goes to the following for numerous productive discussions about film production in Scotland, and for helping me in ways too numerous to list, Belle Doyle and Celia Stevenson (Scottish Screen), Jennifer Reynolds (Glasgow Film Office), Alexandra Stone (Recorded Picture), Christopher Young (Young Films), Pirate Productions, Eimhear McMahon (Sixteen Films), Nicole Gregory, Clare St John (DNA Films), Ros Borland (Gabriel Films), Charles Henri Belleville, Tina Foster (Plum Films), Kali Films, Kris R. Bird (Mothcatcher Productions), Doug Hill

(Scotlandthemovie.com), Clare Andrews, Dina Iordanova, John Hill, Robert Wilson, Bernard Bentley, Fidelma Farley, Karen Lury, Ian Garwood, Dimitris Eleftheriotis, Murdo Macdonald, Christine Geraghty, Sarah Leahy, Peter Hutchings, Philip Drake, Sarah Street, Gerda Stevenson, Simon Miller, Michael Gardiner, Gill Plain and Felicity Marsh. The index was compiled by Yun-hua Chen.

The writing of this book coincided with a rather difficult time, throughout which I was indebted to the kind and generous warmth and support of various friends. My heartfelt thanks go out to the Martin-Jones family, good in a crisis! Especially to my mum and dad, Ro and John, John and Tim, and Dai and Doreen. Furthermore, for invaluable emotional and physical support, Belén and Manuel, Tom and Nat, Leticia, Naomi and Malcolm, Paulina, Ana, French Dave, Gustavo, Bernard, Lynn Buchanan and the entire family Montañez Morillo. Most importantly of all, thank you Soledad, for putting up with all the hours of unsociable writing, and for sitting with me through all the wonderful (and sometimes terrible) films!

Introduction: Fantasy Scotlands

Contrary to what you might expect from its title, this is not a book about Sean Connery. It is, rather, a book about the range of filmmaking in Scotland in the 1990s and 2000s. It examines this extremely productive period in a global context, exploring the different identities on offer in the various fantasy Scotlands created by filmmakers from around the world. I do not directly aim to discuss any of the famous Scots to make it in Hollywood – from directors Alexander Mackendrick (*Whisky Galore!* (1949), *Sweet Smell of Success* (1957)) and Bill Forsyth (*Local Hero* (1983)) to actors like Connery, Brian Cox and Ewan McGregor – or indeed, the extremely talented Scottish directors lauded in Europe for their outstanding art films, like Peter Mullan and Lynne Ramsay. Many of these figures are discussed, although not so much as ambassadors for Scottish cinema (which they undoubtedly are), but rather as players in a context that is envisaged in a broader manner than has previously been the case. As this is a book about filmmaking in Scotland, rather than Scottish cinema, it does not focus solely on films made by Scots, about Scots, for Scots. It does include numerous indigenous Scottish productions, whether on large or small budgets, and whether for domestic or international markets. However, these indigenous productions are considered alongside the coproductions Scotland has been involved in (in particular with the USA), and the location shoots of a number of British, French, US and Indian films in Scotland. It is a book that I felt needed to be written in this way because – it seems to me – many discussions of cinema and Scotland constantly revolve around the same films, and the debates in existence are therefore in need of expansion.

Scotland: Global Cinema consists of ten chapters that examine a different genre or mode (style) of filmmaking. Each begins with a brief history of this specific genre or mode of filmmaking in Scotland, before focusing on key examples from the two decades under consideration. Drawing out the historical background to these films enables a greater understanding of their engagement with recognisable and stereotypical images of Scotland, opening them up to broader debates and facilitating an exploration of their relationship with the global markets at which they aim. In chapter order the genres/modes discussed are: the comedy (*Gregory's Two Girls* (1999), *Festival* (2005)); the road movie (*Soft Top, Hard Shoulder* (1993), *Carla's Song* (1996), *Tickets* (2005)); popular Indian or 'Bollywood' filmmaking and its impact on Scotland (*Kuch Kuch Hota Hai* (1998), *Kandukondain Kandukondain* (2000), *Pyaar Ishq aur Mohabbat* (2001), *Nina's Heavenly Delights* (2006)); the Loch Ness monster movie (*The Secret of the Loch* (1934), *Loch Ness* (1996), *The Water Horse* (2007)); the horror movie, specifically in its werewolf guise (*Dog Soldiers* (2002), *Wild Country* (2005)); the costume drama (*The Governess* (1998)); the gangster film (*American Cousins* (2003), *Danny the Dog* (2005)); the social realist melodrama (*Ae Fond Kiss* (2004), *On a Clear Day* (2005)); the American independent/female friendship film (*Women Talking Dirty* (1999), *Beautiful Creatures* (2000)); and the art film (*Young Adam* (2003), *Red Road* (2006)). These chapters suggest ten different ways of considering the history of cinema in Scotland, and of expanding existing debates concerning the cinematic depiction of Scotland.

If this is not a book about Sean Connery, who are the major figures? One of the most surprising things about writing the book was that one name appeared repeatedly: Peter Capaldi. Capaldi is well known to television viewers across Britain, having appeared in any number of popular shows. He is probably most famous internationally for playing supporting roles in Hollywood productions. Many will remember his face, if not his name, as John Malkovich's manservant Azolan in *Dangerous Liaisons* (1988), or, for those with longer memories, as Mac's (Peter Riegert) sidekick Oldsen, in *Local Hero*. In 2009 he also starred in the British comedy *In the Loop*, a political satire directed by another Scots-Italian, Armando Iannucci. Capaldi is an unsung hero of 1990s/2000s film production in Scotland. Not only did he win an Oscar for the short film which he wrote and directed, *Franz Kafka: It's a Wonderful Life* (1993) (part funded by the Scottish Film Production Fund), Capaldi also wrote the screenplays for two feature films discussed in this book: the road movie *Soft Top, Hard Shoulder* (Chapter 2) and the gangster movie which he also directed, *Strictly Sinatra* (2001) (Chapters 2 and 7). At the time of writing he is working as writer and director on a film starring Ewan McGregor scheduled for release in 2011 with the working title 'The Great Pretender'. Moreover, in the period under discussion, Capaldi starred in the low budget Scottish horror film *Wild Country* (Chapter 5). Capaldi's name is of importance for *Scotland: Global Cinema*, then, because his absence from previous discussions of Scottish cinema is undoubtedly due to the fact that he writes, directs, and stars in low budget genre movies made in his native Scotland. It is unusual for these films to receive much in the way of critical appraisal, and their box office impact is often relatively insignificant, but nevertheless they are indicative of the range of filmmaking currently taking place in Scotland.

A Scots-Italian, Capaldi places his hybrid identity at the forefront of his movies. The 'unsteady' or hybrid sense of Scottishness that often comes across as a result provides another possible reason why his films are often left out of discussions of Scottish cinema and Scottish identity. Yet here, in a book that aims to expand discussion of Scottish cinema to incorporate the diverse range of genre filmmaking in Scotland, Capaldi is a key presence. My point when discussing Capaldi is that if we shift our focus away from the more recognised Scottish directors like Bill Forsyth and Bill Douglas, stop focusing so exclusively on the auteur and the art film and examine as well the works of less appreciated filmmakers, suddenly existing debates are transformed. Thus, in line with the movement in literature towards the study of many literary 'Scotlands'[1] in the 1990s/2000s, *Scotland: Global Cinema* considers the various different cinematic Scotlands produced by filmmakers during this period, both from home and abroad. Such a shift in focus replaces existing discussions of Scottish cinema and Scottish identity with an analysis of Scottish *cinemas*, and Scottish *identities*.

In fact, examining filmmaking in Scotland, as opposed to strictly adhering to Scottish films, expands the range of dramatic personae to include a cast of international players. Contrary to my own expectations when I started writing a book exploring a range of popular genre films, the English director Ken Loach (most well known for making politically engaged social realist films) features in Chapters 2 and 8. Although Loach's work is often associated with 'serious' subject matter (witness the appreciation his films receive on the international festival circuit), Loach is very skilful in his deployment of generic elements in his filmmaking. In Chapter 5, Loach is joined by another, very different, English director, Neil Marshall, who has produced a number of successful horror films in Scotland, including *Dog Soldiers*, *The Descent* (2005) and *Doomsday* (2008). Whilst Loach is well respected in Europe and Marshall in the USA, they are usually considered British, as opposed to Scottish, directors even though they have both made several films set in Scotland. In *Scotland: Global Cinema* I explore how their very varied depictions of Scotland enable a nuanced understanding of the ways Scotland is represented in films that circulate internationally, whether made by Scots or not.

In terms of actors, alongside Hollywood heartthrob McGregor I discuss not only up-and-coming young Scottish actors like Martin Compston, but also two Asian megastars – the Bollywood actor Shah Rukh Khan and the

Chinese action star Jet Li – who have respectively starred in Indian and French productions shot in Scotland in the 1990s and 2000s. Their presence enables a broader examination of the types of identities that exist in contemporary Scotland, in particular in terms of diasporas (dispersed communities of people who live outside their country of origin) and the different types of audiences to which various films appeal by deploying Scotland as a location.

Finally, these male figures are joined by a number of films directed by and/or starring women of various national origins (English, Scottish, US, Indian), again a stark contrast to much previous work on Scotland and cinema. These include: *Festival* (directed by Annie Griffin), *Pyaar Ishq aur Mohabbat* (starring Kirti Reddy), *Morvern Callar* (directed by Lynne Ramsay and starring Samantha Morton), *Nina's Heavenly Delights* (directed by Pratibha Parmar and starring Shelley Conn and Laura Fraser), *The Governess* (directed by Sandra Goldbacher and starring Minnie Driver), *Women Talking Dirty* (directed by Coky Giedroyc and starring Helena Bonham Carter and Gina McKee), *On a Clear Day* (directed by Gaby Dellal) and *Red Road* (directed by Andrea Arnold and starring Kate Dickie).

Scotland: Global Cinema, then, explores how different types of films create a plurality of cinematic and, in many cases, fantasy Scotlands, for various audiences both in Scotland and abroad.

Previous Writing on Scotland and Cinema

Filmmaking in Scotland first received significant critical attention in Colin McArthur's edited collection, *Scotch Reels* (1982). Since then publications on the subject remain relatively sparse in contrast to the number that have appeared on British cinema, which usually discuss predominantly English films and English issues. Whilst things have picked up in the 2000s, the great majority of recent books to appear on cinematic depictions of Scotland have focused on unpacking classic films, like *I Know Where I'm Going!* (1945), *Whisky Galore!* (1949), *The Maggie* (1954), *The Wicker Man* (1973) and *Trainspotting* (1996).[2] However, there has been a slowly growing body of texts that deal with the broader issues concerned with filmmaking in Scotland. To understand how this book integrates itself with the debate, I will begin with *Scotch Reels*.

In *Scotch Reels*, McArthur and several other contributors drew the conclusion that cinematic images of Scotland and Scottish identity had effectively been colonised by filmmakers from Britain and Hollywood. This understandable conclusion was partly a result of the situation in 1982, in which Scottish filmmakers found it very difficult to make films in Scotland, about Scotland. McArthur and his co-contributors searched in vain amidst the numerous English and US films about Scotland for a realistic representation of contemporary Scotland that would stand in contrast to the ubiquitous clichéd myths of Scotland which, they argued, were not a fair representation of modern Scotland. For McArthur the defining myths which were repeatedly found in films made about Scotland (usually by filmmakers from elsewhere) were those of Tartanry and the Kailyard. Images of Tartanry referred to Scotland as a pre-modern wilderness, using the vast, beautiful and often bleak countryside of the Highlands and Islands to stand in for the whole of Scotland. This selective image of Scotland deliberately ignored the existence of the thriving Lowland cities of Edinburgh and Glasgow. Moreover, this myth was constructed in the aftermath of the defeat of the Jacobite rebellion of 1745–6, and was concurrent with the consolidating of the Union of England and Scotland as Britain. As the Highlands were subsequently cleared of their threatening native population, the supposedly wild and hairy Highland clans who rose up twice after the Act of Union of 1707, this image of Scotland as an untamed wilderness was consolidated on the notion of Scotland as a nation lost to, or lost in, the past. Novelist Sir Walter Scott was particularly influential in the construction of this Romantic view of Scotland, both in his literature and due to his defining role in the celebrations of 1822 when Edinburgh hosted King George IV, and the wearing of tartan (previously banned in the wake of 1745–6) became a legitimate practice once again.

In addition to this shortbread tin imagery of a barren but picturesque mountainous wilderness, hairy savages in kilts and red-haired Highland cows, there was the related myth of the Kailyard, or the cabbage patch. Drawn from the literature of J. M. Barrie, the myth of the Kailyard depicted Scotland as a land of isolated, tight-knit communities, of canny natives resisting the modern world and known for putting one over on any visiting city bureaucrats. Classic examples of Kailyard Scotland are found in films like *Whisky Galore!* and *The Maggie*. For McArthur the Kailyard was another debilitating myth that represented Scotland as a lost, preindustrial idyll, a fictional place for the film viewer to visit for a brief wallow in nostalgia.

Throughout the 1990s several critics revisited this argument to reconsider whether all films made or set in Scotland are 'Scotsploitation' films. The shift in emphasis has generally not reexamined the myths themselves, but reconsidered how they are deployed and consumed. Detailed accounts of this development already exist so one or two relevant points are all that is necessary for this discussion.[3] In 1990 the anthology *From Limelight to*

Satellite emerged, greatly broadening the scope of analysis of Scottish cinema. For instance, John Caughie reconsidered the approach of *Scotch Reels* (to which he was one of the original contributors) in its reductive-ness. From his later vantage point, Caughie also developed and clarified Scotland's third dominant myth, that of Clydesideism, which explored the waning role of masculinity in Scottish society after the decline of its ship-building and manufacturing industries in the latter half of the twentieth century. Clydesideism mourned the loss of 'real' masculinity (the myth of the industrialised 'hard man') in the feminising environment of the serv-ices industry. Caughie's major addition to the discussion was to argue that the myths of Tartanry, the Kailyard and Clydesideism were indeed debil-itating in that they each played out 'an epic transformation' (the Union of Scotland and England in the myth of Tartanry, the rapid growth of indus-trialisation in the Kailyard and the shift from a manufacturing to a services industry in Clydesideism) and rendered it as a though a loss. Yet, Caughie countered, these dominant myths also contained 'historical resonances' which could still be felt in the present.[4] For Caughie then, these myths were not always deployed negatively, and were often used to work through issues of contemporary significance to Scottish audiences.

Cairns Craig, also one of the original contributors to *Scotch Reels*, weighed in along similar lines in *Out of History* (1996), a book focused on nineteenth-century Scottish literature.[5] This is a useful book for *Scotland: Global Cinema*, which I examine in detail in Chapter 5. Craig noted that myths like Tartanry could be seen in a more positive light if considered as ways of remythologising a Scottish past which had been deliberately excluded from official, English versions of British history. Similarly, Pam Cook made an important contribution in *Fashioning the Nation* (1996), discussing the potential of the costume drama – no matter if it deploys the dominant imagery of Tartanry, which it often does – to offer audiences a way of rethinking national histories and identities. I shall say more on this in Chapter 6. Finally, McArthur's most recent book, *Brigadoon, Braveheart and the Scots* (2003), departs from his position in *Scotch Reels* twenty years earlier, and discusses the effects on Scottish audiences of the perpetually recurring, 'distorted' Hollywood image of Scotland. McArthur's work in the 2000s, then, illustrates how the field has come to appreciate the various ways in which images of Scotland, no matter how 'distorted', can have a powerful impact on audiences in Scotland and the rest of the world. Our understanding of who 'owns' cinematic images of Scotland (whether filmmakers, audiences or critics, be they from Scotland or elsewhere) has thus become far more nuanced, and indeed far less straightforward, since *Scotch Reels*.

To date, however, the most significant writing in the field has been that of Duncan Petrie, especially in *Screening Scotland* (2000) and *Contemporary Scottish Fictions* (2005). Petrie has continued the move towards rethinking representations of Scotland in a more positive light, beginning with a reconsideration of the use of the three myths initially established in *Scotch Reels*. As Petrie's work is a recurring reference point throughout the book I will not outline his arguments in detail at this stage. Suffice it to say that perhaps his most influential contributions have been to establish Scottish cinema (and more recently, television and popular literature) within the broader contexts of Scotland's political and cultural development in the latter decades of the twentieth century (with particular reference to the changing face of Scotland's film industry), and to begin to chart the influence of broader, indigenous aesthetic traditions – such as the Scottish Gothic tradition – on contemporary production.

In summary, by the late 1990s and early 2000s a more celebratory attitude reigns towards cinematic representations of Scotland than in *Scotch Reels*, whether domestic or international productions, especially in relation to the potential these films offer Scottish audiences to consider their own identities. *Scotland: Global Cinema* continues the reevaluation of images of Scotland in a positive, and often celebratory light. In this it is indebted to the pioneering groundwork of these predecessors, and also to emergent figures like Jonathan Murray, Jane Sillars, Ian Goode and Sarah Neely, whose work I engage with at various points throughout the book.

Popular Genres in a Changing Industrial Context

Currently, Petrie's *Screening Scotland* is the most comprehensive book dedicated to Scotland and cinema. As it was published in 2000, by necessity its analysis stops in the late 1990s, whereas the majority of films I discuss have emerged since then. Moreover, most work on Scottish cinema to date has tended either to focus on the art film or to discuss Scotland's popular genre films in light of the dominant myths of Scotland or as part of broader aesthetic traditions. The first major difference between these approaches and that of the present book is that popular genre films are here discussed *as genre films* rather than as films about Scotland which happen to be genre films. The art film merits one chapter, repositioning it as one of many types of film production currently taking place in Scotland. This approach is partly determined by my own interests in popular genres, but is predominantly a response to a missing dimension in the study of cinematic representations of Scotland.

Genre theory has a long tradition within Film Studies. As Steve Neale demonstrated in 'Questions of Genre' (1990), understanding the different national, cultural, aesthetic and institutional/industrial contexts in which genre films are produced avoids the pitfalls of either problematically homogenising all international genre films or designating some as more 'authentic' than others.[6] As various writers have since shown, this applies to genres as diverse as the Italian spaghetti western and the Japanese horror film. Indeed, many of the popular genres that constitute the history of British cinema have already been examined in depth, even if the examples of these traditions associated with Scotland have not. Unusually, in the case of Scottish cinema the contextual information is already in place. The defining myths of Tartanry, the Kailyard and Clydesideism have been identified and explored, along with their relationship to Scotland's other aesthetic traditions. Moreover, the impact of the changing institutional/industrial conditions on film production in Scotland continues to be charted in the media and the academy. What is missing, then, is a consideration of how the generic elements of these films facilitate their engagement or interaction with the three myths and these other contextual factors. This is the added dimension that *Scotland: Global Cinema* brings to writing on Scotland and cinema.

The most important industrial factor in recent years has been the increase in indigenous production facilitated by the devolution of lottery funding distribution to Scotland in 1995 and the establishment of Scottish Screen in 1997 – which amalgamated several already existing film production and funding bodies and came to oversee the spending of these new finances.[7] In the mid-1990s Scotland suddenly appeared on the global map of cinema due to two unexpected, relatively low budget successes, *Shallow Grave* (1994) and *Trainspotting* (1996). Indigenous production increased during the 1990s and 2000s, and despite the initial success of these US independent-styled alternative films, it was the European art film model that came to exemplify Scottish production. Home grown directors Lynne Ramsay and Peter Mullan (and later David Mackenzie and Andrea Arnold) gained international prestige at film festivals, and were conferred auteur status within discussions of an emergent New Scottish Cinema. Amongst other accolades Mullan's *Magdalene Sisters* won the Golden Lion at Venice in 2002, and Arnold's debut feature *Red Road* garnered the Special Jury Prize at Cannes in 2006.

Because of the low budget nature of indigenous production in Scotland and the need to court international audiences to recoup production spend, the art film model is often considered the most appropriate by film financers. Through the international film festival and independent cinema distribution circuits these niche films have a chance of competing with the global dominance of Hollywood and the multiplex. However, even with this emphasis, there has been a great deal of activity in terms of popular genre filmmaking. As the profile of Scotland as a filmmaking nation has risen internationally, enticing more film production companies to the country (whether to locate, make coproductions or location shoot), the skills base has increased accordingly, again furthering indigenous production. One example of this is the success of director David Mackenzie. His major breakthrough was the art film *Young Adam*, which is discussed in Chapter 10, but his first feature was the very low budget *The Last Great Wilderness* (2002). This international coproduction, part financed by Zentropa (Lars von Trier's Danish film production company), combined generic elements from the road movie, horror and gangster films to reexamine existing myths of Scotland as a murderous wilderness full of weird locals, as previously found in *The Wicker Man* (1973). Although *The Last Great Wilderness* did not register in the way that *Young Adam* later would, it gave Mackenzie the start he needed in the industry. In this new production context, then, where skills are required in making films on low budgets, popular genres can provide the necessary generic frameworks within which filmmakers can cut their teeth. More importantly perhaps, low budget genre movies are often considered more likely to recoup their production costs than art films, and are therefore able to attract international finance (albeit sometimes meagre) on the promise of a likely return.

Finance from television has also had an impact. In this respect, the international coproduction *The Water Horse* illustrates how increased television production in Scotland has not only increased production of the Scottish art film (see chapter ten) but also popular genre filmmaking. *The Water Horse* was produced by Ecosse Films, London, who were previously responsible for the long-running BBC television series set in Scotland *Monarch of the Glen* (2000–5), and who had also produced the made for television feature-length BBC costume drama *Mrs Brown* (1997). *Mrs Brown* was an unexpected international success, obtaining a US theatrical distribution deal with Miramax, who would subsequently participate in the development of *The Water Horse*. Thus, not only has television production in Scotland provided an increased skills base for both art and genre cinema (several of the directors discussed in later chapters started out in television) and a substantial financial input to certain films, it has also demonstrated the potentially lucrative nature of genre filmmaking in Scotland to international financiers.

Famously, in *European Cinema* (2005) Thomas Elsaesser argues that Europe's popular genre cinemas effectively ended in the 1960s.[8] Yet,

although the same scale of industry is admittedly no longer present, as contemporary filmmaking in a country as small as Scotland demonstrates,
popular genre films continue to be produced all over Europe.[9] Their relative lack of budget in comparison with Hollywood films (and indeed, many
European art films) means they may not always be as well known. Even so,
the cult audiences that have followed films like *Dog Soldiers* have ensured
the development of the careers of directors like Englishman Neil Marshall,
with his follow up, *The Descent* (2005), recouping its costs of production in
European markets alone.[10] Indeed, as the role of the DVD becomes of even
greater importance than theatrical release (for which competition is fierce
and mostly controlled by Hollywood)[11] there is an increased market for
popular genre films.[12] This is true both of successful cult horror films like
Dog Soldiers and *The Descent* and also of straight to DVD releases like the
Scottish werewolf movie *Wild Country*, which have the potential to facilitate
lower level local engagement with issues of importance to audiences within
the nation. As Andrew Higson noted in 1989, a national cinema is defined as
much by the films that people in the nation watch as by the films it produc-
es.[13] Accordingly, it is often through the DVD that different sections of the
population, such as Scotland's Non-Resident Indian community (see
Chapter 3), engage with films that address concerns specific to their lives,
even if they do not always necessarily qualify as 'Scottish' films.

Thus, along with the art cinema that Elsaesser favours, there are
numerous ways in which genre films can be financed and can circulate in
competition with Hollywood; the global reach of filmmaking in Scotland
is thereby equally demonstrated by popular cinema. I should be clear,
however, that I am not saying that we should ignore Scottish art cinema
any more than we should popular genre films. It is often frustrating to read
discussions of 'British' cinema that note the supposed demise of the art
film by citing the waning popularity of previously famous England-based
auteurs of the 1980s and 1990s (Derek Jarman, Sally Potter, Peter
Greenaway) or the lack of apparent continuation of their legacy. These
Anglocentric accounts can seem either unaware of (or possibly in denial
of) the emergence of a new base for the art film, no longer in London, but
in Glasgow. Thus, whilst acknowledging the individual works of new
Scotland-based auteurs (Peter Mullan, Lynne Ramsay, David Mackenzie,
Andrea Arnold), the coexistence of this emergent talent in the new centre
for art cinema is often ignored. There remains much ground to be covered,
then, in analysing and celebrating the Scottish art film if these entrenched
perceptions are to be challenged.

Even so, because of the popular emphasis of this book, I will not be following Petrie in his description of contemporary Scottish filmmaking as

either a 'devolved British cinema', or even as constitutive of a 'new Scottish cinema'.[14] These labels, whilst helpful when discussing certain Scottish films, are not accurate enough when the broader context of filmmaking in Scotland is examined. A term like 'New Scottish Cinema' suggests a new wave of film production and is often attributed to filmmaking that considers itself alternative or oppositional to other forms of mainstream cinema. Positing the emergence of a 'New' national cinema is often done to position a small national cinema as a niche product within the global market for art cinema. Although entirely applicable to the Scottish art film (and very welcome in light of the lack of acknowledgement that Scottish art cinema has received), neither of these cases applies to the majority of films discussed in this book. Moreover, this type of focus can predetermine the outcome of analysis of films made in Scotland, which may be judged in terms of whether they are culturally or 'only' industrially important for Scotland, based on a desire to champion Scottish filmmaking internationally at the expense of much of the filmmaking taking place in the country. Instead, then, inspired in part by Mette Hjort's exploration of Danish cinema in *Small Nation, Global Cinema* (2005), I examine Scotland as a 'global cinema'. By this I mean both a youthful film industry with a global impact and a small nation in which the global film industry makes films (in both instances often with the assistance of indigenous organisations like Scottish Screen and the Glasgow Film Office). As a global cinema, Scotland is understood as a country that exists in the midst of, and interjects in various ways with, the increasingly decentralised flows of film production and distribution that circulate the globe.

Popular Genres in a Changing Cultural and Political Context

The increase in film production in Scotland in the 1990s and 2000s, especially the newfound institutional and financial independence of Scotland's filmmakers, exists within a broader political context. Perhaps most important in this respect is the impact of political and cultural devolution in Scotland. Put briefly, over the course of the twentieth century there was increasing disillusionment in Scotland surrounding its position as 'junior partner' to England within the Union of Britain. With Scotland's industries in gradual decline in the second half of the century there was growing dissent over Westminster's governance of Scotland. In 1979 a referendum was held to establish whether Scotland should be governed by a devolved assembly. Although the vote was narrowly in favour, it was not passed due to a stipulation that the referendum would be ratified only if forty per cent of the population voted yes. The fairly low turnout for this first referendum is often considered to be due to the lack of control the new assembly would have had over taxation in Scotland. This, coupled with the fact that the referendum was not passed thanks to a political contrivance, ultimately fuelled the desire for devolution in Scotland. In *Contemporary Scottish Fictions* Petrie argues that in the following two decades this failed referendum bolstered Scottish cultural outpourings against what was to rapidly become Thatcherite Britain.[15] In elections in 1997 New Labour defeated the Conservative Party, which had held power since 1979. A measure of Scottish dissatisfaction with the way they had been ruled from London was the complete defeat of all Tory candidates north of the border. Not one single Conservative MP was returned in Scotland in the 1997 general election. A second referendum on devolution was held in 1997, and this time a clear majority voted for a devolved parliament with limited powers to alter taxation in Scotland.

The coincidence, within a few very concentrated years in the mid-1990s, of political devolution and the devolution of lottery money for filmmaking to Scotland (plus the establishment of Scottish Screen, the international success of *Shallow Grave* and *Trainspotting* and the two high-profile Scottish-set Hollywood costume dramas *Braveheart* (1995) and *Rob Roy* (1995)) ensured that Scottish filmmaking blossomed within a resurgent cultural and political environment. As McArthur shows in *Brigadoon, Braveheart and the Scots*, filmmaking in Scotland played a major role in shaping this environment. Thus, for David McCrone, in his second edition of *Understanding Scotland* (2001), even though Scotland is not (yet) a fully independent nation state, it does have an identity based upon what Benedict Anderson described as an 'imagined political community'[16] (that is recognisable both to its inhabitants and to outsiders), through which many nations make sense of their identities.[17] For this reason, when examining filmmaking in Scotland, an integral part of the construction of this imagined community, it is necessary to ask along with McCrone, 'not only "When was/is Scotland?" but "Where is Scotland?" and "Whose Scotland?"'[18] It is here that the many, varied Scotlands – and fantasy visions of Scotland – depicted in popular genre films become increasingly important.

At the time of writing there is great uncertainty in the sector over how filmmaking will be affected by the introduction of Creative Scotland, the Scottish Executive's new cultural development agency that is to encompass Scottish Screen. The situation has been made more uncertain by a further shift in government from Labour (a Unionist party) to the Scottish

National Party (SNP), which became, in elections in 2007 the ruling party in Scotland (albeit with around a third of the popular vote, and a minority administration in Holyrood) and has the aim of independence for Scotland. The SNP argues that Scotland should become fully independent from the state of Britain, increasingly comparing Scotland to other small European nations to make this case.

Despite this uncertainty, the ground has been laid for film production to continue to flourish in Scotland, a strong component of which is indigenous filmmaking in its myriad formats. This is evidenced by such factors as the gradual development of training and infrastructure, as demonstrated by the establishing of Film City in Govan, Glasgow (a production facility and film studio based on Zentropa's Filmbyen, Copenhagen) with £3.5million from the European Regional Development Fund;[19] the establishing of the Skillset Screen Academy Scotland, at Napier University in Edinburgh, to facilitate the training of filmmakers in Scotland;[20] the introduction of The Director's Lab at the Edinburgh International Film Festival to assist budding young directors as they begin to establish themselves in the industry; the increased promotion of the BAFTA Scotland awards as a recognisable brand labelling quality Scottish film for international consumption;[21] dedicated funding provided by Scottish Screen for filmmakers to attend international festivals (Sundance, Cannes, etc) and promote their films;[22] and so on.

In this slowly transforming industrial landscape numerous small independent film production companies survive, many of who focus on genre filmmaking, or include genre films alongside their art film productions. This remains a volatile business in which companies can fold unexpectedly, but despite the sad end of Paddy Higson's Antonine Films in 2001 the sector remains active. Production companies of the 2000s include Sigma Films (see Chapter 10), Gabriel Films (Chapter 5), Black Camel Pictures (Chapter 5), Crab Apple Films, La Belle Allee, Pure Magic Films and Broken Spectre, all based in Glasgow, as well as Makar Productions, Plum Films, Elemental Films, Mead Kerr Productions and Mothcatcher Films (Chapter 5) in Edinburgh, Young Films on the Isle of Skye (Chapter 1) and Roaring Fire Films in Aberdeen. Numerous others can be found at www.filmbang.com. I would not want to ignore the impact of certain London based firms either, like Ecosse Films (directed by Scotsman, Douglas Rae), which has produced several Scottish-based films and television series (Chapter 4), and Ken Loach's Sixteen Films (Chapters 2 and 8). As I argue throughout, although companies like Sigma Films may aim at the Cannes and Sundance festivals, many others look towards less high-profile international markets in genre films. This is before we even consider the animation sector (Edinburgh's Red Kite Productions, for example), the digital media industry in and around Dundee (most famous internationally for the *Grand Theft Auto* computer games) and documentary filmmakers like Nick Higgins (Lansdowne Productions, Glasgow), all areas which must, regrettably, remain beyond the scope of this particular work. It is because of these changing conditions, then, that *Scotland: Global Cinema* emphasises the study of Scotland's art films alongside its various popular genres (and the international markets they aim at), to ascertain the extent to which films made in Scotland after devolution and the break up of Britain enable, in Michael Keating's words, 'a rediscovery and modernization of historical identities . . . in the global era.'[23,24]

(Fantasy) Tourism/Fantasy Scotlands

Adding to the increase in indigenous production within the broader context of cultural devolution came the influx of international productions in the wake of *Braveheart*. In 1997 the Hydra Report analysed the impact on tourism of three films, *Rob Roy*, *Braveheart* and *Loch Ness*. The report was commissioned by the British Film Commission, Scottish Screen Locations and the Scottish Tourist Board, and was entitled 'The Economic and Tourism Benefits of Large-scale Film Production in the United Kingdom'. Perhaps unsurprisingly the report found that these films had not only increased income into Scotland at the site of production (production spend), but had directly affected the decision of tourists to visit Scotland. With an estimated £7million – 15million of tourist revenue being attributed to the fabled '*Braveheart* effect', in the wake of the report both the Scottish Executive (since renamed the Scottish Government by the SNP) and Visit Scotland (the Scottish Tourist Board) took steps to both encourage international film productions to locate to Scotland and to increase distribution of indigenous films portraying Scotland's touristic vistas. These measures affected several of the films discussed in this book, not least of which was the sudden arrival of Bollywood productions.

Scotland has a long tradition as a tourist destination since the Highland clearances of the eighteenth and nineteenth centuries – as a sporting paradise (shooting, fishing, mountaineering, golf) especially for wealthier visitors, including the British royal family; a Romantic pre-modern idyll for 'literary tourists'[25] in the wake of James MacPherson's Ossian poems (see below) and again with Scott's novels; and, increasingly, in the nineteenth, twentieth and twenty-first centuries for sightseeing, hill walking, skiing, cycling, canoeing and various other adventurous outdoor activities. Post-Hydra Report, Scotland set about marketing its natural attractions through cinema.

For this reason, in several cases I examine whether individual films are set in Scotland, or use Scotland as a film set. This is a continuation of the debate which began in *Scotch Reels*. However, here the manner in which this occurs is examined in relation to the particular pleasures offered by different genres and modes of filmmaking and individual films are considered in their global context of production and distribution. I argue that the question of whether films made in Scotland engage with the locations in which the narratives take place or simply use Scotland as a scenic backdrop does not necessarily have to have a 'negative' (in the sense of 'colonising' or otherwise ideologically regressive) answer. In the majority of instances, using Scotland as a film set can have as much of a positive impact on the types of identities constructed in the film as is the case in narratives that firmly establish themselves in Scotland. It is no longer sufficient, then, to condemn the stereotypical, mythical constructions of Scotland isolated in *Scotch Reels*. Rather, they need to be examined in relation to the specific films in which they appear, and the ends to which they function.

The contemporary films under discussion are also examined in light of similar films produced in other countries. This facilitates a reconsideration of exactly how locally oriented Scottish films are in their representation of Scotland and Scottish identities and whether many of them have begun to represent Scotland differently in response to the growing international market for films set in Scotland. This is a major advantage of the genre-based approach. For instance, in Chapter 3 comparisons are drawn between *Nina's Heavenly Delights* and various Bollywood films; in Chapter 4 between *Loch Ness* and US monster films *Jurassic Park* (1993), *Anaconda* (1997) and *Lake Placid* (1999); in Chapter 5 between *Dog Soldiers* and *Wolfen* (1981), *Wolf* (1994) and *Ginger Snaps* (2000); in Chapter 6 between *The Governess* and *A Room With a View* (1985) and *The Portrait of a Lady* (1996); and in Chapter 7 between *American Cousins* and *The Godfather* (1972) and *The Sopranos* (1999–2007). As I demonstrate, in many cases the role played by tourism has led to a knowing construction of Scotland as a fantasy space to which the viewer is temporarily transported for the duration of the film. Although it is resonant with the myths identified in *Scotch Reels*, the ends to which this fantasy space are used are not necessarily ideologically regressive, even if they do not always directly address Scottish concerns. This book, then, demonstrates how a cinematic fantasy space is the perfect place to explore different and new types of identities, be they national (Scottish, British, English or otherwise), transnational, global/local, diasporic, gendered, and so on.

This examination of fantasy Scotland is not new in itself. In relation to indigenous Scottish productions, in a much-quoted statement from 1995, Adrienne Scullion argues that the development of the Scottish imagination in certain art forms has facilitated a 'sophisticated engagement with the fantastic that some cultures might celebrate as magic realism'.[26] Scullion's position falls in line with the aforementioned critiques of *Scotch Reels* (including Caughie, Craig, Cook and Petrie), in which there is a greater appreciation of fantasy's positive effect on the way audiences (both in Scotland and potentially elsewhere) construct their identities in relation to popular genres. Thus the particular pleasures associated with different genres facilitate an expanded awareness of how certain defining myths can be deployed in the fantasy space of cinematic Scotland and consumed in a far less negative way than was previously thought. Admittedly, the tricky issue surrounding fantasy remains that first isolated by *Scotch Reels* of whether we are examining a locally constructed fantasy of Scotland or another culture's (and film industry's) view, and, indeed, what position on Scotland ('positive' or 'negative') we might argue to be taken by these different cinematic constructions. Even so, this is not an insurmountable problem if we acknowledge that this is not a black and white issue but a matter of perspective.

Autoethnography

One way of attempting to solve this problem is to examine the practice of autoethnography. It is possible to explore Scottish production in a similar way to that used to approach other 'small' film producing nations that require a degree of international success to be financially viable. In *Imperial Eyes: Travel Writing and Transculturation* (1992), Mary Louise Pratt developed the concept of 'autoethnography', by which colonised cultures on the periphery of Europe's colonial expansion took stereotypical images of themselves produced by the metropolitan centre, repackaged them and sold them back to the colonial culture.[27] The clearest example of this practice of 'transculturation' is the tourist souvenir, a hybrid that is partly an authentic product of the indigenous culture and partly a reflection of the tourist's conception of what a typically 'ethnic' product is.[28] This idea has already been integrated within film studies, for example, through an examination of Chinese art cinema in Rey Chow's *Primitive Passions* (1995), in relation to the spaghetti western in Dimitris Eleftheriotis's *Popular Cinemas of Europe* (2002) and the European heritage film by Elsaesser in *European Cinema*. In all these instances autoethnography in cinema is considered a cunning strategy through which filmmakers can self-consciously 'auto-exoticise', thereby giving international audiences what they expect (reassuring them with stereotypical images of the nation) whilst simultaneously addressing issues of interest to local audiences. Indeed, as part of this process, Eleftheriotis identifies the scope of cinematic fantasy tourism evident in the spaghetti western, albeit with a different emphasis to the argument I am making here.

It is not unusual for critics nowadays to view Scottish cinema as willingly collaborating in its own exploitation. After all, Scotland has a long history of cashing in on stereotypical notions of Scottishness. James McPherson's invention of the third-century 'Scottish' bard, Ossian, is one famous example of this practice. In the 1760s, McPherson pretended to have discovered Ossian's epic poetry and translated it from the original Gaelic. As historian T. M. Devine notes, the widespread popularity of Ossian at that time was due to the concurrent rebranding of the Highlands of Scotland as a primitive wilderness on the edge of a Europe that increasingly considered itself 'modern'.[29] Thus, once indigenous cinematic representations of Scotland began to appear they were likely to be self-conscious attempts to grapple with these pre-existing, clichéd stereotypes. This technique has already been noted by Jane Sillars in Scottish television programmes like *Hamish Macbeth* (1995–7) in which stereotypical images of Scotland are deployed, but framed ironically to target international audiences and simultaneously address local viewers with a knowing wink, inviting complicity in the sale of national stereotypes.[30]

However, the practice of autoethnography, whilst evident in certain Scottish productions, is problematised by the number of 'Scottish' films that are coproduced with funding from outside Scotland. Where do we situate the 'auto' if the film is British (perhaps produced in London, even if shot on location in Scotland) as opposed to Scottish? Again, how do we examine 'runaway' Hollywood productions (Hollywood-funded films outsourced to British production companies), or French, English, US or Indian productions that originate outside Scotland even whilst often involving Scottish production companies, employing Scottish personnel and filming on location in Scotland?

Take *Rob Roy*, for example. It is possible to consider this £16million Hollywood production alongside previous US costume dramas to adapt Sir Walter Scott's novel. For example, Sue Harper notes the way US filmmakers in the 1950s used the Scottish landscape as a stand in for the US frontier, in which a virile masculinity was necessary to conquer the rugged country.[31] Hence, in US films like *Rob Roy, the Highland Rogue* (1953), Scotland became a film set for 'a celebration of an energetic and classless masculinity',[32] and 'Scottish rebellion against British rationality' (especially in films about Jacobite rebellion) functioned as a 'prequel' of the American War of Independence. Seen in this way, *Rob Roy* appears just another in a long line of Hollywood remakes that use Scotland's landscape and history as a substitute for the USA.

On the other hand, we might focus on the role played by writer Alan Sharp and director Michael Caton-Jones, both Scotsmen working in the Hollywood film industry, and follow Petrie's conclusion that Sharp has written into a film which otherwise seems to follow the pattern of a revenge western 'the cultural tensions and conflict' of 'Scotland after the Act of Union'.[33] In this sense, *Rob Roy* seems a work of authoethnography, even if the 'auto' is established by émigrés working in Hollywood. We could therefore view the film as similar to the Asian blockbuster *Crouching Tiger, Hidden Dragon* (2000) in that the debates that accompany Taiwanese director Ang Lee's film hinge on what kind of national identity (if any) it can be said to construct. For example, as Christina Klein argues of *Crouching Tiger, Hidden Dragon*'s vision of ancient China, we might similarly consider *Rob Roy* an emigrant's or diaspora's invented dream or fantasy of a (homeland) Scotland which only exists in the imagination of the outsider.[34] For certain US audiences, then, both films may function a little like the classic Hollywood musical *Brigadoon* (1954). *Brigadoon* is about an enchanted Highland village that only emerges from the mists of time for one day every 100 years, and can be understood as a tourist's or diaspora's fantasy of Scotland.[35] In *Brigadoon* and *Rob Roy*, then, the 'auto' that is addressed is not indigenous to Scotland, the cinematic Scotland on display targeting instead an outsider's conception of (fantasy) Scotland.

In any case, as images of Scotland continue to be sold on the international market examining the extent to which a film is *auto*-ethnographic (as opposed to simply deploying an ironic framing around stereotypes of Scotland in a generally post-classical fashion) becomes extremely problematic. As Mike Wayne has argued, when 'the imaginings by which the community comes to understand itself are no longer primarily self-generated' it is as important to consider the 'perceptions of the nation that are held by *others*' as they too 'are a key determinant in the kinds of imaginings produced'.[36] Thus, for instance, as I examine in relation to the Loch Ness monster movie in Chapter 4, it is possible to consider the way in which a (touristic) fantasy view of Scotland is presented to the viewer (whether Scotland is deployed as setting or as film set) in a manner that addresses different audiences nationally and internationally.

In short, *Scotland: Global Cinema* examines the different imagined, or, as I prefer to consider them, fantasy Scotlands that are constructed by different genres and modes of filmmaking and the various types of identities they explore. By examining filmmaking in Scotland, this thorny issue no longer requires a 'positive' or 'negative' judgement to be made, as it did in *Scotch Reels*. Rather, the position taken on the issue really depends on where (in the world) you are looking at Scotland from.

Scotland: Global Cinema

The issue of identities is the dominant theme that traverses the different chapters that follow, as the diverse genres and modes collectively illustrate the lack of one singular, 'authentic' Scottish identity in favour of many cinematic Scotlands. Increasingly it is in popular genre films made and set in Scotland that non-national (ethnic, sexual, gendered, diasporic, transnational, global/local, regional) identities are often explored, despite the reputation that art and social realist films have for tackling 'serious' subject matter. In part this is because of a need to appeal to as broad an audience as possible, including those beyond the nation. However, it is also a positive side effect of the appeal of generic structures, and the seemingly 'innocent' viewing pleasures they offer, which also enable the examination of more weighty issues as though under cover of being, for instance, 'just a comedy'. If these films reach out beyond the nation in their subject matter, then, their constructions of a fantasy Scotland (or anywhereland-Scotland), is aided by the resonance of this particular nation with pre-existing myths of Scotland (of its many Brigadoons) as a place of transformation for the visitor, a location in which renegotiations of different identities have always taken place on the silver screen.

I begin Chapter 1 with Bill Forsyth's comedy *Gregory's Two Girls*. The emergence in the 1990s and 2000s of internationally well regarded Scottish art cinema directors – such as Peter Mullan, Lynne Ramsay, David Mackenzie and Andrea Arnold – has led to a repositioning of Bill Douglas as the originator of indigenous Scottish cinema, or at the very least, of New Scottish Cinema. However, this kind of historicising functions retrospectively, and is a reflection of the current state of film production in Scotland. In a certain sense, without Ramsay's *Ratcatcher* (1999) there is no lineage from Douglas's *My Childhood* (1972). Accordingly, if we examine the various genres currently being produced in Scotland, then we can consider the other labyrinthine pasts that might account for contemporary film production in Scotland. A return to Forsyth in Chapter 1 functions as a reminder that throughout the 1980s it was Forsyth (rather than the then unappreciated Douglas) who was considered the father of Scottish cinema, whilst simultaneously deconstructing the manner in which the name of directors like Forsyth and Douglas are used as labels that sell this emergent small national cinema internationally. When questioning where Scottish film history starts, it is more appropriate, I contend, to posit a variety of answers, the comedy (like the art film) being one amongst many. This chapter, then, examines the comedy, as a mode of film production and the global/local identities that are constructed in *Gregory's Two Girls* and *Festival*.

Chapter 2 expands this discussion to include the road movie, which has shifted its emphasis since the early 1990s, from films about returning to Scotland (*Soft Top, Hard Shoulder*) to films about leaving Scotland and the transformation of Scottish identities in broader global contexts (*Carla's Song, Tickets*). Chapter 3 then positions Scotland as a film location into which global flows of film finance pour (to mutual benefit) with the arrival of Bollywood location shoots in the 1990s. Here I examine the correlation of this movement with the growth of the tourist industry and the existence of the global Non-Resident Indian diaspora. The chapter concludes by examining the way in which the Scottish film *Nina's Heavenly Delights* constructs a Bollywood inflected aesthetic to examine the identities that are constructed by these flows as they interact within Scotland. Chapter 3 is pivotal in that it establishes the groundwork for many chapters that follow, both in relation to the creation of Scotland as a touristic fantasy-land and the transnational flows that intersect within Scotland (both to produce films, and as represented in films). By placing Bollywood early on in the discussion I illustrate the multifaceted picture of the various cinematic Scotlands now being produced whilst also demonstrating how contemporary filmmaking in Scotland coincides and interlinks with broader global movements (of people, expertise, trade and finance) since the end of the Cold War, as is typical of transnational cinema globally.[37]

Indeed, for the purposes of this book it is important to understand early on the impact of tourism (for example, on Bollywood film productions in Scotland) for what this tells us about other representations of Scotland, such as that of the Loch Ness monster in Nessie movies – whether British (*The Secret of the Loch*), US/UK (*Loch Ness*) or US/UK with the majority of it filmed in New Zealand (*The Water Horse*). Chapter 4 explores how these Loch Ness monster movies autoethnographically construct touristic fantasy Scotlands for international consumption. Chapter 5, on the horror film, develops the link between such fantasy Scotlands and the use of the wilderness myth to reach the US market in films like *Dog Soldiers* and local markets with *Wild Country*. Chapter 6, on the costume drama focuses on the use of Scotland as a fantasy anywhereland in which to construct 'new' identities (in this instance, Jewish diasporic identity in *The Governess*), and

Chapter 7 continues the exploration of the diaspora (a theme examined in Chapter 2 on the road movie) with the Scots-Italian gangster film *American Cousins*, as well as the use of Scotland as a setting in which to examine globalization in *Danny the Dog*, a film produced by a French production company and starring Chinese martial arts star Jet Li. Chapter 8 moves on to the social realist film, exploring its use of a melodramatic mode to examine familial stories of multicultural and diasporic identities in *Ae Fond Kiss*, and more universal issues surrounding post-industrial masculinity in *On a Clear Day*. Chapter 9 continues the discussion of gender in a universalised Scotland, as both tourist Edinburgh (*Women Talking Dirty*) and post-industrial Glasgow (*Beautiful Creatures*) provide the backdrop against which women discuss their existence without men. Finally, Chapter 10 explores the shift in emphasis in the construction of a Scottish art cinema that aims at the international film festival circuit, from a European art cinema (*Young Adam*) to a 'world cinema' aesthetic (*Red Road*).

As these chapters variously demonstrate, films that take place in similar locations do not necessarily deal with identities in the same manner or from the same point of view, as we might expect following the myths (themselves based on specific regions of Scotland) identified in *Scotch Reels*. For example, *The Governess*, set on the Isle of Skye, has more in common with the urban gangster films *American Cousins* and *Danny the Dog* (both set in Glasgow) through their shared exploration of diaspora, than it does with films set in the Highlands and Islands (for example, *Loch Ness* and *Dog Soldiers*). Rather than there being a regionally specific focus, then, many interlocking themes criss-cross the chapters. The subject of diaspora appears in the chapters on the comedy, road movie, Bollywood, gangster films, costume dramas and social realist melodramas. Tourism is examined in relation to Bollywood, Loch Ness monster and female friendship films, whilst discussions of global/local identities appear in practically every chapter but are particularly focused on in the comedy, road movie, Bollywood and gangster chapters. Examination of US interaction with Scotland appears most clearly in the Loch Ness monster, horror and gangster chapters, whilst Scotland's position in relation to Europe arises in discussions of the road movie and art film. The reworking of more traditionally 'Scottish' themes can be found in chapters on the Loch Ness monster movie, the horror film and the costume drama (Tartanry, the Highlands as wilderness) and the gangster movie, social realist melodrama and the art film (Clydesideism) respectively. Finally, as gender is often sidelined in discussions of Scottish cinema, chapters on Bollywood, gangster, costume, social realist melodramas and female friendship films all deal with this issue.

In 1986, Julian Petley famously noted the 'lost continent' of British cinema, in particular the popular genres (as opposed to realist movements) that had yet to receive critical attention.[38] There are now numerous books on British cinema's popular genre cinemas. In the chapters that follow I explore Scotland's lost continents, or perhaps a more apt metaphor would be Scotland's Brigadoons, its numerous forgotten cinematic 'traditions', and the engagement they offer with different identities.

Notes

1. Robert Crawford, 'Dedefining Scotland', in Susan Bassnet (ed.), *Studying British Cultures* (London: Routledge, 1997), pp. 83–96, p. 93.
2. Murray Smith, *Trainspotting* (London: BFI, 2002), Pam Cook, *I Know Where I'm Going!* (London: BFI, 2002), Colin McArthur, '*Whisky Galore! and The Maggie* (London: I. B. Tauris, 2003), Colin McArthur, *Brigadoon, Braveheart and the Scots* (London: I. B. Tauris, 2003), Jonathan Murray, Lesley Stevenson, Stephen Harper and Benjamin Franks (eds), *Constructing The Wicker Man* (Glasgow: University of Glasgow, Crichton Publications, 2005).
3. See for instance the introduction to Duncan Petrie, *Screening Scotland* (London: BFI, 2000).
4. John Caughie, 'Representing Scotland', Eddie Dick (ed.), *From Limelight to Satellite* (London: BFI & SFC, 1990), pp. 13–30, p. 20.
5. Cairns Craig, *Out of History* (Edinburgh: Polygon, 1996).
6. Steve Neale, 'Questions of Genre', in Barry Keith Grant (ed.), *Film Genre Reader II* (Austin: University of Texas Press, 1995), pp. 159–83.
7. A detailed account of all the institutional changes that occurred during the 1990s can be found in chapter eight of Duncan Petrie's *Screening Scotland*.
8. Thomas Elsaesser, *European Cinema* (Amsterdam: Amsterdam University Press, 2005), p. 489.
9. Mary P. Wood, *Contemporary European Cinema* (London: Hodder Arnold, 2007), p. 83.
10. Ibid., p. 96.
11. Linda Ruth Williams, *The Erotic Thriller in Contemporary Cinema* (Edinburgh: Edinburgh University Press, 2005), p. 8.
12. Wood, *Contemporary European Cinema*, p. 5.
13. Andrew Higson, 'The Concept of National Cinema', *Screen*, 30: 4 (1989), pp. 36–47.
14. Petrie, *Screening Scotland*, p. 186; Duncan Petrie, 'Scottish Cinema: Introduction', *Screen*, 46: 2 (2005), pp. 213–16, p. 215.
15. Duncan Petrie, *Contemporary Scottish Fictions* (Edinburgh: Edinburgh University Press, 2004), pp. 2–3.
16. Benedict Anderson, *Imagined Communities* (London: Verso, 1983).

17. David McCrone, *Understanding Scotland: The Sociology of a Nation,* 2nd edn (London: Routledge, 2001), p. 52.
18. Ibid., p. 51.
19. Film City website: http://www.filmcityglasgow.com/ (02/08/08).
20. Skillset Screen Academy website: http://www.screenacademyscotland. co.uk/ (02/08/08).
21. BAFTA Scotland website: http://www.bafta.designiscentral.com/ (02/08/08).
22. Scottish Screen website: http://www.scottishscreen.com/content/sub_ page.php?sub_id=142 (30/10/08).
23. Tom Nairn, *The Break Up of Britain* (London: Verso, 1977).
24. Michael Keating, *Nations Against the State* (London: Macmillan, 1996), p. 218.
25. John R. Gold and Margaret M. Gold, *Imagining Scotland* (Aldershot: Scolar Press, 1995), p. 54.
26. Adrienne Scullion, 'Feminine Pleasures and Masculine Indignities', in Christopher Whyte (ed.), *Gendering the Nation,* Edinburgh: Edinburgh University Press, 1995), pp. 169–204, p. 201.
27. Mary Louise Pratt, *Imperial Eyes* (London: Routledge, 1992), p. 7.
28. Ibid. p. 6 ('transculturation' defined), pp. 141–3 (example of the tourist souvenir as hybrid export art).
29. T. M. Devine, *The Scottish Nation 1700–2000* (London: Allen Lane, 1999), p. 242.
30. Jane Sillars, 'Drama, Devolution and Dominant Representations', in Jane Stokes and Anna Reading (eds), *The Media in Britain* (MacMillan, 1999), pp. 246–54.
31. Sue Harper, 'Bonnie Prince Charlie Revisited: British Costume Film in the 1950s', in Robert Murphy (ed.), *The British Cinema Book,* 2nd edn (London: BFI, 2001), pp. 127–34, p. 130.
32. Ibid.
33. Petrie, *Contemporary Scottish Fictions,* p. 201.
34. Christina Klein, '*Crouching Tiger Hidden Dragon*: A Diasporic Reading', *Cinema Journal,* 43:4 (2004), pp. 18–42, p. 22.
35. McArthur, *Brigadoon, Braveheart and the Scots,* pp. 117–21.
36. Mike Wayne, 'The Re-invention of Tradition: British Cinema and International Image Markets in the 1990s', *EnterText,* 2: 1 (2001/2), pp. 38–66: http://arts.brunel.ac.uk/gate/entertext/issue_2_1.htm (19/06/08).
37. Sheldon H. Lu, 'Crouching Tiger, Hidden Dragon, Bouncing Angels', in Sheldon H. Lu and Emilie Yueh-yu Yeh (eds), *Chinese-Language Film* (Honolulu: University of Hawaii Press, 2005), pp. 220–33, p. 222.
38. Julian Petley, 'The Lost Continent', in Charles Barr (ed.), *All Our Yesterdays* (London: BFI, 1986), pp. 98–119.

CHAPTER 1

Comedy: Global/Local Identities

This chapter examines film comedies made and set in Scotland. It explores why comedies are either ignored in academic debates surrounding cinema in Scotland, or their comedic aspect downplayed in favour of more 'serious' topics dealt with by individual filmmakers. Through indepth analysis of *Gregory's Two Girls* (1999) and *Festival* (2005) I argue that Scottish filmmakers use comedy as a mode of film production, with certain contemporary Scottish films deploying their comedic elements to construct an 'edgy' comedy, designed to make audiences laugh, whilst dealing with serious issues that are perhaps more recognisable, if not more relevant, in Scotland than elsewhere. These two films in particular use a comedic mode to examine Scotland's changing national (or rather, local) identity in an increasingly global context.

Film Comedy in Scotland

A number of films made and set in Scotland are comedies or have a strong comedic element. These include: *The Secret of the Loch* (1934), *The Ghost Goes West* (1935), *Whisky Galore!* (1949), *Laxdale Hall* (1953), *The Maggie* (1954), *Brigadoon* (1954), *The Battle of the Sexes* (1959), *What a Whopper* (1961), *The Prime of Miss Jean Brodie* (1969), *The Wicker Man* (1973), *Gregory's Girl* (1981), *Local Hero* (1983), *Comfort and Joy* (1984), *Restless Natives* (1985), *Trainspotting* (1996), *Loch Ness* (1996), *Orphans* (1997), *Gregory's Two Girls* (1999), *The Match* (1999), *Women Talking Dirty* (1999), *American Cousins* (2003), *Festival* (2005), *On a Clear Day* (2005) and *GamerZ* (2005). Many of these films will be discussed in later chapters in relation to other genres and types of cinema, but all are comedies of one sort or another.

The comedy plays an integral role in the history of home grown Scottish filmmaking. As I discuss in Chapter 10, although indigenous filmmaking in Scotland can be argued to have begun in the 1970s with Bill Douglas's *Childhood Trilogy* it was Bill Forsyth's second feature, the comedy *Gregory's Girl* (1981), which really brought Scottish cinema to mainstream British audiences. For over a decade Bill Forsyth's name was synonymous with debates surrounding an emergent Scottish cinema, a reputation that was solidified internationally with another comedy, *Local Hero* (1983). What is puzzling, then, is that although Forsyth's films have received critical attention, they have not been examined as comedies or, indeed, in relation to the tradition of comedies set in Scotland. To begin to do so it is worth noting initially how previous films in this tradition, many of which are best described as British rather than Scottish films – in that they were – shot on location in Scotland by London based studios, previously functioned in debates over how Scotland is represented in cinema.

In *Scotch Reels*, Colin McArthur examined two comedies set in Scotland, *Whisky Galore!* and *The Maggie*. These are films in which small Scottish communities triumph over the interests of larger, potentially intrusive powers, such as the bureaucratic British government in *Whisky Galore!* and (US) capitalism in *The Maggie*. These communities outwit representatives of these outside forces through their cunning, wily, folksy ways. McArthur discusses these films in terms of their reiteration of the myth of Kailyard Scotland, noting their 'detestation of modernity as it related to the city and to the power of capital . . . and particularly to the power of central government bureaucracy'.[1] Here Scotland's isolated position on the edge of 'civilised' Europe is evoked to suggest a magical land seemingly untouched by, and indeed – due to its wily Kailyard folk-wisdom – *resistant* to, modernity. It is from the mythical assumptions evoked by the use of Scotland as a location (if not a film set) representative of the Kailyard that the comedy is derived. When the street-smart English or US citizen arrives in Kailyard Scotland they are transformed into a different person, a process which entails laughter at their expense. Yet, because these fish-out-of-water comedies represent Scotland as the last bastion of a pre-modern way of life, the conclusions that McArthur draws correspond to critical interpretations that emphasise these films' 'negative' outsider's view of Kailyard Scotland. Scotland remains a land without its own voice or identity, a fact that is insidiously transmitted to the viewer under cover of seemingly innocent laughter.

The critical denial of the potentially 'positive' role played by Scotland as a location in these films continues to this day. In *Film Comedy* (2002), Geoff King positions Forsyth's Scottish comedies of the 1980s in relation to British film comedy, noting in particular their closeness to the Ealing comedies of the post-war years (including *Whisky Galore!* and *The Maggie* but also *Passport to Pimlico* (1949), *Kind Hearts and Coronets* (1949), *The Titfield Thunderbolt* (1953) and *The Ladykillers* (1955)). King draws on Charles Barr's earlier work on Ealing comedies in *Ealing Studios* (1977) noting that what marks them out as distinct from other strains of British comedy (such as the vaudeville style of George Formby's comedies, or the slap-stick *Carry On* films) is their attempts to construct a consensual, middle-class, liberal view of British identity.[2] Yet does this mean that Forsyth's Scottish comedies simply provide further examples of the Ealing spirit, depicting Scotland not as a country in its own right but as a space in which to examine the impact of modernity on British life in general? Do they provide any further insight into Scotland than *Whisky Galore!* or *The Maggie*? As I will show momentarily by analysing *Gregory's Two Girls*, I believe there is more to Forsyth's comedies than this.

Viewing Scottish comedies since Forsyth enables a break from discussions of such representations of Scotland as 'positive' or 'negative' (effectively 'Scottish' or 'British') in relation to the debates surrounding Kailyard Scotland instigated by *Scotch Reels*. Instead, in line with Jonathan Murray's analysis of Forsyth's *Local Hero* (1983),[3] I believe that indigenous Scottish comedies can be understood as 'edgy' comedies, at once aware of their use of existing stereotypes or other identifying markers of Scottishness that appeal universally whilst simultaneously exploring serious themes under the cover of often rather uncomfortable laughter. Before continuing any further, then, it is necessary to understand the manner in which these films should be understood as comedies.

Comedy as Mode versus The *Auteur*

It is usual to consider 'film comedy' a genre, in spite of its potentially very fluid borders, as seen in the existence of related genres like the romantic-comedy. In cinematic terms, however, comedy can also be considered a mode of film production that potentially crosses the boundaries of individual genres. Discussing film as a mode means referring to the elements of style or expression (be they aesthetic, stylistic or rhetorical) that we usually associate with a generic label like 'comedy'.

The notion that film comedy can be discussed as a mode has already been explored in relation to contemporary British comedies of the 1990s (for example, *Four Weddings and a Funeral* (1994), *The Full Monty* (1997)), in Nigel Mather's *Tears of Laughter* (2006). Mather considers these films to deploy humour

> for dramatic and emotional effect in the context of scenarios dealing with such seemingly non-comic subjects as mass unemployment, failed or uneasy relationships, bitter family disputes, or instances of racial tension and conflict in British society . . . [T]he interaction of comic and dramatic modes of narration within the films discussed proved to be a dynamic creative mechanism in 1990s British cinema.[4]

This 'interaction of comic and dramatic modes of narration' prompts Mather to label such films 'comedy-dramas', noting in passing the increasing use of comedy in British films that deal with gritty social subject matter.[5] In *Gregory's Two Girls* and *Festival* this argument enables a consideration of their at times rather serious (if not dark) subject matter, which is rendered in a comic way. Understanding these films as at once light and dark, then, facilitates a reconsideration of the conclusions of previous approaches to the works of Forsyth.

Critics writing on Forsyth very often disavow (briefly acknowledge and then proceed to sideline or ignore) their comic element in favour of a more 'serious' discussion of their darker themes and the aesthetic concerns of the director. For example, in *Scotch Reels*, McArthur, discussing Ealing comedies like *Whisky Galore!* and *The Maggie*, argues that 'the objective function of popular cinema is very often to paper over the cracks in the society, to mask contradictions'.[6] Popular genres like the comedy, then, are often dismissed because of their seeming avoidance of the contradictions in society, such as issues of class, race, gender and sexuality. In contrast to popular genres, the influence or genius of the director is discussed as part of the discourse surrounding the figure of the auteur, a director who plays a major creative role in the filmmaking process (perhaps also writing the script and/or editing the film).

The auteur is a figure comparable to a great writer or artist, someone apparently capable of transcending the supposed creative 'limitations' of film industries and their ideologically conservative popular films. Yet this construction of the director as auteur is part of a much larger, complex interplay of industrial, marketing and distribution, journalistic and academic discourses around the existence or 'identity' of European cinemas (and in fact, world cinemas), in a Hollywood dominated marketplace. Smaller filmmaking nations, especially in Europe, are often unable to compete in a global marketplace dominated by Hollywood's filmmaking and distribution practices. Instead, they establish themselves as niche products that appeal to different audience demographics. For instance, European art cinema offers a different kind of movie-going experience to the Hollywood blockbuster, and is distributed through the international film festival circuit and independent or art house cinema chains. In order to differentiate themselves from Hollywood films (usually marketed through the name of the star), European art films are associated with great directors, or auteurs, who are critically elevated above the status of directors working in the Hollywood studios. Thus, when Forsyth appeared on the scene making comedies in Scotland, the British film industry, film critics and academics downplayed the comedy of his films in favour of a discussion of his status as a director worthy of international renown. Although many of Forsyth's films, in particular *Gregory's Girl*, *Local Hero* and *Gregory's Two Girls* contain a significant comic element – including visual gags, awkward or embarrassing situations, puerile humour, stylised comic acting and so on – these films are treated as though they were art films rather than comedies.

A good example of this practice is found in an early piece by Allan Hunter from 1990, in which Forsyth's position is declared that of an 'artist, not an entertainer'.[7] Hunter emphasises Forsyth's 'healthy disinterest in the mythology of the film industry', stressing his place 'in the modest ranks of filmmaking mavericks who dream in celluloid'.[8] Here the discourse surrounding the auteur structures Hunter's prose, as he denigrates industrial production, praising Forsyth's maverick genius instead. Problematically, Hunter's article is mostly based on Forsyth's own statements in interview, in which he attempts to position himself within the pantheon of great directors from Europe; discussing his love of French auteurs like Louis Malle and Jean-Luc Godard,[9] and comparing the reception of his films (because of their association with comedy) to what he considers the more favourable treatment received by those of German director/auteur Wim Wenders.[10] The difficulty with taking these remarks at face value is that Forsyth, whilst undoubtedly expressing an honest opinion, is of necessity positioned within the realm of film marketing in a global context, and has a vested interest in establishing himself as an auteur.

Nevertheless, in the 1980s, Forsyth came to signify Scotland in terms of international cinema distribution just as directors like Jean-Luc Godard or François Truffaut had France, Roberto Rossellini or Federico Fellini, Italy, Glauber Rocha, Brazil, Akira Kurosawa, Japan and, since then, Abbas Kiarostami, Iran, Wong Kar-wai, Hong Kong and so on. Thus, Hunter's approach attempts to critically 'salvage' the auteur status of a filmmaker whose output was often received as comedy, in order to confirm the existence of a small, emergent, niche national cinema in Scotland. In doing so, Hunter deliberately disavows the comedic aspect of Forsyth's films, noting that

> Forsyth believes that his films are universally misinterpreted and misunderstood; viewers latch on to certain obvious elements and assume they have unlocked the door to his entire psyche, never looking beyond the qualities of charm and humour to examine the recurring themes of loss, loneliness and isolation.[11]

The discourses of marketing and promotion of small national cinemas under the banner of the recognisable auteur with which Forsyth engages are echoed by Hunter, and the comedic aspect of Forsyth's films brushed away as though a façade, in favour of 'uncovering' the more weighty subject matter that laughing might somehow obscure.

This stance on the director is not uncommon. It is apparent, for example, in Philip Kemp's book-length celebration of director Alexander Mackendrick, in which Kemp defends *Whisky Galore!* for its use of the baser 'conventions of comedy' in relation to the otherwise more weighty considerations of Mackendrick's *oeuvre*.[12] Not surprisingly, then, Hunter was not the only one to take this approach to Forsyth. In 1983, John Brown's *Sight and Sound* review of Forsyth's *Local Hero* begins with an immediate disavowal of the importance of such key industrial figures as the producer (David Puttnam) and the star (Burt Lancaster), who are typically used to market genre films, focusing instead on 'Scotland's first completely home-grown film-maker',[13] his 'persistently cool and detached style' and his 'ironic bitterness'.[14] This is no surprise from *Sight and Sound*, a journal produced by the British Film Institute, whose laudable aim is to keep alive the notion of British cinema as a distinct category that circulates alongside other niche world cinemas. The same thought processes had previously structured Gilbert Adair's 1981 review, in the same journal, of *That Sinking Feeling* and *Gregory's Girl*, Adair comparing Forsyth to 'the early *nouvelle vague*' and the work of French auteurs Eric Rohmer and François Truffaut.[15] Indeed, in *Screening Scotland* (2001), focusing on the themes of loss, loneliness and isolation that Hunter identified, Duncan Petrie discusses Forsyth's works as Scottish art films, comparing *Gregory's Girl* to the 'playful absurdity of the early French nouvelle vague and the Czech "new wave"'.[16]

Whilst the approach of writers like Hunter, Brown and Petrie maps out a territory within which Scottish cinema can be taken seriously in a global context, even so, an equally engaging discussion can be raised by considering the way these films use a comedic mode to enhance their discussion of serious issues. This is not to say that I do not consider Forsyth an auteur necessarily, but rather that I think a film can be worth studying because, rather than in spite of, it being funny. After all, the theatrical comedies of Shakespeare or Aristophanes have yet to be disregarded for being (more or less) humorous. Understanding these edgy comedies as operating in a comedic mode circumvents some of the complex politics behind these previous approaches whilst also enabling us to break free of the potentially stultifying 'positive' or 'negative' conclusions so often reached by discussions of filmic representations of Scotland introduced by *Scotch Reels*.

Gregory's Two Girls (1999)

Gregory's Two Girls was Forsyth's eighth feature. His early career started in Scotland with *That Sinking Feeling* (1980), followed by *Gregory's Girl* (1981), *Local Hero* (1983) and *Comfort and Joy* (1984). Forsyth then departed for Hollywood, to make *Housekeeping* (1987), *Breaking In* (1989) and the £13 million flop, *Being Human* (1993). *Gregory's Two Girls* marked his return to Scotland. It was a Young Lake production, from Scotland-based producer Christopher Young, made on a budget of £3.5 million drawn predominantly from Film Four (Channel 4 television's filmmaking division, who also distributed the film), the Scottish Arts Council Lottery fund and Kinowelt of Germany.[17]

Gregory's Two Girls (1999) offers an upbeat view on life in the new town of Cumbernauld, a satellite town constructed to alleviate the housing crisis facing Glasgow in the post-war era. It is the sequel to *Gregory's Girl* (1981), Forsyth's breakthrough film, which used the new town setting to gently explore shifting gender roles amongst teenagers at a local school. In the former film, as a setting for the story of loveable young Gregory (John Gordon Sinclair) – a schoolboy goalkeeper in love with a worldly-wise female striker – the 'newness' of the new town environment gelled with the 'newness' of the film's gender politics. In *Gregory's Two Girls*, the now much derided (sub)urban periphery of the new town is revisited, finding Gregory a teacher at the same school but still stuck in a state of immature adolescence. He is besotted with a young female student, and, whilst keen, as his catchphrase 'Don't spectate, participate' encapsulates, to extol the benefits of political intervention in the face of global capitalism that he gleams from watching videos of Noam Chomsky and reading *New Internationalist*, he himself is not involved in any such activities.

In addition to *Gregory's Girl*, *Gregory's Two Girls* also revisits *Local Hero* (Forsyth's most famous film) in its exploration of the influence of global corporate finance on Scotland. *Local Hero* depicts a US oil company's attempts to buy up an entire Scottish community, demolish it and build an oil refinery. In *Gregory's Two Girls* the focus is on the use of Scottish labour in 'Silicon Glen', the high-tech electronics and computing industries (often funded by global corporations based in the USA, Japan or elsewhere abroad), that settled in Scotland in the latter decades of the twentieth century. This politically contextualised (and indeed, simplified) analysis of Scotland's interaction with global capitalism is figured through the self-made entrepreneur Fraser Rowan (Dougray Scott), Gregory's old school friend. Fraser is a Scot who has made good since leaving for the USA, and now runs Rowan Electronics, employing over 400 people in the local community with significant financial backing from the British government. Alongside its production for profit, however, Rowan Electronics also supplies humanitarian aid to Africa in the form of reconditioned computers. This seeming benevolence covers its covert supply of electronic torture equipment to an African dictatorship.

Gregory's Two Girls explores how meaningful political action can take place in contemporary Scotland. It conflates the maturation of its protagonist to adulthood with his embrace of localised resistance to the global corporate hegemony symbolised by Rowan. In *Gregory's Girl* a 'fresh', regional Scottish setting provided an alternative to the mythical Scotlands of the Kailyard, Tartanry or Clydesideism. In *Gregory's Two Girls* this regional identity is seen – through the late blossoming of the now adult Gregory into a world citizen – to develop into adulthood. In this way *Gregory's Two Girls* addresses the late-twentieth-century transformation of Scottish identity from a national model into a local, regional (in this case, new-town) 'Scottishness' that interacts with the global forces that would otherwise shape its destiny. What is important for this study is that the puerile teen comedy of much of the film is entirely in keeping with this intention, to invite audiences to experience this development, along with Gregory, from a state of immaturity (both sexual and political) to the position of engaged world citizen. In so doing, the film both discards previous images associated with the nation, such as Tartanry, and opts instead for a regional or local identity that interacts with the deterritorialised flows of globalisation, and that resonates with both Scottish audiences and viewers in comparable small European nations.

It's a 'Bella' World

In the only existing article on *Gregory's Two Girls*, Jonathan Murray, to some extent replicating the above tradition of academic criticism of Scottish cinema that unfavourably compares genre films with art cinema, discusses what he considers to be the film's 'selective, essentializing and self-defeating . . . reading of Scottish-American cross-cultural exchange'. Murray argues that '*Gregory's Two Girls* diagnoses US hegemony as an impossible and intractable bind for the Scottish national sphere: regressive in all its fundaments, yet too powerfully entrenched to contest locally with any realistic hope of success.'[18] By contrast, Murray offers a more positive account of Lynne Ramsay's *Ratcatcher* (1999), emphasising its sophisticated, peripheral negotiation of US cultural hegemony. However, Murray's reading of *Gregory's Two Girls* cites evidence mostly drawn from the opening of the film and does not take into account its deployment of a comedic mode. In comparison, analysis of key points that occur as the narrative develops (not least of which is the ending), suggest that this popular genre film is as involved in the same process of peripheral identity negotiation under globalization as *Ratcatcher*, and that the edgy comedic tone is an important dimension in this process.

The opening scene of the film establishes the mood of edgy comedy. Gregory is initially obsessed with one of his pupils, Frances (Carly McKinnon). We open in Gregory's dream, but are not immediately aware of this. In his dream Gregory is having sex with Frances in the school gym, only to be interrupted by the headmaster at the door with two policemen. Humour is used to signal the dreamlike quality of this fantasy, thereby detracting from its serious implications. This is achieved both through the incongruous use of romantic violin and harp music on the soundtrack to accompany the close ups of the red and sweating faces of Gregory and Frances, and in the headmaster's hilariously banal 'threatening' statement that he has sent the caretaker Mr McAlpine to fetch the master key! As the headmaster finally enters the gym, Gregory ejaculates, awaking to find that he has stained his sheets.

The topic of Gregory's sexual desire for his pupil is extremely provocative, but the treatment of this subject through comedy enables it to demonstrate the road to maturation of Gregory. Through the narrative of his personal development, Gregory is identified with an 'inactive' national identity that develops along with Gregory (at a local level, in the new town), into a productive, global/local identity. This is an identity defined at a local level through engagement with the forces of global capitalism as they impact upon Cumbernauld. In this respect the first words spoken by Frances in Gregory's dream are telling: 'This has to stop . . . All this looking, all that not touching, I can't take it anymore. Its time to touch, Greg, touch me.' As the film progresses, Gregory's desire – expressed for him in his dream by Frances – to stop looking and to 'touch', replicates Gregory's shift of emphasis from an observer of the inequalities of global capitalism to a (local level) political activist, a 'toucher' as it were. In his own terms, Gregory develops from one who spectates to one who participates. Ultimately his inappropriate sexual desire, which provides so much of the comedy, is channelled into both a productive adult relationship with Bel (Maria Doyle Kennedy), and (by extension) his newfound engaged political activism, ensuring that his personal maturation reflects a vision of national (or in fact, global/local) coming-of-age under globalization.

Key to this process is the scene in which Gregory's dream is replayed in reality and he begins to move in to a more mature stage in his development. Here the comedic mode is again vital. Two policemen arrive at the

Figure 1.1 Global/Local Awakening: Gregory's (John Gordon Sinclair) desire matures from teenager to adult in *Gregory's Two Girls* (1999)

school to question Gregory in the presence of the headmaster, after Frances's father has discovered Gregory and Frances in a local park late at night. Throughout his flurried, hastily constructed cover story about badgers being sighted in the park, shots of the incredulous faces of his various audience members are intercut with that of the blundering Gregory. The editing emphasises how his embarrassment increases in intensity under their watchful gaze, until he finally blurts out the Freudian slip, 'I've never actually seen Frances's beaver.' The script then milks this highly embarrassing moment for all it is worth, Gregory flusters onwards in the silence, 'beaver, it's a bit of a mouthful' (etc.), before revealing a suspicious-looking (although completely innocent) stain on the inner thigh of his trousers. This set piece comedy is the real-life correlative of his adolescent wet dream, and afterwards it is the headmaster who (after several prolonged fits of laughter) sets Gregory on the adult path to a relationship with Bel. The edginess of this comedy consists less in Gregory's desire for Frances (which is really a symptom of his situation) and more in his fear of leaving his safe, detached perspective on the world and actually doing something to affect his environment. Gregory's need to mature into adulthood, then, is dealt with in a comedic manner to facilitate engagement with larger, national issues.

Gregory's maturation (both personal and political) continues with the arrival of Jon, Gregory's sister's American fiancé. Although Gregory assumes that Jon will be an uninformed American (thanks to the anti-American stance he has adopted from Chomsky), it transpires that Jon was taught by Chomsky whilst studying at the Massachusetts Institute of Technology (MIT) and has worked for the UN. The three take a road trip to various nearby heritage sites, enabling the film to outline its position on the status of the new town as part of a global, rather than a national context. At Dumbarton Castle, Jon comments on the present state of Scotland as he sees it:

> I suppose you're lucky really, living in an old, safe, dead country like this. Makes for a comfortable life . . . old castles, look at your river here, its dead, no connections with the world anymore. You go to Africa, Asia, you won't find a dead river like this. Your battles are hundreds of years behind you, and all your heroes are statues.

Filmed in a site of national heritage splendour, this conversation seems to affirm the mythical assertion of Tartanry that Scottish identity is 'lost' to the past. However, as the conversation progresses both Gregory and Jon advocate local, individual action over hero worship. Thus it is the identity of the nation, in particular as a site of resistance to the hegemony of corporate globalization, which is ultimately at question. In its place, there is participation in politics at a grassroots level, suggesting that national identity has been (or for Forsyth, should be) replaced by a local/global identity. In this process the film's edgy humour is again important, as the dialogue that accompanies the road trip further demonstrates.

Gregory's passivity towards direct political action is the result of his belief in a 'dead' national identity that stymies any meaningful attempt to create change. This is confronted when he is questioned by Jon at Stirling Castle. Jon shows his ignorance of Scottish history by asking 'Did Wallace and Rob Roy get along?' Gregory sarcastically replies that 'The intervening four hundred years limited any meaningful relationship . . . it's like asking if Christopher Columbus was pally with, Popeye.' Yet the joke is lost on Jon, and it is his final question that is the most telling: 'You can understand me, Greg; why can't I understand you?' Gregory may know his own national history, but as yet he is unable to communicate with others from around the world. He is as cut off as his dead country, with its dead heroes and dead river. In this instance, then, the comedy aimed at the ignorant yank stereotype backfires, challenging Gregory's preconceptions and furthering the somewhat tense mood as we, like Gregory, are unable to laugh at the serious implications of Jon's words. This mood is enhanced when the three visit an Italian restaurant, and whilst Gregory's sister and

Jon speak Italian with the waiter, Gregory is left embarrassedly repeating the only Italian word he knows, 'Bella! Bella!' The reappearance of this catchphrase from his teenager persona in *Gregory's Girl* reemphasises his lack of maturation in relation to the two global citizens, foregrounding his role as the unknowing clown of the piece.

Santiago de Cumbernauld

Gregory finally finds his new identity after he meets Dimitris (Martin Schwab), the ex-political journalist, torture victim and now wandering human rights activist. Dimtris' national identity is left purposefully unclear, to demonstrate that this is no longer of as much importance as the lesson he teaches Gregory about getting involved at a local level. Dimitris is instrumental in showing both Gregory and the viewer that Cumbernauld is not simply a Scottish new town. Along with the global nexus of corporate wealth evoked by the presence of Rowan Electronics is its correlative, global citizens like Dimitris, the UN worker Jon, the Italian waiter in the restaurant and the Chilean exiles living in Cumbernauld who Dimitris introduces to Gregory. The Chileans have lived in the new town for over twenty years, since the Pinochet dictatorship (or as Dimitris describes it, since 'the CIA were screwing Chile'), even though Gregory has been ignorant of their presence. Through his visit to the Chileans' home, a dead national history is contrasted with a submerged, multicultural local history.

Gregory is pictured surrounded by the exiles having a family get together. His awkwardness is comical. He sits on the edge of the sofa, holding a half-finished beer in one hand and a maraca in the other, as all around sing in an accented South American Spanish which he cannot understand or join in with. The irony of this situation is deliberate, as earlier on in the film Gregory was seen pontificating to his English class about Chile, by reading from Chomsky. The humour derives from the incongruity between his professed opinions and his knowledge of the world. Even though Gregory is in his home town he is suddenly the fish out of water who comically attempts to accommodate himself to this new community. His blushes are saved when the Chileans break into a rendition of 'Flower of Scotland' for his benefit. The tension in the scene is now broken, as Gregory is able to join in, but the edginess of the comic moment demonstrates his inability to interact with other inhabitants of the global village. The Chileans' identity is presented as a hybrid or accented (both literally and figuratively) Scottishness. This is emphasized in particular as the camera lingers on the three generations all proudly

singing the unofficial Scottish anthem together. This identity exists somewhat invisibly to the Scottish inhabitants of the new town, even though
they are connected to the global flows of deterritorialised people like
Dimitris, the political undercurrents who proliferate under globalization.
Through the Chileans, *Gregory's Two Girls* suggests that it is possible for
a regional identity to connect to global politics through the interactions
between different deterritorialised flows of people in different (localised)
parts of Scotland.

Finally, the film's conclusion sees Gregory and Frances, having been
rebuffed by the British government's Scottish Office in this pre-devolution
story, take direct political action. They hijack the shipment of computers
containing electronic parts for torture equipment before it can leave
Scotland, throwing the computers off a cliff. The film's final image is of
dawn breaking over smashed electronic hardware washed in the tide,
accompanied by upbeat music. Direct action at a local level, then, affects
the global trade in torture equipment, as two peripheral characters from
the Scottish new town derail the global flow of illicit trade between supra-
national corporations and their clients. Comedy is again crucial in creating
this optimistic tone to the ending. As Gregory and Frances prepare to bed
down in the back of the stolen van, Gregory makes it clear that nothing
must happen. Frances, acquiescing, teases him, saying, 'You can be like
Ghandi, he used to sleep next to naked young virgins to test his will
power.' Gregory replies, 'That was his excuse.' The ending, then, maintains the film's edgy comedy as the adult Gregory goes to sleep alongside
a teenage schoolgirl, one of his own pupils, whom he has drawn away from
her family home and embroiled in illegal activities. The appropriate
behaviour he demonstrates towards her is humorous in relation to his previous desires at the start of the film, but a question mark remains over the
'legality' of the type of action in which he has involved her. Direct political
action, it is suggested, necessitates a rather dangerous relationship with
the law. This is seen through the evocation of the actions of Ghandi, the
Indian political leader who famously opposed the British Empire. The
point being made, however, is that at least now Gregory is 'being like'
Ghandi (in his willingness to take direct political action), rather than just
talking about him.

Murray's critique of *Gregory's Two Girls* concludes that the film is
entirely pessimistic about the damage caused to Scotland by corporate
capitalism.[19] By contrast, I argue that it displays a studied ambivalence
over this matter, acknowledging the rejuvenating jobs (not to mention the
increased communication with the outside world) that Rowan has brought
to Cumbernauld whilst questioning the price that local communities may

be paying (or indeed, dishing out to the rest of the world) for their 400 jobs. The earnest freshness of students like Frances suggest that the 'newness' of new town Scottish identity seen in *Gregory's Girl* is still possible twenty years on, as long as the new town is considered as a 'global anywhere' rather than a depressed region of Scotland. The nation may be 'dead', the film contends, but the potential of the new town is alive. The nondescript spaces of Cumbernauld in which the film takes place (parks, grey concrete housing blocks, anonymous school, electronics factory, luxury country house, etc) could be, literally, anywhere. Thus an international dimension exists in the film's *mise-en-scène*, enabling a globally applicable story of local resistance to corporate globalization. This 'serious' consideration of identity, however, is packaged in a comedic format, to make it palatable to wider audiences than other much darker, realist films that feature new towns, like *Ratcatcher* or *Sweet Sixteen* (2002).

Thus, viewing *Gregory's Two Girls* as a film that operates in a comedic mode enables us to consider its existence on the 'edge' between a serious reconsideration of Scottish national identity in a global context (including corporate power, third-world dictatorships and the trade in instruments of torture) and the embarrassing scrapes experienced by an immature adult, Gregory, struggling to outgrow his adolescent desires. A similarly precarious process of negotiating global/local interaction through comedy is found in *Festival*.

Festival (2005)

Set during the annual Edinburgh Festival and its vast, unofficial 'Fringe' (together comprising comedy, theatre, music, film and various other festivals within the greater festival), *Festival* follows a number of parallel and occasionally intertwining small stories of characters at the event. The ensemble cast includes the earnest young actress Faith (Lyndsey Marshal), in Edinburgh with her one-woman play about Dorothy Wordsworth; Brother Mike (Clive Russell), a Catholic priest struggling with paedophilic tendencies and performing a one-man play about a Catholic priest struggling with paedophilic tendencies; several comedians, including Irish journeyman Tommy O'Dwyer (Chris O'Dowd); Joan Gerard (Daniela Nardini) an arts correspondent for BBC Radio Scotland; Sean Sullivan (Stephen Mangan), a famous British comedian and impressionist on the verge of breaking into the US market; a theatre troupe of three young, pretentious Canadians; and a family of caricatured Edinburgh New Town (in this case an integral, wealthy area of the city as opposed to a satellite town) elite who hire out their luxury town house to the Canadians

– including a haughty bourgeois lawyer, baby, depressed wife, Micheline (Amelia Bullmore), and her overbearing mother. *Festival*'s interweaving plot lines are similar to those of the Robert Altman comedies *Nashville* (1975) and *Prêt-à-Porter* (1994), and are used to demonstrate the chaos, complexity and carnivalesque environment of the Edinburgh Festival.

Like *Gregory's Two Girls*, *Festival* was also produced by Christopher Young. A Young Pirate Production (Young Films and Pirate Productions), *Festival* was made on a budget of £1.8 million from the UK Film Council, Film Four, Scottish Screen and the Glasgow Film Office. It was distributed by Pathé.[20] The scriptwriter and director, Annie Griffin (American by birth, but resident in Scotland since 1981), had previously worked in television, achieving success with the Channel 4 comedy set in Glasgow, *The Book Group* (2002–3). *Festival*, then, was scripted and directed by a newcomer with a television pedigree and shot on a low budget using a cast who were unknown in cinematic terms, although well known to British television audiences. Its narrative structure, although comparable to Altman's famous film comedies, could equally be considered akin to television comedies like *The Book Group*. It is interesting, therefore, given the film's local televisual pedigree and look, that most of its British press coverage focused on the writer/director Annie Griffin, echoing the discourse surrounding the auteur previously seen in relation to Forsyth.

Coinciding with the launch of the film, the *Guardian* newspaper printed a lengthy interview with Griffin in which she discussed her experiences as a budding actor on the fringe, and her inspiration for the film.[21] Here the voice of the director is given free reign (it is effectively a monologue), and, typically for any treatment of an auteur, her biographical inspirations for the film are placed centre stage. The *Sight and Sound* review for its part discussed *Festival* in comparison with Altman's *Nashville*, but less to stress its comedic nature and more to establish the director's credentials within the pantheon of world cinema auteurs. Jonathan Romney attempts a serious comparison of the two as 'state of the nation' films, but is unable to adequately illustrate how *Festival* engages with the national beyond a rather vague description of Edinburgh offered by a quotation from Griffin.[22] Although Romney praises *Festival* for being, precisely, an edgy comedy (a 'cruel, highly intelligent and often bitterly hilarious comedy of showbiz manners'),[23] he is quick to assert that it is a comedy for adults and different from 'the dominant playground pulp', as he dismisses the rest of the genre.[24] Finally, Romney notes it 'surprising' that Griffin's 'first feature film . . . should be in some senses so approachably mainstream',[25] flagging the director's 'experimental background'[26] as though to ward of any suggestion of skilful genre filmmaking in favour of that of an auteur experimenting with the 'limitations' of genre for adult gratification. As with Forsyth, then, Griffin is thrust into the spotlight as emergent director, shifting attention away from the film itself onto the auteur. In this process, the comedic nature of the film is qualified through praise of its 'seriousness'. Yet what these journalists fail to address is the manner in which *Festival* uses its provocative, adult comedy to address the 'state of the nation', or more accurately, the state of Edinburgh.

Sexy Auld Reekie

Like *Gregory's Two Girls*, *Festival* does not so much examine national as global/local identity. In this, the comedic mode that *Festival* deploys – albeit in an adult, as opposed to the teen register of *Gregory's Two Girls* – demonstrates how Edinburgh (during the festival at least), becomes a nodal point in the globe wherein international flows of people, cash and culture briefly intersect, mingling as they do so with the respective local flows that traverse the city year round. Its edgy comedy focuses on sex and ambition and the potentially inclusive roles they play in international success, both for the festival's performers and the city itself.

Festival is not the first film to examine such themes in Edinburgh. In *Screening Scotland* (2000), Duncan Petrie isolates two dominant urban representations in films set in Scotland: the 'historical city', usually associated with Edinburgh, and the modern or contemporary, industrial city of Glasgow.[27] For Petrie, the former is often depicted through a particularly 'Gothic vision of Edinburgh where under the surface of bourgeois respectability there lurks a dark and macabre world of terror and criminality'.[28] Petrie breaks up Edinburgh-based films into two camps, those that represent a 'light' view of the bourgeois New Town, and those that stress the dark underbelly of the Old Town (in particular a number of body snatcher films, see Chapter 5). To some extent it is possible to argue that *Festival* conforms to this notion of a city of dark and light, especially in the plotline of its suicidal paedophile priest with guilty thoughts about the young boys with whom he plays football in the park (dark) and its depressed New Town housewife and mother (light and dark). Yet I believe it can be understood slightly differently, as belonging to a much smaller tradition of Edinburgh based films. In its use of comedy, *Festival* traces its lineage back to such films as *The Battle of the Sexes* (1959) and *The Prime of Miss Jean Brodie* (1969), which Petrie places in the 'light' category. Like *Festival*, these particular Edinburgh-based films are comedies in which the topic of sex (if not sex *per se*) plays a key role. Moreover, these are films in which, unlike the body snatcher tradition, the links between Edinburgh and the outside world are emphasised, as they are in *Festival*.

The Battle of the Sexes begins with a close up of a couple kissing and proceeds to conflate the 'battle' between the sexes with the interaction of the mass production of US market capitalism (coded as modernity/femininity) and the craftsmanship of Scottish tweed manufacture (coded as tradition/masculinity). This struggle is rendered comic through the interaction of Martin (Peter Sellers), the representative of a fading, stuffy but wily (Kailyard) Scotland, and Angela Barrows (Constance Cummings), an industrial consultant from the USA who sets out to modernise a small, traditional Scottish business. In *The Prime of Miss Jean Brodie*, schoolteacher Miss Jean Brodie (Maggie Smith) instructs her charges in their identity stating, 'You are citizens of Edinburgh, the city of Hume and Boswell. You are European.' Unfortunately, she is caught up in a scandal surrounding her vocal support for European dictators Franco and Mussolini, whilst her star student Sandy (Pamela Franklin) has an affair with her former lover, art teacher Mr Lloyd (Robert Stephens). In both instances the topic of sex is combined with comedy and used as a medium through which to approach larger issues of Edinburgh's status in relation to the rest of the world. The same process is seen in *Festival*.

The titles of *Festival* play over military drumming. The film opens with an image of a bagpiper's face, red and inflated, as he plays this most traditional of Scottish symbols for the benefit of tourists. Within seconds, extra-diegetic music, specifically, high pitched trumpets, cuts in on the sound track. This creates a discordant effect with the bagpipe music and drumming, a jarring musical theme that recurs throughout the film to illustrate how Scottish tradition (the bagpipes and drums are evocative of the Tartanry of the Edinburgh Military Tattoo) is invaded during the festival by the outside world. In this way, stereotypical views of national identity, like that of Tartanry, are rendered unstable in the environment of the festival, which brings together people from all over the world. For the months when these guests visit Edinburgh, Scottish identity is no longer national, but a fusion of the global and the local.

The opening introduces scenes of the carnival in full swing throughout Princes Street, the Mound and on the scenic Royal Mile as hopeful performers attempt to drum up interest in their shows by parading their costumes and talents in the streets. Having set the scene, *Festival* then introduces the characters and their interweaving plotlines in rapid succession, thereby illustrating the international flows traversing Edinburgh. First to arrive is Faith, just off the bus from England. Then the three actors from Canada, the Irish comics and finally Sean Sullivan, a British (English) comedian whose agenda at the festival (aside from sitting on a comedy jury) is to snare a high-flying Los Angeles-based manager Arnold Weiss (Stuart Milligan) who is in town for the festival. The destabilising of established identities by these various international flows is most clearly seen in the interaction between the three Canadians and the Scottish characters they encounter.

The young Canadian, Rick (Jonah Lotan), is initially attracted to the very notion of being in Scotland. Looking at the city skyline from the window of the town house they are renting he states, 'Cool . . . Scotland.' His romantic besottedness is possibly due to the historical links between the two countries (Canada received a large influx of Scottish immigrants during the eighteenth and nineteenth centuries),[29] and the fact that Canada's Scottish diaspora still retains its interest in Scottish culture. Rick develops a relationship with the depressed wife of the family whose house they are renting, Micheline. Initially mirroring each other, gradually they exchange and merge identities, Micheline finally dressing in Rick's jacket, and Rick donning one of her kimonos. This process of identity interchange demonstrates the destabilising nature of these international flows onto 'normal' Scottish life.

To illustrate this further, the discordant music again plays over the interior of the family home, from which Micheline is absent, her stern-looking husband working at home on his laptop and caring for their crying baby. Micheline is then discovered outside in the night, looking in at the Canadians, rather than staying at home with her stultifying family. Ultimately she abandons them to leave town with the Canadians, running away, as it were, with the circus, but also replicating the movement of dispersal of so many Scots in previous centuries who left their homes for Canada. This association of Micheline with the émigré is further established when she is depicted in hilly countryside overlooking the city as a Gaelic song plays on the soundtrack. In Micheline, then, are encapsulated the possibilities of 'Other' Scottish identities (Gaelic, diasporic, Scottish-Canadian) that exist due to the transnational movements of its populations beyond the boundaries of the nation.

In addition, Canadian actress Dina (Megan Dodds) has a brief fling with a local Edinburgh scallywag, Mark (Chris Alexander), who elects himself as their guide. Their conversations are extremely humorous and illustrate how *Festival* attempts to broaden its appeal beyond solely local audiences. When they first meet, speaking rapidly in a thick north Edinburgh accent, Mark asks Dina, 'You'se here for the festival? You and yer pals doing a show, eh?' To which she replies: 'Do you also speak

English?' Again, much later in the film Mark and Dina, by now lovers, have the following conversation:

MARK: You got yerself a lumber the night.
DINA: (imitating Mark's accent) 'A lumber the night.' What does that mean?
MARK: It means yer a lucky bird.
DINA: 'A lucky bird. It means yer a lucky bird.'

These humorous exchanges work on two levels, making them accessible to both local and international audiences. For the local audience there is a knowing recognition of both the local dialect and language ('a lumber' meaning sex) and for the international audience (starting with many English people), the same feeling of perplexity that Dina has when encountering 'English' that sounds like a foreign language. For actress Dina, the exotic Scottish accent is something she is happy to experiment with (although incomprehending she continues to repeat, 'a lucky bird' in imitation of Mark's accent), as though trying on a new identity in the fantasy space of the festival.

This attempt at a dual address is present in a number of other ways throughout the film, from the in-jokes specific to a very small part of Scotland (such as Tommy O'Dwyer's remark about 'pig ignorant' Fifers) to the skilful use of attractive Edinburgh settings (the castle at night, the Meadows, the Royal Mile and various distinctive exteriors of famous comedy clubs and theatres) which would be recognisable to anyone who has visited the city or indeed, the festival. What is most interesting, however, is the way that *Festival*, whilst 'selling' the city of Edinburgh to these different audiences, also critiques this very process of self-promotion through its humorous depiction of sex.

Several characters use sex as a tool to foster their own ambitions, the film's sex scenes commenting upon the way in which the Edinburgh festival 'sells', or transforms its own identity in the process of attracting the global flows depicted in the film. Most noticeable in this respect are the sex scenes involving Tommy O'Dwyer and Joan Gerard, and Sean Sullivan and emergent comedienne Nicky Romanowski (Lucy Punch). Both temporary couples form because Gerard and Sullivan are jury members, and O'Dwyer and Romanowski are each nominated for the comedy award as a result of their affairs. In these sex scenes the comedic mode is again apparent, being used to make more palatable the exploitative nature of the sexual interaction taking place. For instance, the first time Sullivan and Romanowski sleep together she begins to practice her act (which deploys a Jewish mother stereotype) whilst masturbating him. Sullivan, disappointed, asks her to pretend to be a Thai prostitute instead, and when she does not, begins to impersonate the role himself. The close-in two-shot of their heads, as each performs their respective routines, illustrates how isolated they each are in their individual desires and ambitions. Their sexual act is interrupted by the ever practical Petra (Raquel Cassidy), Sullivan's personal assistant, who bursts into the hotel room to collect Sullivan for his meeting with Weiss. At this point, Sullivan's penis, until then out of shot whilst being massaged, suddenly rears into view at the bottom of the shot as his climax is comically interrupted by his desire for international fame.

Thus *Festival*, whilst equally involved in the process of ambitious self-promotion as Sullivan, O'Dwyer, Romanowski and the other characters – offering Edinburgh's tourist vistas and its landmark festival to international audiences – packages this desire in an edgy, critical comedic mode that exposes this very process of self-exploitation. Like Altman's *Nashville*, *Festival* is simultaneously a comic critique *and* celebration of a specific place and its industry. This comparison, however, functions as much on the level of the film's comedic register as it does to conflate Griffin with Altman. *Festival* is not an art film that somehow transcends the boundaries of genre. Rather, like *Gregory's Two Girls*, *Festival* engages with serious issues in a comedic mode. Indeed, in both films a self-conscious understanding of Scottish identity as a matter of global/local negotiation mirrors the same realisation on the part of the resurgent film industry in the 1990s and 2000s as does the potential appeal to local and international audiences. In all these respects the role of comedy is vital.

Notes

1. Colin McArthur, 'Scotland and Cinema', in Colin McArthur (ed.), *Scotch Reels* (London: BFI, 1982), pp. 40–69, p. 47.
2. Geoff King, *Film Comedy* (London: Wallflower, 2002), pp. 157–63.
3. Jonathan Murray, 'Straw or Wicker? Traditions of Scottish Film Criticism and *The Wicker Man*', in Jonathan Murray, Lesley Stevenson, Stephen Harper and Benjamin Franks (eds) *Constructing the Wicker Man* (Glasgow: University of Glasgow, Crichton Publications, 2005), pp. 11–36.
4. Nigel Mather, *Tears of Laughter* (Manchester: Manchester University Press, 2006), p. 2.
5. Ibid., p. 6.
6. McArthur, 'Scotland and Cinema', p. 49.
7. Alan Hunter, 'Bill Forsyth: The Imperfect Anarchist', in Eddie Dick (ed.), *From Limelight to Satellite* (London: BFI, SFC, 1990), pp. 151–62, p. 151.
8. Ibid.
9. Ibid., p. 152.

10. Ibid., p. 158.
11. Ibid., p. 156.
12. Kemp, Philip, *Lethal Innocence* (London: Methuen, 1991), p. 27.
13. John Brown, 'A Suitable Job for a Scot', *Sight and Sound*, 52: 3 (1983), pp. 157–62, p. 157.
14. Ibid., p. 158.
15. Gilbert Adair, 'One Elephant, Two Elephant: *That Sinking Feeling* and *Gregory's Girl*', *Sight and Sound*, 50: 3 (1981), pp. 206–7, p. 206.
16. Duncan Petrie, *Screening Scotland* (London: BFI, 2000), p. 154.
17. Young Films website, *Gregory's Two Girls* webpage: http://youngfilms. typepad.com/blog/gregory.html (13/11/07).
18. Jonathan Murray, 'Kids in America? Narratives of Transatlantic Influence in 1990s Scottish Cinema', *Screen*, 46:2 (2005), pp. 217–25, p. 221.
19. Ibid., p. 225.
20. Young Films website, *Festival* webpage: http://youngfilms.typepad.com/ blog/festival_2005/index.html (15/11/07).
21. Annie Griffin, 'Let Me Entertain You', the *Guardian*, 8 July 2005: http:// film.guardian.co.uk/edinburgh2005/story/0,,1544938,00.html (15/11/07).
22. Jonathan Romney, 'Edinburgh Cringe', *Sight and Sound* 15: 8 (2005), pp. 26–9, p. 28.
23. Ibid., p. 26.
24. Ibid., p. 28.
25. Ibid., p. 29.
26. Ibid.
27. Petrie, *Screening Scotland*, p. 74.
28. Ibid.
29. See T. M. Devine, *Scotland's Empire 1600–1815* (London: Penguin, 2003), pp. 188–220.

CHAPTER 2

Road Movie: Scotland in the World

This chapter explores the place of the road movie in Scottish cinema. It begins with a brief introduction to existing literature on the genre. The history of road movies featuring Scotland is then discussed, in particular the dominant trend in British films to depict Scotland as an end point for journeys featuring English protagonists. The remainder of the chapter charts a shift in emphasis that became apparent in the early 1990s to road movies featuring Scottish protagonists. *Soft Top, Hard Shoulder* (1993) follows a Scot returning to Scotland, simultaneously emphasising a rejuvenation of Scottish national identity and a nuanced appreciation of its ethnic complexities. For their part, Ken Loach's *Carla's Song* (1996) and his contribution to the portmanteau film *Tickets* (2005) depict Scots on the road in wider, global contexts. Refusing to homogenise Scottish national identity, these films illustrate the similarities between certain sections of the Scottish populace (especially the working classes) and various manifestations of the growing global underclass. Like Lynne Ramsay's *Morvern Callar* (2002), Loach's films use the pretext of a journey to explore the evolving nature of Scottish identity within the broader context of globalization.

Road Movies and Scotland

The road movie only began to receive serious academic recognition in the 1990s. After Timothy Corrigan's influential discussion in *Cinema Without Walls* (1991), further works include two coedited volumes (Steven Cohan and Ina Rae Hark's *The Road Movie Book* (1997) and Jack Sargeant and Stephanie Watson's *Lost Highways* (1999)), and David Laderman's *Driving Visions* (2002).[1] In these texts the road movie is a prime vehicle for exploring the changing cultural landscape at specific points in a country's national history. For Cohan and Hark, drawing on Corrigan's examination of the US road movie as a post-war phenomenon, 'the road movie provides a ready space for exploration of the tensions and crises of the historical moment during which it is produced', especially 'in eras where the culture is revaluating a just-closed period of national unity'.[2] Similarly, for

Sargeant and Watson, 'the road movie has emerged as a genre that exists as broadly critical of society and hypothesizes geographical movement as allied to cultural shifts both in America and beyond'.[3] For Laderman, 'the driving force propelling most road movies . . . is an embrace of the journey as a means of cultural critique'.[4] Perhaps unsurprisingly these books predominantly examine road movies within national contexts, providing in-depth discussions of the US road movie and the numerous themes it explores (entirely understandable considering the US is the country from which the majority of road movies emerge), although they do devote space to road movies from various other nations. However, subsequently this national emphasis has begun to shift to a more transnational view of the road movie.

Ewa Mazierska and Laura Rascaroli's *Crossing New Europe* (2006) moves beyond the confines of national identity and examines the contemporary European road movie as a transnational genre.[5] Their aim is to

> examine the ways in which recent European travel films have mirrored and explored the complex question of movement in and through Europe in the last thirty years. Our intention is to determine to what extent travel films have engaged with the notion of a changing European social-geographical space, which has in turn produced new forms of national and transnational identity.[6]

Mazierska and Rascaroli argue that European road movies date back to the travel films of the early silent era like Georges Méliès' *Voyage dans la lune/Voyage to the Moon* (1902).[7] They also note that it is more typical in European road movies, which lack the vast geographical expanses of the North America continent, to emphasise the crossing of borders, or the changing landscapes ('from deprived to wealthy areas, from the country to the city') that characters encounter.[8] This shift of critical emphasis from the national to the transnational matches the movement of Scottish road movies – from explorations of the nation and national identity to examinations of Scottishness beyond national borders (a transnational, or border crossing Scottishness in a global arena) – around the time of cultural and, eventually, political devolution from the state of Britain.

A number of British road movies pass through or conclude in Scotland, including *The 39 Steps* (1935), *I Know Where I'm Going!* (1945), *What a Whopper* (1961), *Hold Back the Night* (1999) and *The Last Great Wilderness* (2002). This tradition typically sees an English character cross the border into Scotland, and is part of a broader trend of films depicting outsiders (usually English or US characters) either stepping off the boat or plane in Scotland. This tradition includes: *Whisky Galore!* (1949), *Laxdale Hall* (1952), *The Maggie* (1954), *Brigadoon* (1954), *Trouble in the Glen* (1954),

Rockets Galore! (1957), *Local Hero* (1983), *Loch Ness* (1996), *The Rocket Post* (2004) and *Made of Honor* (2008). In many of these films, in particular the road movie, the outsider is either humiliated or rejuvenated (or both) by their experiences in Scotland. Moreover, their experiences often reflect upon the changing relationship between England, Scotland and the USA at different points in history.[9] However, in the 1990s/2000s things have changed. Coinciding with the increasingly contested issue of Scotland's cultural and political devolution from the state of Britain (following the failed referendum of 1979) and the impetus towards indigenous expression created by Forsyth in the 1980s, the Scot finally emerged as the central character in a road movie in *Soft Top, Hard Shoulder* (1993).

Going Home/Finding Home: *Soft Top, Hard Shoulder* (1993)

Soft Top, Hard Shoulder follows Gavin Bellini (Peter Capaldi), a struggling artist of Italian-Scottish descent (a Scots-Italian) who lives in London. Gavin is visited one day by his uncle Salvatore (Richard Wilson), who suggests that, should he return to Glasgow in time for his father's sixtieth birthday party, he may inherit a share of the family's wealth. The Bellini family's backstory is quickly sketched in, using a photo album, old postcards, black-and-white film footage (both real and recreated) of the 1920s, and, finally, a home movie of a Bellini family gathering, including baby Gavin, firmly locating these Italian immigrants in Scotland. Gavin's voiceover reveals that the Bellini family, arriving in Scotland from Italy in the 1920s, prospered by selling ice cream in Glasgow. This is a recurring story (with a basis in fact) in popular genre cinema in Scotland that I return to in Chapter 7. Gavin's grandfather never admitted to the family back home that he had not reached the US, instead maintaining the myth that he was in New York. In the present, with a £30 loan for petrol from his uncle, Gavin attempts the journey to Glasgow in his battered old Triumph Herald car. Along the way he picks up a hitchhiker, a young Scottish woman called Yvonne (Elaine Collins). After a series of mishaps and delays typical of the road movie (a lost wallet, breakdowns, a mistaken arrest by police etc), they arrive in Scotland. Just in time for the party, Gavin has a sudden change of heart, and rather than line his pockets seeks out Yvonne on a bridge overlooking the Clyde. There they realise their mutual affection, and Yvonne accompanies Gavin to the birthday party, where he refuses his share of the inheritance.

In *Screening Scotland* Duncan Petrie criticizes *Soft Top, Hard Shoulder* for its shortcomings as a road movie, noting that it fails 'to overcome the

basic obstacle facing any attempt at a British road movie: how to spin out
a relatively short and unexciting journey – in this case the 400 miles from
London to Glasgow – into a credible and engaging feature film'.[10] Whilst
this is true to a certain extent, there is more to this road movie. For one
thing, it illustrates the continuation of the indigenous drive behind
Scottish film production that emerged after Forsyth in the 1980s. *Soft
Top, Hard Shoulder* was written by and starred Peter Capaldi, who had
previously appeared in *Local Hero* (1983). As Philip Kemp noted in *Sight
and Sound* at the time of the film's release, the film contains several
knowing 'nods' to its predecessor, including 'a rabbit on a deserted
Scottish road, and an isolated red phone box by the seashore'.[11] Although
Soft Top, Hard Shoulder counted on the support of Gary Stone at
Shepperton (the studios provided space and facilities), Capaldi was the
creative impulse behind the original concept, and the film was made on a
tiny budget (around £200,000), over half of which was donated by a single
private investor. The cast and crew were on deferrals (receiving expenses
only, and no fee until the film began to make a profit), the lead roles were
played by a husband and wife team (Capaldi and Collins), and no pre-sale
agreements were made because 'the team were not prepared to sacrifice
control over the production or lose sight of profit from "the back end" by
entering into pre-sale agreements'.[12] *Soft Top, Hard Shoulder*, as Steve
McIntyre noted at the time of its release, is an example of low budget
genre film attracting investment owing to the likelihood of backers seeing
a return on their money.[13] It demonstrates how the road movie is the
perfect genre if your budget is limited, as the majority of filming can take
place with extremely minimal production facilities. With this genre in
particular, then, it is possible to make independent statements concerning
issues that impact upon society, such as the changing condition of national
identity in Scotland.

It is tempting to view Capaldi's story of the return of a Scot from an
unpromising life in London to claim his inheritance in Glasgow as a
comment on the state of the two nations in the early 1990s. It could be
argued that the film represents another instance of the increasing sense of
cultural devolution of the era, as Scots grew dissatisfied with the state of
the union with England. Yet caution is required as the film does not
actively encourage such a reading. *Soft Top, Hard Shoulder* is not a film
about the need for a triumphal return to Scotland (or even, a return in a
Triumph) to reclaim one's heritage. It is not a film about going home (as
the title of Mark Knopfler's musical theme from *Local Hero* suggests), but
about 'finding home', a process of journeying that may not necessarily
stop on arrival at your destination. Instead, *Soft Top, Hard Shoulder*

explores the complexity of Scottish identity by examining the hybrid identity of Scots-Italian Gavin Bellini (who, as his name suggests, is half Scot, half diasporic Italian) on his journey from London to Glasgow, neither of which is a city in which he feels at home.

The notion of a hybrid, Scots-Italian diasporic identity is foregrounded from the very beginning when the home movie of Italian immigrants in Glasgow is accompanied by Chris Rea's pop version of the classic song of diasporic longing (usually associated with the Irish diaspora in the US), 'Danny Boy'. On one level, this tune illustrates the humour of the situation, as Gavin's grandfather settles in Glasgow rather than the city more usually associated with the song because of its large Irish diaspora, New York. On another it equates the longing for home of the diaspora with Gavin's grandfather, and, by extension, Gavin, as the theme recurs throughout the film as an accompaniment to his return 'home' from England.

Gavin does not conceive of himself as Scottish with any great sense of pride. He was desperate to leave Scotland for London to pursue his dreams. Indeed, we see him, whilst a starving artist in London, sitting in the kitchen of his flat eating porridge. This meal, traditionally associated with Scotland, is here a marker of poverty rather than of a proud heritage, and is contrasted with the succulent chicken leg enjoyed by his English flatmate and landlord John (Jeremy Northam), to whom Gavin owes back rent. When explaining the origin of his name to Yvonne, Gavin proudly proclaims that Bellini comes from the 'sun drenched slopes of Italy', but when she asks him about Gavin he replies distractedly that it is 'Scottish, I suppose'. Thus, Gavin's hybrid identity is not straightforwardly Scottish (even if by the conclusion he has learned to love his Scottish side), and nor is it incidental to the film, which uses it to explore the potentially hybrid nature of Scottish identity.

As he is not content with being Scottish, Gavin's journey 'home' is one of self-discovery in which he comes to terms with being himself not by arriving but by being on the move with Yvonne (once in Glasgow he only rings the bell of the family home before disappearing to find Yvonne). Through the course of the film he discovers an identity in transit that has roots in Scotland (both he and Yvonne express joy when crossing the border into Scotland) yet is also part of a larger world. For this reason, he is finally depicted, not in the bosom of his family home raking in his inheritance, but taking a chance on a new life with Yvonne. Significantly they become a couple whilst standing on a bridge (by definition a transitory structure) over the river Clyde, where its waters leave Scotland. Historically the Clyde has seen the departure of Scots for other lands, particularly the

Figure 2.1 Hybrid Hitchhiker: Scots-Italian Gavin Bellini (Peter Capaldi) en route from England to Scotland in search of home. *Soft Top, Hard Shoulder* (1993)

USA. As I will demonstrate further, momentarily, it is in this sense that *Soft Top, Hard Shoulder* is the precursor of more recent Scottish road movies that explore Scottishness and Scottish identity in a global context.

Scotland, the Final Frontier

In the process of examining identity in transit, the film's references to the US road movie tradition are significant. In his review, Philip Kemp notes that the film is somewhat derivative, and that 'the bickering fellow travellers who finally fall for each other have been showing up regularly ever since *It Happened One Night*' (1934).[14] Yet it is not sufficient to denigrate this film for 'borrowing' from this US film tradition (and indeed, the western) as it does so to self-consciously reflect upon a hybridised and transitory sense of Scottishness, both within and beyond the confines of the nation.

Soft Top, Hard Shoulder has great fun with its references to the USA. For instance, Gavin's Triumph is called Crazy Horse (the name of a famous nineteenth-century Sioux Indian chief), and was a reward given to him by a country and western band for some graphics he provided for them. The notion of the freedom of the open road that Crazy Horse evokes is humorously illustrated by the musical flourish that accompanies the unveiling of its battered form, and the excited revving guitar chords on Gavin's departure for Scotland. Yet the promise of discovering a new frontier in the car is undermined by its dishevelled and miniature appearance, because it is regularly overtaken by lorries in the inside lane, and indeed, by the gag which immediately follows Gavin's departure as he is discovered stuck in a traffic jam before he has even left London. These references to the Old West in relation to the freedoms supposedly offered by the car are no coincidence, for, as Stephanie Watson has shown, the US road movie has its origins in the western genre, and evokes the same explorative, frontier drive as the western, which 'wraps American history beneath a myth of origin which forwards a historical fight for personal freedom and liberty set against the hardships of an expansive landscape of extremes'.[15] There are numerous other playful references to the western genre and the US road movie throughout, but what is important is the reason for this evocation of the US genre, which is revealed once Gavin and Yvonne finally arrive in Scotland.

Attempting to find a room for the night, the travellers approach a Scottish inn, only to be greeted by a tight fisted (Kailyard) Scottish innkeeper stereotype. They are granted entrance only after they have agreed payment in cash, and the room, to put it mildly, lacks all mod cons. In the morning, however, Yvonne and Gavin bond in the breakfast room. Against a background of a stuffed boar's head and two sets of mounted antlers on the wall, they dance the Slosh (a Scottish line dance then popular in and around Glasgow) to rock music playing on the radio. Here the film examines a hybrid identity that can replace such previously defining stereotypes as the Kailyard, as the confluence of traditional Scottish and US dancing – embodied by the synchronised movements of the two young protagonists – plays across the foreground of the Kailyard's more traditional decor. Once again, Scottish identity is considered a hybrid of the local and the global, as this road movie evokes the US genre (incongruously) in a Scottish setting.

Capaldi would later examine the same theme in a gangster film based in Scotland that he wrote and directed, *Strictly Sinatra* (2001), a £4 million production for DNA Films (see Chapter 7). This later film contains the same backstory of an Italian immigrant, this time a restaurant owner called Aldo (Alex McAvoy), who stops off in Glasgow on the way to New York and never resumes his journey. The protagonist, Toni Cocozza (Ian Hart) is a third-rate crooner who hangs out in Aldo's restaurant, his obsession with Sinatra mirroring Aldo's persistence in the belief that he is actually in New York. The idea that a little bit of New York exists in Glasgow propels the story, as Cocozza, after becoming embroiled in the affairs of a local mobster, enjoys a rise to fame akin to Sinatra's, only on a humorously miniature scale. At the film's conclusion, on the run from the mob, Toni completes Aldo's journey to New York, where he finds happiness being himself rather than an imitation of another. *Strictly Sinatra* can perhaps be considered a sequel, or alternative version, of *Soft Top, Hard Shoulder*. In this later film Gavin's move from England to Scotland is completed, as it were, by a movement onwards again, by Toni, from Scotland to the USA.

As was the case in the comedies explored in the previous chapter, then, in these two Capaldi films Scotland is a place immigrant flows travel to and from. The nation is not conceived of as a stable entity, or as having an essential national identity. Rather, it is a node or intersection of global flows of people and trade. Thus, whilst Gavin's refusal of his share of the inheritance at the end of *Soft Top, Hard Shoulder* could be interpreted as a rejection of his (Scots-)Italian side, or at least, an acknowledgement of his Scots(-Italian) side, the development of this story in the later film, *Strictly Sinatra*, implies that any return of the wanderer to Scotland in the early 1990s does not necessarily preclude a later decision to move on again into the wider world. After all, Gavin's grandfather's story of his arrival in Scotland in the 1920s is presumably based on historical fact – many Italian immigrants were deceived into thinking they were buying a ticket to the USA, only to find themselves dumped off the boat in Scotland[16] – but it could also have been a cover story told to his family that elided the increased difficulties immigrants faced getting into the USA after quotas were imposed in the wake of World War I.[17] In this case, *Soft Top, Hard Shoulder* is less a Scottish film reflecting cultural devolution than it is an expression of a diaspora that continues to move from rural poverty in Italy, across Europe via Scotland, to the USA, over the course of several decades.

It is possible, then, to extend an argument that both Duncan Petrie and Steve Blandford have made about *Prague* (1992) – a somewhat contentious film that used Scottish Film Fund money to film on location in Europe – to its contemporary, *Soft Top, Hard Shoulder*. *Prague* is also a film about a young Scotsman and his relationship with grandparents from elsewhere in Europe. As Petrie and Blandford point out, films like *Prague* can be understood as attempts to imagine Scottish identity in a broader context than the nation, in this instance in Europe. In 1996 Petrie argued that re-exploring Scotland's relationship with Europe, both past and present, allows a space for the articulation of an identity, itself necessarily hybrid, diverse and outward looking – eschewing equally the regressive and parochial tropes of popular representation, and the essentialist embattled posture associated with British Europhobia.[18]

For his part, in 2007 Blandford states that '*Prague* is arguably reflective of a widespread pre-devolutionary feeling that Scotland should associate itself more and more with Europe, as it were "beyond" Britain.'[19] Indeed, this would tally with the position of the Scottish National Party during the 1990s and 2000s (prior to their election as the nation's first party), who argued that Scotland should become an entirely independent nation and function in Europe alongside countries like Ireland, Norway and so on. We might argue, then, that *Soft Top, Hard Shoulder*'s emphasis on Gavin's Scots-Italian identity reflects a similar desire to that of *Prague*, to examine contemporary Scottish identity in the larger context of Europe.

Yet it is equally possible to view *Soft Top, Hard Shoulder*, whose primary concern is less with Europe and more with transatlantic connections and the immigrant's dream of the USA, as an example of what Jonathan Murray called the '"devolved" *American* cinema' that emerged in Scotland in the 1990s.[20] Murray was responding to Petrie's contention, in *Screening Scotland*, that 'new Scottish cinema' after the 1990s should be understood as a 'devolved British cinema' because of its continued reliance on British (that is, London-based) funding.[21] Murray drew this different conclusion by examining films as diverse as *Rob Roy* (1995), *Trainspotting* (1996), *Gregory's Two Girls* (1999) and *Ratcatcher* (1999), and the defining ways in which they deploy their generic and aesthetic borrowings from US cinema to depict (and in some cases, examine or interrogate) Scottishness and ways of representing Scotland. In either case, however, understanding Scottish identity, especially in recent Scottish road movies, means considering Scottishness beyond previous cinematic stereotypes of the nation, beyond (or 'after')[22] Britain, and indeed, beyond the geographical borders of Scotland. Accordingly, the remainder of this chapter explores contemporary Scottish road movies in which Scots characters are depicted exploring other countries, focusing on two films by Ken Loach.

Leaving Home/Finding Home: *Carla's Song* (1996) and *Tickets* (2005)

Ken Loach is an English director whose films have, at times, crossed the border into Scotland. His Scotland-based collaborations with screenwriter

Paul Laverty are of particular interest for this discussion: especially *Carla's Song*, *My Name is Joe* (1998), *Sweet Sixteen* (2002), *Ae Fond Kiss* (2004), and the Loach/Laverty section of *Tickets*, which follows Scottish characters even though not actually taking place in Scotland. Laverty was born in India of a Scottish father, spent time studying and practicing law in Scotland and worked as a human rights lawyer in Nicaragua in the 1980s. Laverty and Loach have collaborated on a number of projects together, including two feature films not set in Scotland, *Bread and Roses* (2000) and *The Wind that Shakes the Barley* (2006). Their mutual interest focuses on class interaction and class struggle within certain sectors of Britain (including Scotland), and especially under globalization. Alongside the use of Scotland as a location, Laverty's various travels in the Americas and elsewhere contributed not only to the Nicaraguan sections of *Carla's Song* but also to *Bread and Roses*, which explores the conditions faced by Central American immigrant workers in Los Angeles.

It might be considered a little unusual to find two of Loach's films examined as road movies. He is commonly discussed in terms of British social realism, a topic I return to in Chapter 8. However, critics are increasingly viewing Loach in a different light. For instance, in *The Cinema of Ken Loach* (2002), Jacob Leigh discusses how Loach interweaves his social realist cinema with melodrama, in order to make his 'serious' political messages more palatable to wider audiences. Leigh uses an analysis of *Carla's Song* to make this point.[23] This generic element of Loach's work should not be a surprise. After all, *Carla's Song* uses the romance between George and Carla as a catalyst for its examination of the conflict in Nicaragua. It is not a fabulous stretch, then, to note that *Carla's Song* and *Tickets* are both road movies.

Loach's films demonstrate that defining a film as 'a social realist film', 'an art film' or 'a road movie' can be limiting. In the introduction to *Crossing New Europe*, Mazierski and Rascaroli rightly note that the distinction so often drawn between a 'unified' genre of the road movie in US cinema, and a diverse body of auteur films from elsewhere that just happen to be road movies, does not adequately describe either the multiple and various types of US road movies or the potential that exists for European road movies to be examined in the same way, as a 'unified' genre of travel films.[24] Thus, acknowledging the legitimacy of studying Loach's two films as road movies (by reconciling their existence as both works of genre and auteur cinema), is of key importance to this chapter.

Carla's Song was an international coproduction with a budget of £2.8 million, funded by Channel Four Films (UK), Road Movies Dritte

Produktionen (Germany) and Tornasol Films (Spain). Laverty also received script development funds from the Glasgow Film Fund, the European Script development Fund, and the Scottish Film Production Fund.[25] *Carla's Song* is set in 1987 and begins in Glasgow, where bus driver George Lennox (Robert Carlyle) meets a Nicaraguan dancer living in exile, Carla (Oyanka Cabezas). George pursues Carla and, after saving her from a suicide attempt, travels to Nicaragua with her to confront the unresolved issues from her past. In Nicaragua George learns of the guerrilla war being waged against the Sandinista government by the US-backed Contras, and Carla's history unfolds as they travel through the countryside in search of her partner, Antonio (Richard Loza). His brutal torture by the Contras was witnessed by a wounded Carla and is the source of her post-traumatic stress. The film concludes with Carla and Antonio reunited, at which point George returns home to Scotland.

The three-part portmanteau film *Tickets* is also an international coproduction in terms of production, cast and directors. It was made on a budget of $4.3 million (€3.5 million), seventy per cent of which came from the Fandango and Medusa production companies of Italy and the remaining thirty per cent from London-based Sixteen Films and the UK Film Council.[26] The idea for the film came from Iranian director Abbas Kiarostami, and the three sections were directed by the Italian Ermanno Olmi, Kiarostami and Loach, in that order. The film is set on a border-crossing train journey from Austria to Rome.[27] The Laverty/Loach section charts the adventures of three Scottish teenagers – Celtic Football Club supporters Jamesy (Martin Compston), Frank (William Ruane) and Spaceman (Gary Maitland) – who are travelling to a European Champion's League football match again Roma. Jamesy has his ticket stolen by an unnamed Albanian boy (Klajdi Qorraj). Frank demands the ticket back, aggressively interrogating and threatening the boy and his family. However, when the boy's sister (Blerta Cahani) pleads for her family, Frank gives them his ticket, even though he knows it will likely mean imprisonment in Italy and may cost him his job in Scotland. On arrival in Rome, however, Frank and his friends escape from railway guards and the Italian police, making their getaway through the crowds with the assistance of some Roma Football Club fans waiting in the station.

Writing on another recent Scottish art-film-cum-road-movie in which Scottish characters are depicted on the road abroad, John Caughie discusses Lynne Ramsay's *Morvern Callar* (2002) in the context of Scottish devolution. For Caughie, this tale of a young woman who leaves Scotland for Spain does not so much express an attempt to establish a new Scottish identity as it does a sense of experimentation with 'a disassemblage of unity into an assemblage of disunities, not just trying on national identities but imagining not having one'.[28] Caughie makes his argument by examining how *Morvern Callar* avoids fixing an image of national identity. He discusses the casting of English actress Samantha Morton (playing an Englishwoman who happens to be in Scotland) as Morvern; the lack of agency attributed to Morvern by the narrative; the decision not to provide the viewer with a stable point of view with which to identify; and the lack of any redemptive resolution in the sections set in Spain. Caughie's reading of the film tallies with that of Mazierska and Rascaroli, who consider it to play with the different 'tourist identities' that become possible when home is 'both here and elsewhere, or perhaps in neither place'.[29] In both interpretations the intent to examine a potentially hybrid Scottish identity in the global context seen in *Soft Top, Hard Shoulder* has here exploded into an eradication of any geographically specific Scottish identity within a broader conception of European identity (or perhaps non-identity), in which characters inhabit non-nationally specific hinterlands (supermarkets, raves, holiday resorts, anonymous countryside) that are neither definitively Scotland or Spain.

Yet, significantly, it is to *Morvern Callar*'s art cinema credentials (a mode of film practice that typically aims at a very specific, but pan-European, niche market) rather than its status as a road movie that Caughie looks when making this argument. Indeed, in this he takes the same approach as any number of reviewers to compare Ramsay's film to European auteurs and other art cinema predecessors, such as Luis Buñuel, Andrei Tarkovsky and Bill Douglas;[30] Carl Dreyer;[31] Michelangelo Antonioni, Agnès Varda and Jean Cocteau.[32] For Mazierska and Rascaroli, on the other hand, when viewed in the broader context of the European travel film, *Morvern Callar* is considered a more hybrid form of European art film, road movie and horror genre. This hybridity is what enables its exploration of changing identities. Thus, Caughie's and Mazierska and Rascaroli's readings of *Morvern Callar* provide a useful backdrop against which to examine *Carla's Song* and *Tickets*, in which the exploration of Scottish identity on the road in South America and Europe is specifically tied to Loach and Laverty's examination of the global working class (or even, underclass), to which a certain section of the Scottish population belongs. If we take an approach akin to that of Mazierska and Rascaroli, then, it is possible to examine these social realist films as road movies, and in doing so to see how their border crossings facilitate a larger examination of the changing identity of certain sections of the Scottish population in an increasingly global context.

Uniting the Global Working Classes

There is already a substantial body of work on *Carla's Song* that notes the similarities between the two halves of the film, the opening in Glasgow and the second half in Nicaragua. In *Loach on Loach* (1998) the director notes,

> The fact that George is a bus driver was obviously not an accident because the kind of people he gets on his bus and enjoys meeting and jokes with are exactly the same kinds of people he meets in Nicaragua. Except for the fact that they've all got guns, the girl soldiers he is chatted up and kidded by are just like his sister and her schoolfriends. We tried to thread all those little resonances into it.[33]

Thus, although George's journey is one of discovery in which he learns at first-hand about a violent situation in a far off country, there is a sense of potential equation between the lives of certain sectors of the populations of the two countries. George's actions in the first half of the film (in Glasgow) are clearly mirrored by his undertakings in Nicaragua. When George and Carla take a bus from the capital, Managua, into the country-side, they replay in jest their initial meeting in Glasgow when she sneaked onto his bus without paying. Again, a scene in which George dances to live music with his girlfriend in a crowded pub in Glasgow is replayed when he dances with Carla amidst her family and friends in Nicaragua. Most importantly, in Glasgow, George abuses his position as bus driver to take Carla into the countryside to visit a rainy spot on a Scottish hillside, effectively stealing a bus to do so. In Nicaragua, this event recurs when George steals a bus to chase after Carla through hostile territory as she attempts to find Antonio. Finally, George's dislike of authority figures is expressed in the same way in both Glasgow and Nicaragua when he gives an inspector, in Glasgow and then later, in Nicaragua, ex-CIA agent turned aid worker Bradley (Scott Glenn), a humorous caricature he has drawn of them.

This mirroring suggests that the British working classes, figured here through the actions of George and the people of Nicaragua involved in their revolutionary struggle, have a degree of commonality in spite of their vast differences of circumstance. Although it is dangerous to reduce Loach's complex work to a soundbite, his message seems to be a variation on the old Communist slogan, 'workers of the world, unite', derived from Karl Marx and Friedrich Engels' *The Communist Manifesto* (1848).[34] The message of *Carla's Song* can perhaps be described as: 'workers of the world, become aware of your affinities.' Loach made this intention clear in an interview in *Cineaste* in 1998, stating that he was discussing 'internationalism at the rank and file level'.[35] When asked explicitly if he sees a connection between the struggles of the British working classes and 'the situation in the Third World chronicled in *Carla's Song*', he notes,

> Well, it's all part of the same context; they're all pieces in the same jigsaw. It certainly relates. We've become more and more of a global economy with one superpower putting its finger in every pie. The plight of the working classes in Britain relates to what American capital is doing, and furthermore, has a relationship with what's going on in Nicaragua. You can trace a cause and effect, even if it does seem rather random and arbitrary at times.[36]

Admittedly Laverty and Loach's perspective is not the only way to view this situation. Academics engaging with Loach's recent films, especially *Land and Freedom* and *Carla's Song*, have noted their pessimism about the ability of individual working-class characters to effect meaningful political change. For instance, John Hill, as part of a larger argument concerning representations of the working classes in British cinema of the 1990s, considers George's actions in *Carla's Song* as akin to an 'individual alienated act of defiance' that is unfavourably contrasted in the film with 'the Nicaraguan revolution of the 1980s'.[37] Hill's argument is entirely persuasive in terms of the large context that he distils and comments on in his usual expert manner. However, in relation to this particular film, a fine point of debate arises from his analysis. Hill cites as evidence for his argument George's failure to become involved in the revolution.[38] Yet, unlike David Carr (Ian Hart) in *Land and Freedom* (1995) (Hill's other example), it is debatable whether George ever intended to become involved in the revolution, or indeed, whether his desire to return home from a rather dangerous warzone necessarily signals a failure on his part, or on the part of Britain's working classes. It is equally possible to argue that it is when George becomes aware of both the brutal torture suffered by Antonio at the hands of the Contras (his back was broken, his tongue cut out and his face burned with acid), and the USA's role in funding and orchestrating the Contras' guerrilla campaign, that he takes meaningful, decisive action. At this point in the film, when he is on the verge of returning home disillusioned, he finally becomes involved, stealing a bus and driving into hostile territory to help Carla. Far from signalling the failure of George (and the British working classes), this moment suggests that George's skills as a bus driver and a self-styled anti-authoritarian friend of the common people are equally as effective in each context. As was the case with *Gregory's Two Girls*, then, Scottish identity in a global context is a matter of global/local action at an individual level. When seen in this light, *Carla's Song* may actually succeed in its attempt to illustrate an equation (or at least, coexistence), between the British working classes and those in other parts of the world.

Figure 2.2 Global Gadabout: Working-class Glaswegian George (Robert Carlyle) loses himself in Nicaragua with Carla (Oyanka Cabezas) in *Carla's Song* (1996)

However, what is important for this discussion is not whether Loach and Laverty are 'right' or 'wrong', if their films are 'pessimistic' or 'optimistic', but rather, that certain of their films – specifically those which take the form of road movies that transport Scottish characters beyond the nation – conceive of a worldwide struggle occurring under globalization to which the Scottish working classes are either drawn, or at the very least, exposed. *Carla's Song*'s road movie structure facilitates this discussion of 'internationalism at a rank and file level' not only due to the border crossing it enables but also through the didactic manner in which it transports George (and the viewer) through the political landscape of Nicaragua in 1987. The history lesson begins with a conversation between George, Carla and several Nicaraguan farmers who are travelling on a bus, in which George learns of the collectivisation and land reforms undertaken by the revolution. It continues with a visit to a hospital treating the civilian victims of the war followed by one to a school established as part of the revolution's literacy programme where adults are slowly learning to write their names. The journey enables the story to move into contested territory so that George can witness the horror of war when the Contras ambush Carla's village, targeting the school and health centre. Finally, it provides an opportunity for an associative memory trigger that facilitates Carla's confrontation with her past in a manner that goes beyond the conventional methods of flashback and dream sequence that the film also deploys. This occurs when a man has his face burned by boiling water whilst trying to fix a steaming bus engine. His cries of pain trigger Carla's memory of Antonio's torture by acid.

Thus, through its border crossing, and its didactic travels through the Nicaraguan countryside, this road movie suggests that what is happening to the working classes, whether in Scotland or elsewhere in the world, is part of a much bigger picture, even if the linkages 'seem rather random and arbitrary at times'. This is what marks *Carla's Song* and *Tickets* out as different from Loach and Laverty's other Scottish films, including *My Name is Joe* and *Sweet Sixteen*, although less so than *Ae Fond Kiss* (see Chapter 8). The crucial element in this distinction is that these films enable such an international parallel to be drawn specifically because they are road movies.

Working Classes Football Club

In *Tickets* the world has moved on, but the issues remain the same. In addition to their strong accents, the distinctive colours of their Celtic football tops identify the three lads as Scottish. In fact, their shirts demonstrate that they belong to a minority within Glaswegian society, because of Celtic Football Club's association with Catholicism and its roots in Glasgow's Irish diaspora. They also belong to the post-industrial working classes, as – like Morvern Callar before them – they are supermarket workers. On the road (or more accurately, rails) in Europe they encounter an Albanian family travelling to Rome. Initially their response to the family is extremely friendly. Seeing their hunger, Spaceman shares their stock of sandwiches with the family. As the tension increases over the stolen ticket, however, the three agonise over whether to donate their ticket to the Albanian family or shop them to the police.

This situation plays out contemporary discussions taking place throughout Europe as to the intentions and fate of immigrants into western Europe. The three lads are confronted with a dilemma: they are unable to pay the requisite fine for the stolen ticket, yet they face potential imprisonment should they not retrieve it from the Albanian family, who would then, themselves, be imprisoned for theft. Putting forward one point of view, Jamesy argues with Frank and Spaceman: 'See if it was my fuckin' family in that position I'd steal a ticket, I'd have fuckin' stole it, and so would you, so would you.' By contrast, Spaceman retorts that 'There's fuckin' hunnerds a refugees. We're only fuckin' three supermarket workers man, we cannae fuckin' look after 'em all.'

In the end, their decision hangs on whether or not they should believe the story that the unnamed Albanian girl tells them of the reasons for their visit (to meet their father in Rome) and the mistreatment they have received which has left them without enough tickets. Significantly, helping the boys with their dilemma, the young woman is a typically Loachian working-class heroine (beautiful, strong willed, earnest and emotional), her faltering tale accompanied by slow, solemn music to enhance the melodrama of her family's position. Moreover, Frank's decision to trust the girl is vindicated when, on arrival in Rome, the three witness the family reunited with their father (to the same emotive musical accompaniment). Thus the need for a collective identity amongst the working classes of different nations, 'internationalism at the level of the rank and file', is again stressed by Loach and Laverty. The final escape of the three lads from the authorities provides a note of hope for the future, once more advocating the need for trust and understanding between the workers of the world.

In *Tickets*, as in *Carla's Song*, the Scottish working classes are figured as part of a much bigger context than the nation in which they connect up with class counterparts from other nations also on their travels. In this respect it is noticeable that the three young Scottish actors were last seen together in Loach and Laverty's *Sweet Sixteen*, a bleak portrayal of post-industrial working-class life in Greenock, a town just outside Glasgow. *Sweet Sixteen* concludes with Martin Compston's character, Liam – a victim of circumstance – facing imprisonment, having failed to keep together his family or maintain his friendship with Pinball (William Ruane). In contrast to this dark and pessimistic film, in *Tickets* an alternative version of the same story is offered, with the teenagers' travels beyond the nation enabling a more upbeat conclusion. The difference is that this time the discourse surrounds Europe (and its different classes), rather than the nation or its various depressed localities.

In the first section of *Tickets*, the Albanian family appear in the background of a parable about the compartmentalising (through military force) of certain different people within and without Fortress Europe. A military captain instructs his troops to move the family out of the dining car, away from its wealthy inhabitants. Here we are shown the economic compartmentalisation – be it through the establishment of borders that mark off Fortress Europe from the rest of the world, or through the wealth differences within Fortress Europe – that segregate the classes and condemn the working-class immigrant to relative poverty. Yet, in the Loach/Laverty conclusion, *Tickets* stresses the need for the working classes to reach out and help their counterparts, those who are also (and in this case, literally) 'excluded from the banquet'. When the young Celtic fans make a selfless gesture towards solidarity with the Albanian family we see two global flows of people, both of whom (albeit for very different reasons) are absent from their nations of origin, interacting and finding common ground. This is the difference between *Tickets* and *Carla's Song*. One or the other of Carla and George is always on home soil, but in *Tickets* both sets of people interact on foreign territory, illustrating the increasingly deterritorialized flows of people that exist under global capitalism. Loach's 'internationalism at the rank and file level' thus morphs into a 'transnationalism at the rank and file level' as a global working class, or underclass, is identified to which the Scottish working classes belong.

The theme of football emphasises this global interaction, and the contradictions it raises in terms of wealth and class. In contrast to the three Celtic fans, the nameless Albanian boy wears a Manchester United football top bearing the name of David Beckham. When asked how he knows English he replies that he learned the language at school and from watching football on television. Here, in spite of its association with the global entertainment industry, the brand of Beckham that was used to make Manchester United famous (not to mention to sell merchandising bearing his, and the club's, name) worldwide is figured as part of a unifying force that can bring people together. When the three friends escape from the police at the close of the film this potential for football to unite different peoples is again demonstrated. The red shirts and flags of the Roma fans as they blockade the police are filmed in a manner that evokes propaganda films of a Communist protest, with triumphal music playing as close-ups on individual singing faces at crowd level, arms aloft, are intercut with aerial shots of the immovable wall of fans meeting the running forms of the police. Thus, football, a globalised profit-making form of entertainment is seen, perhaps appropriately given its working-class heritage, to bring together the working classes in a seeming triumph over both the authorities that control Fortress Europe, and indeed, the divisive suspicions of 'fellow travellers' that have increased in the post-Cold War era.

In conclusion, as in certain of Loach's other films, including *Ladybird Ladybird* (1994), *Land and Freedom* and *Bread and Roses*, in both *Carla's Song* and *Tickets* characters who cross borders between nations and cultures demonstrate the similarities between the lives of the working classes from two different locations. This Loachian emphasis on global working-class solidarity distances these two road movies from a host of other films that depict a travelling Scot, from the classic comedy *The Ghost Goes West* (1935) to Bill Forsyth's big budget Hollywood flop *Being Human* (1993), the comedy *The Big Tease* (1999), the Bollywood film *The Rising: Ballad of Mangal Pandey* (2005) and the thriller *The Last King of Scotland* (2006). Instead, it places them alongside art films like *Prague* and *Play Me Something* (1989), films in which Scotland is positioned as a global 'periphery' which people travel from, or return to.

Importantly, however, Scotland is not contrasted with some sort of 'centre', be it metropolitan or national. Rather, both films examine the deterritorialized, decentred, increasingly transnational border-crossing flows of people with which the Scottish working classes increasingly intersect and interact. In the context of other border-crossing road movies to emerge from a number of different contexts, such as *Cold Fever* (1995), *Calendar* (1993) and *In this World* (2002), these road movies, like the comedies of the previous chapter, are part of a more general move to use genre cinema to try to understand globalization, its deterritorialized flows of people, and the new, potentially transnational, identities it generates.

Anywhere but Aberdeen

As I have shown, in a nascent film industry like that of Scotland the road movie remains a useful genre for exploring questions of pertinence surrounding Scottishness and Scottish identity. A close contemporary, of *Soft Top, Hard Shoulder*, the experimental digital movie *Work, Rest and Play* (1994) by the Glasgow-based Autonomi explored the changing face of Britain (in terms of class, commerce and the impact of US culture) in a non-narrative mode loosely evocative of an existential road movie. More recently the low budget film *The Last Great Wilderness* (2002) (an international coproduction between Glasgow's Sigma Films and Lars von Triers' Zentropa (Denmark)) examines Scottish/English relations around the time of devolution.[39] The question remains, however, as to whether the increase in road movies that emphasise Scottishness and Scottish identity in a global context will consolidate in any one particular direction.

At the time of writing, the 'micro-budget Scottish road movie'[40] *The Inheritance* (2007) has been awarded the Raindance Award at the British Independent Film Awards. A sixty-minute film, *The Inheritance* cost a meagre £5,000 to make and was shot over only eleven days in the Highlands. The film's plot is similar to *Soft Top, Hard Shoulder* – it concerns a young man returning to Scotland from London to claim an inheritance – but is otherwise a much darker movie. In *The Inheritance*, most of the travelling takes place within Scotland. The journey to Scotland is reduced to a montage of shots of David (Tim Barrow) in a train, in a manner reminiscent of the train journey in *I Know Where I'm Going!* In *The Inheritance*, Scotland is integral to the narrative, and locations (like

Skye and the Forth Rail Bridge) are explicitly named and discussed. There is a great deal of talk between the two brothers about the relevant lifestyles they can expect to enjoy when in Scotland or England, and, accordingly, whether or not their futures belong in the land of their child-hoods. As in *The Last Great Wilderness*, then, a low-budget road movie offers the opportunity for an exploration (no matter how minimal) of the border-crossing potential of the travel film for examining Scottishness and Scottish identity.

Yet in the Scotland/Norway coproduction *Aberdeen* (2000), a £3.8 million production, something else happens entirely. *Aberdeen* is the story of a strong willed, successful young Scottish woman, Kaisa (Lena Headey), who experiences a nightmare journey while transporting her alcoholic father Tomas (Stellan Skarsgård) from Norway to Scotland. They race against time as Kaisa's mother Helen (Charlotte Rampling) is dying of cancer in hospital in Aberdeen. Although supposedly a road trip begin-ning in Norway and heading towards Aberdeen, the majority of the film was shot in Glasgow. The city's streets are recognisable to a local's eye and create an unwitting sense of alienation in any spectator who knows these locations, especially as it takes the characters so long to leave the city, even when they claim to have done so. At one point Kaisa confidently pro-claims, 'we're in Edinburgh' whilst they are still standing in Glasgow city centre.

The film further defamiliarises Glasgow into a Scottish anywhereland as many scenes take place in unidentified or anonymous locations, including airports, a caravan park, a cathedral ruin, cafes, bars, a prison, a hospital, a police station and so on. In *Aberdeen*, then, Scotland becomes a film set through which a road movie travels, enabling a story of family, parenting and responsibility to be rendered apparently universally applicable. In this particular film, with no attempt made to integrate characters and locations, the degree to which it is engaged with Scottishness is minimal, its transna-tionalism taking the form of a universalising non-national specificity. Thus the effect of increased international coproduction activity in Scotland, whilst it may in some cases further considerations of Scottish identity, may in others lead to an avoidance of anything specifically Scottish. It remains unclear at present, then, whether the Scottish road movie is more at home in Scotland or abroad, and indeed, whether road-movie Scotland is to be a specific location or a film set. As I will examine in Chapter 3, this question of how Scotland is employed, as film location or film set, and to what end, is of increasing importance generally, thanks to the impact on this small global cinema of the very international flows of trade, finance and people depicted in these road movies.

Notes

1. David Corrigan, *Cinema Without Walls* (New Brunswick, NJ: Rutgers University Press, 1991), pp. 137–60; Steven Cohan and Ina Rae Hark (eds), *The Road Movie Book* (London: Routledge, 1997); Jack Sargeant and Stephanie Watson (eds), *Lost Highways* (Washington, DC: Creation Books, 1999); David Laderman, *Driving Visions* (Austin, TX: University of Texas Press, 2002).
2. Steven Cohan and Ina Rae Hark, 'Introduction', in Cohan and Hark (eds), *The Road Movie Book*, p. 2.
3. Jack Sargeant and Stephanie Watson, 'Looking for Maps', in Sargeant and Watson (eds.), *Lost Highways*, p. 6.
4. Laderman, *Driving Visions*, p. 1.
5. Ewa Mazierska and Laura Rascaroli, *Crossing New Europe* (London: Wallflower, 2006).
6. Ibid., p. 1.
7. Ibid., p. 4.
8. Ibid., p. 5.
9. David Martin-Jones, 'Sexual Healing: Representations of the English in Post-Devolutionary Scotland', *Screen*, 26: 2 (2005), pp. 227–33.
10. Duncan Petrie, *Screening Scotland* (London: BFI, 2000), p. 158.
11. Philip Kemp, 'Soft Top, Hard Shoulder', *Sight and Sound*, 3: 1 (1993), pp. 51–2, p. 52.
12. Carolyn Hooper, 'Art of the Deal', *Screen International*, 869 (1992), pp. 7–9, p. 9.
13. Steve McIntyre, 'Inventing the Future', *Scottish Film and Visual Arts*, 5 (1993), pp. 17–19, p. 19.
14. Kemp, 'Soft Top, Hard Shoulder', p. 52.
15. Stephanie Watson, 'From Riding to Driving', in Sargeant and Watson (eds), *Lost Highways*, pp. 22–37, p. 22.
16. Joe Pieri, *The Scots-Italians* (Edinburgh: Mercat Press, 2005), p. 36.
17. Ibid., pp. 2–3.
18. Duncan Petrie, 'Peripheral Visions', in Wendy Everett (ed.), *European Identity in Cinema* (Exeter: Intellect, 1996), pp. 93–101, p. 101.
19. Steve Blandford, *Film, Drama and the Break-Up of Britain* (Bristol: Intellect Books, 2007), p. 67.
20. Jonathan Murray, 'Kids in America? Narratives of Transatlantic Influence in 1990s Scottish Cinema', *Screen*, 46: 2 (2005), pp. 217–25, p. 218.
21. Petrie, *Screening Scotland*, p. 227.
22. Tom Nairn, *After Britain* (London: Granta, 2000).
23. Jacob Leigh, *The Cinema of Ken Loach* (London: Wallflower, 2002), pp. 5–22.
24. Mazierska and Rascaroli, *Crossing New Europe*, p. 4.
25. Petrie, *Screening Scotland*, p. 174; Anon, 'New Films', *Vertigo*, 6 (1996), pp. 12–16, p. 12.

26. Melanie Rodier, 'Tickets: Strangers on a Train', *Screen International*, 1472 (2004), p. 22.
27. Ibid.
28. John Caughie, '*Morvern Callar*, Art Cinema and the "Monstrous Archive"', *Scottish Studies Review*, 8: 1 (2007), pp. 101–15, p. 103.
29. Mazierska and Rascaroli, *Crossing New Europe*, pp. 194–6.
30. Graham Rae, 'A Corpse for Christmas', *American Cinematographer*, 38: 9 (2002), pp. 74–81, p. 75.
31. Allan Hunter, 'Morvern Callar', *Screen International*, 1360 (2002), p. 30.
32. Chris Darke, 'Has Anyone Seen This Girl?', *Vertigo*, 2: 4 (2003), pp. 16–17.
33. Graham Fuller, ed. *Loach on Loach* (London: Faber & Faber, 1998), p. 109.
34. The original source is often translated as, 'Working Men of all Countries Unite!'. See Karl Marx and Friedrich Engels, trans. A. J. P. Taylor, *The Communist Manifesto* (London: Penguin, [1848] 1967), p. 121.
35. Susan Ryan and Richard Porton, 'The Politics of Everyday Life', *Cineaste*, 24: 1 (1998), pp. 22–7, p. 27.
36. Ibid.
37. John Hill, 'Failure and Utopianism', in Robert Murphy (ed.), *British Cinema of the 90s* (London: BFI, 2000), pp. 178–90, p. 179.
38. Ibid.
39. David Martin-Jones, 'Sexual Healing', *Screen*, 26: 2 (2005), pp. 227–33.
40. Scottish Screen, 'Scottish Wins at the British Independent Film Awards 2007', *eroughcuts*, 140 (November 2007), pp. 2–3, p. 3; and *The Inheritance* website: http://www.theinheritancethemovie.com/ (07/12/07).

CHAPTER 3

Bollywood: Non-Resident Indian–
Scotland

This chapter analyses representations of Scotland's Non-Resident Indian (NRI) communities in popular Indian, or 'Bollywood' films, and *Nina's Heavenly Delights* (2006), a Scottish film influenced by Bollywood.[1] I contrast how Scotland is depicted in fantastical song and dance sequences in the international Indian hits *Kuch Kuch Hota Hai* (1998) and *Kandukondain Kandukondain* (2000) with its more narratively integrated representation in *Pyaar Ishq aur Mohabbat* (2001). The latter is the first Bollywood film set entirely in Scotland, although its vision of NRI life articulates an ideological view of the diaspora propounded by the Indian filmmaking centre of Mumbai. Its ideological position is typically Indian, rather than Indian-Scottish or Scottish-Indian, as it participates in Bollywood's recent attempts to construct cinematically a consensual view of the global Indian middle class.

The chapter then explores *Nina's Heavenly Delights* (2006), a recent Scottish film influenced by Bollywood cinema, but also closely linked to such British predecessors as *Bhaji on the Beach* (1993), *East is East* (1999), *Bend it Like Beckham* (2002) and *Bride and Prejudice* (2004). *Nina's Heavenly Delights* fuses aspects of Bollywood into its otherwise recognisably British cinematic aesthetic to reflect the narrative's examination of blended or hybrid identities within Scotland's NRI community (whether queer or straight) be they inter-racial or inter-national.

Why Scotland?

The study of Bollywood cinema is now widespread, with countless books on the subject emerging in the 1990s and 2000s. It is therefore surprising that, amongst the academic coverage of the upsurge in film production in Scotland during this period, nothing exists on the influx of Bollywood filmmakers in the 1990s. In the 2000s the trade journal *Screen International* presected several pieces on the growth of filmmaking in Scotland, particularly in feature articles by Allan Hunter.[2] However, whilst these are significant for the attention they focus on Scottish film production, the many

Bollywood films shot in Scotland do not warrant much discussion in comparison. Even so, international hits like *Dilwale Dulhania Le Jayenge* (1995) (hereafter *DDLJ*) and *Kuch Kuch Hota Hai* (hereafter *KKHH*) contain scenes shot in Scotland and have brought considerable revenue into the country, as has *Pyaar Ishq aur Mohabbat*.

Unlike the trade press, the popular press is very keen to discuss the explosion of Bollywood production in Scotland. The consensus of opinion is that the major benefit it brings to Scotland is financial, rather than cultural. Juliette Garside's pronouncement, alluding to the Hydra Report, in the *Sunday Herald* (2002) is typical in this respect:

> There is no doubting the power of film to boost tourism. A 1997 report for the government agency VisitScotland claimed that the mist and heather blockbusters *Braveheart* and *Rob Roy* were responsible for £15 million of tourism income. Between 1995 and 1997, visits from Americans, Europeans and Scots to the Wallace monument shot up from 66,000 to 197,000. Bollywood films could soon be pulling in tourists from the subcontinent too. Of the 22 Indian films made in the UK in the 1990s, 12 were shot on location in Scotland. By the end of 2001, a further 12 had been made here. Already 9000 people from India visit Scotland each year.[3]

The impact of the so-called '*Braveheart* effect' was not lost on the British Tourist Authority (BTA) or the Scottish Executive, with the 2002 *Review of Scottish Screen* by the Scottish Executive listing promoting 'Scotland as a location for film making',[4] second only to promoting the growth of the indigenous sector. Accordingly, Scottish Screen Locations, an arm of Scottish Screen, is charged with facilitating the use of Scotland as a location by international productions. The BTA has been extremely proactive in promoting Scotland as a film location. It knows that Scotland's scenic landscapes will draw tourists from the huge global market for Bollywood films. In 2000 the British Film Commission and the BTA sent representatives to India in the wake of successful films like *KKHH* and *Mohabbatein* (2000), to court interested Indian producers.[5] The BTA also produced a Bollywood map to guide tourists around the British locations in which their favourite films were shot,[6] which joined a number of websites offering similar maps.[7] In 2002 the *Guardian* reported that 'around 55,000 Bollywood location maps of Britain have been distributed in India and the Middle East'.[8] Finally, the Scottish Executive's 'Friends of Scotland' website – whilst ostensibly discussing cultural exchange – promotes the revenue flowing into Scotland from the Indian subcontinent, including film productions.[9] Analysing these films, then, enhances our understanding of the current state of film production in Scotland and India, and the transnational flows of capital that have shaped Bollywood films shot in Scotland.

There are three major ways in which Bollywood films bring money into Scotland. Firstly, at the site of production there is location spend. In 2000, location spend in Scotland rose from around £14m (where it had stayed since 1997) to £20m. According to the Scottish Executive this rise was 'partly explained by the increase in the number of large budget features shot in Scotland by Indian and US production companies'.[10] In 2003, the *Audit of the Screen Industries in Scotland* noted that the producers of *KKHH* alone 'spent an estimated £85,000 in Scotland'.[11] To facilitate the inflow of this revenue the UK Film Council published an 'Indian Producer's Guide to Filming in the UK' on its website in the early 2000s.

The second major source of revenue Bollywood productions bring is from the box office. Although the only figures available are for Britain, they are still informative. Of the huge market that Bollywood films reach Britain is one of the largest with at least 1.3 million potential viewers.[12] In 2005, UK cinemas saw over 2.5million people attend Hindi-language films, which 'accounted for about 16% of all UK releases'.[13] Since the global success of films like *DDLJ* and *KKHH* the market for films aimed at diasporic audiences has been recognised by the Indian film industry. In 1998 *KKHH* was placed in the UK top ten charts (and the US/Canada top twenty), and grossed over $1 million at the British box office alone.[14] In 2001 *Kabhi Khushi Kabhie Gham* (hereafter *K3G*) was number three in the UK top ten and grossed over £2 million.[15] Films like *K3G*, *DDLJ* and *KKHH* showed that box office revenue could be gained by enabling Bollywood films to shoot scenes in locations familiar to diasporic audiences. Thus *KKHH*'s famous theme song includes scenes shot in Eilean Donan Castle in Scotland. This landmark is easily recognisable internationally due to its prominence in any number of world famous films (many of them from Hollywood), including, in recent decades, everything from *Highlander* (1986) to *Elizabeth: The Golden Age* (2007). Moreover, to British audiences (indigenous and diasporic alike) it would have been equally well known even if they had never visited Scotland because for several years it featured on a between programmes 'Ident' on BBC television showing the BBC hot air balloon icon hovering over the castle on the loch.

The third revenue source from these productions is tourism. The 2003 Scottish Executive *Audit of the Screen Industries in Scotland* states that 'the encouragement of tourism' is a key component in supporting filmmaking in Scottish locations, even if the films made do not necessarily provide box office revenue. They argue that it is worth supporting indigenous productions that do not succeed at the box office, but which reach the American market as video rentals.[16] The same principal obviously applies to Bollywood films shot in Scotland. These films reach a diasporic audience of 11 million outside India,[17] not to mention the millions more in the Indian subcontinent and non-Indian audiences across Asia, Africa, the Middle East and Europe. Director Dev Anand (who filmed in Dundee in 1998) confidently asserts a directly causal link between Bollywood films and tourism: 'I do know that people liked what they saw of Scotland in *Main Solah Baras Ki*, and went to that country.'[18] If more concrete figures are required, a *Guardian* article of 2002 stated that there were 'more than 200,000 Indian tourists spending £140m a year in Britain, and the influx [is] growing by 13% a year'.[19]

Thus, despite the shift of Bollywood productions away from Scotland towards cheaper location in Eastern Europe since the mid-2000s, location shooting of Bollywood productions is sought by the Scottish Executive and BTA because it brings production units, followed by box office revenue, and finally tourists into Scotland.[20] Accordingly, the UK has signed seven different deals with India, each one offering tax breaks in the hope of enticing Bollywood productions into Britain, resulting in over 400 Indian productions being shot, to some degree or other, in the UK.[21] For this reason, as I will show using *KKHH* and *Kandukondain Kandukondain*, Scotland is represented in many Bollywood films as a tourist destination.

Why India?

The increased location shooting of Bollywood films in Scotland, Switzerland, Australia, New Zealand, Holland, Singapore and New York is not simply due to the desires of these countries for the revenue these films bring. This phenomenon is also a product of conditions in India which have also impacted upon the Indian film industry. A need for new locations emerged in 1989 when an increase in violent disturbances in the politically disputed region of Kashmir rendered it unsafe for filming. As Switzerland was becoming an over-used location in Bollywood films, the net was cast further out. Shooting in Scotland seemed extremely beneficial for Indian productions, the scenery being an obvious audience draw, especially with countries like Scotland bending over backwards to facilitate shooting.

More significant, however, is the change in India's economic standing since the 1990s. This is primarily a result of political and economic changes in India, especially of free market reforms leading to, Ravinder Kaur notes, 'economic liberalisation'.[22] It is in this context that we can understand Scotland's attempts to appeal to the Indian tourist. The removal of 'numerous restrictions on imports and foreign exchange' designed to encourage 'international traffic',[23] have allowed conditions to emerge that favour foreign travel for Indian citizens. Kaur clarifies this situation further: 'A small measure like raising the level of foreign exchange issued for travel abroad from US$500 to US$2000 p.a. served as an incentive for many Indians to travel.'[24] Indeed, Vijay Mishra argues that this is part of a larger movement since the 1970s, during which time a 'travel culture'[25] has developed, facilitating movement between India and its diasporas. Thus, those same conditions that have led to increased 'international traffic' between India and its diasporas have also influenced the growth of overseas location shooting.

Along with encouraging greater international trade, this situation has facilitated the growth of the Indian middle classes. As Rachel Dwyer has shown, the middle classes are increasingly the dominant demographic in India, both in 'their size, which is said to be as great as 100 million or 10 per cent of the total population, but is more probably 4 million households or 25 million people'[26] and their ability to generate 'much of India's popular culture'.[27] For Ravinder Kaur, this demographic has recently developed 'consumption patterns typical of their counterparts in developed countries', with economic liberalisation facilitating the emergence of a 'globalised Indian middle class'.[28] For this reason many Bollywood films of the 1990s are aspirational in tone, *K3G*, for example, celebrating the wealth that market capitalism can create and equating the economic success of NRIs with that of India's middle classes. This acknowledges the dual markets (home and abroad) at which many recent Bollywood films aim. Such films, however, also stress that despite their financial success, India's diasporas have held onto 'traditional' values. For Dwyer these values are typically depicted through 'a form of the feudal family romance in a new, stylish, yet unmistakably Hindu patriarchal structure'.[29] Raminder Kaur, although critical of Indian cinema's tendency to essentialise the diaspora,[30] concurs with Dwyer: 'Whilst the ornamental gloss of consumption is craved, "traditional" values based on family honour and female chastity appear to remain intact.'[31] Equating the diaspora with the homeland in this dual way (both financially and culturally) creates an image of one unified Indian people, one global Indian middle class, in spite of its geographical separation.

The economic motivation for this is clear. The global Indian middle class is a huge market. As Andrew Wills notes, 'the audience outside India can now account for around 65 percent of a film's total earnings'[32] and, although this is not all a diasporic audience, its 11 million strong diasporic element is still a considerable market. To attract this diverse audience, one successful method is a strategic deployment of touristic views of countries where NRI populations exist. Focusing on those aspects of Scotland familiar to both the NRI diaspora and the overseas visitor (including those visiting friends and relatives in Scottish NRI communities), furthers the notion of middle-class Indians – at home and abroad – as one people.

Fantasy versus Tourism – Fantasy Tourism

I have so far shown how location shooting in Scotland is beneficial from both a Scottish and an Indian perspective. I will now demonstrate how the flows of international trade and tourism between the two countries have affected the aesthetics of two popular Indian films with scenes shot in Scotland, *KKHH* and *Kandukondain Kandukondain*.

The prevailing consensus is that when Bollywood films incorporate foreign locations into their song and dance routines they are used as unreal backdrops, fantasylands to which characters are temporarily transported for the duration of the song. This stance is entirely understandable, as these locations often suddenly appear in a narrative which takes place in India. Proponents of this view include Tejaswini Ganti, who argues that 'most foreign locations have no relevance to the plot and function as pure spectacle',[33] and Andrew Wills, who notes that in *KKHH* 'the use of Scottish locations . . . help[s] create a fantastic, unworldly setting that does not correspond to any "real" experience of any audience'.[34] Mishra also argues that North American and European landscapes are presented in *KKHH* 'with no geographical specificity as the globe simply becomes an extension of India'.[35] However, although fantasy recreations of Scotland, these recurring images of certain recognisable Scottish locations do indeed provide 'geographical specificity', and correspond precisely to the 'real' experience of the tourist.

In both *KKHH* and *Kandukondain Kandukondain* the establishing shot that begins each of the theme songs is of Eilean Donan Castle, the distinctive castle on the loch. Along with its use in *Highlander* and its appearance as a BBC 'Ident', this location is so often associated with Scotland that in the run up to the General Election in April 2005, the Scottish National Party began their party political broadcast with an establishing shot of Eilean Donan Castle, accompanied by a Sean Connery voiceover, thereby conjoining Scotland's two more internationally recognisable aspects. An instantly recognisable establishing shot, Eilean Donan has become to Scotland what Monument Valley was to the USA in John Ford westerns, its medieval appearance and surrounding lochs and mountains identifying it precisely with the Tartan tradition of mists and heather noted by the Hydra Report, in 1997.

The use of Eilean Donan Castle in these films ensures that, although these songs take place in a fantasyland otherwise disconnected from their narratives, this location is definitely recognisable as Scotland. The appearance of Eilean Donan Castle establishes 'geographical specificity', and it does so for a particular reason. Although these films do not directly address the NRI's everyday experience of life in Scotland, they appeal to the 'real' experience of audiences who have visited (or who might in future visit) these sites, including weekend-break or daytripping British NRIs and visiting Indian tourists. For this reason, Scotland is used as a film set, but in a manner that has distinctive resonances for different audiences.

In *KKHH*, the theme song is established as a fantasy, as the two main characters are transported to Eilean Donan Castle after wishing on a star. As they sing and dance around the medieval castle their everyday contemporary brand name clothes render them as tourists, suggesting that in the new economic context of the 1990s their fantasy of visiting Scotland is readily attainable. This effect is compounded as they are effortlessly transported to a number of other tourist destinations (including ruins, mountain landscapes and stereotypical white cottages), filmed at Glen Coe, Inchmahome Priory and Tantallon Castle. Moreover, the presence of stars Shah Rukh Khan and Kajol, clean cut representatives of the new global Indian middle class, in these locations reaffirms their attainability.

In *Kandukondain Kandukondain* a similar outcome is achieved in a slightly different manner. Again Scotland appears as a fantasy, but this time directly after a proposal of marriage. It is as though it were a honeymoon destination to which the couple travel in their imagination. Once again, the fantasy is shown to be achievable, and once again the establishing location is Eilean Donan Castle. Here Meenakshi (Aishwarya Rai) is fortressed, as her fiancé Srikanth (Abbas) attempts to breach her walls. The 'Indianized' period costumes they wear, and the presence of shaggy, 'medieval' costumed Western guards (complete with helmets and axes) suggests that Meenakshi and Srikanth are exploring Scotland's heritage as tourists. They play roles associated with the medieval castle (princess and suitor), as though trying them on, and – perhaps fittingly for an Indian adaptation of Jane Austin's *Sense and Sensibility* – they cast the locals in supporting roles in their fantasy.

Using Scotland as a film set in this specific manner, in line with the economic agendas of both Scotland and India, these films locate their theme songs in Scotland through the strategic deployment of recognisable tourist locales. This promotes the locations in question, underscores the international nature of the production and emphasises the ability of Indian capital (here, film production) to interact with other fully modernised parts of the globe. It also appeals to a global audience (specifically the Indian middle classes in India and its international diasporas) which now have the economic capability to travel to Scotland. Thus, although there are many examples that do fit the prevailing consensus (for instance, the use of Edinburgh's distinctive Scott Monument and the Princes Street Gardens as part of a montage sequence that supposedly introduces London in *Yeh Hai Jalwa* (2002)), these particular scenes shot on location in Scotland are used to very specific (fantasy/tourist) ends.

Pyaar Ishq aur Mohabbat (2001)

Despite this particular depiction of Scotland, the existence of Scotland's NRI community is mostly ignored by *KKHH* and *Kandukondain Kandukondain*. Although nowadays it is not unusual for a Bollywood film to transport characters to Europe as part of the narrative, it is still unusual for a Bollywood film to be set in Scotland. As the examples above show, the country's tourist vistas are usually most attractive for Indian filmmakers, not its NRI community.

Pyaar Ishq aur Mohabbat stands out in its use of Scotland as a setting for its narrative and because it was shot entirely outside India – mostly in Scotland but with a sizeable portion in Switzerland and one or two scenes in New Zealand. The main difference is that although it represents Scotland as a tourist destination, it also uses its locations to explore the relationship between the South Asian diaspora's financial success, and their maintenance of middle-class Indian values in a foreign environment. Whilst the film's focus on an extremely wealthy demographic does not altogether reflect the 'real' experience of all diasporic life in Scotland, it still demonstrates a commitment to examining the lives of Scotland's NRIs, a fact that was reflected in the choice of Govan, Glasgow, for its world premiere.[36]

Pyaar Ishq aur Mohabbat follows Isha Nair (Kirti Reddy), a young, middle-class student who gains a scholarship from an Indian college to study medicine at the University of Glasgow. Her stated aim it to return to India afterwards and use her knowledge to benefit the nation. The film revolves around her experiences of life in Scotland (and on a short holiday in Switzerland) and the machinations of the three middle-class men who amorously pursue her: Yash (Sunil Shetty), Taj (Aftab Shivdasani) and Gaurav (Arjun Rampal).

The most useful sequence to analyse for this discussion is Isha's immediate arrival in Scotland. As her plane touches down an establishing shot

shows Glasgow's Prestwick International Airport with its sign prominently on display. As Prestwick is a small, fairly unattractive, airport this
seems a little strange. Presumably any airport could have been used, with
a subtitle informing the viewer of the location. However, *Pyaar Ishq aur
Mohabbat* strives for realism of location (this airport would have been
experienced by many of Scotland's NRI community) even as it paradoxically has Isha picked up by Taj (the son of the wealthy banker, Lord
Bhardwaj) in a shiny red Ferrari! Taj ferries Isha to his father's 8,000 acre
country estate, actually the impressive Blairquhan Castle in Ayrshire.
There she is greeted by Lord Bhardwaj, who is shooting clay pigeons on
his ample lawn. Bhardwaj is resplendent in a red tartan suit jacket. Behind
him is a rugged highland clansman on a white horse, who appears to have
wandered off the set of *Braveheart* (1995). Flanking Bhardwaj are his wife,
and various dog and bird handlers (the latter complete with hawk). Their
Scottish servants are lined up to one side, with several bagpipers in full
tartan regalia on the other. Bagpipe music on the soundtrack accompanies
this tableau, soon joined by upbeat drumming, to give it an 'Indianized'
feel. After a brief introduction, during which Lord Bhardwaj proclaims
the benefits of Indians only marrying other Indians, Isha and her hosts
move into Bhardwaj Hall. Lord Bhardwaj states, 'I came here with only
five pounds in my pocket. Fifty rupees in those times. Mahesh [Isha's
father] says I am an Englishman. But you see, after all these years I haven't
forgotten my India.'

This self-consciously humorous postcolonial scene is interesting for a
number of reasons. It can be seen as an exaggerated expression of the
wealth that several generations of Indian immigrants have attained in
Britain. As Lord Bhardwaj says, he arrived with only fifty rupees (£5), but
now he is lord of the manor. Moreover, the stereotypical tartan regalia of
Lord Bhardwaj, the bagpipers, and the kilted Highlander also express the
diaspora's appropriation of the symbols of Britain's previous imperial
power. Not only indicative of the myth of Tartanry, this tartan regalia is
also closely associated with the British military regiments that previously
occupied India. Thus there has been a postcolonial role reversal, the colonial servants becoming the NRI masters. However, as the mixing of the
bagpipes with Indian drumming illustrates, although the NRI have appropriated the symbols of their new home nation they have retained their own
identity along with it.

This sequence can also be interpreted as the postcolonial reversal that
has recently surrounded Bollywood film production, which sees countries
like Scotland opening their sites of heritage to Indian filmmakers. Now
they are the wealthy lords who are courted by the governments of these

Western countries. Thus in this scene the film displays, albeit in an overtly spectacular fashion, the experiences of both NRIs and Indian filmmakers in Scotland.

Love and Money

The film is at pains to point out that financial success in Europe has not diminished the characters' adherence to the values of India's global middle class. Despite the wealth of the NRI characters in *Pyaar Ishq aur Mohabbat*, 'love' is considered more valuable than money, although here love is a term that really describes filial obedience to a strong but benevolent patriarchal lord who upholds family honour with his shotgun as effectively in a Scottish castle as he would in an Indian village. Notwithstanding Bhardwaj's imperial notion of British identity (let alone Scottish identity) as 'English', the important point is his remembrance of 'Indian' values, that is the values of the global Indian middle class.

This is made clear on many occasions in the film. For instance, consider Isha's first visit to the University of Glasgow, which immediately follows her arrival at Bhardwaj Hall. Isha is introduced to Dr Alam (also an NRI) on the steps of the university's distinctive Gilby-Scott building (its oldest building, we are informed by Taj). This takes place in front of a sign for the university chapel, ensuring that the several centuries of wealth symbolised by the university is tied to a religious heritage. The location emphasises that although this is a situation in which wealth can be created it is also a spiritual place and this wealth is not necessarily a corrupting influence on the Indian diaspora.

Scotland is also depicted as a location in which the NRI community lives entirely segregated from the local population. Isha interacts with her host family, Dr Alam and her NRI friends, the 'mini India' group. When Caucasian Scots are seen in *Pyaar Ishq aur Mohabbat* they are in the background (servants, students, backpackers, extras in a film shoot) and rarely have a speaking part. Indeed, the streets and public transport systems of Scotland are eerily empty, as though the NRI characters live a life that bypasses the other residents of Scotland. Any suggestion that NRI identity has been hybridised, or 'contaminated', by interaction with the Scottish population is absent. In fact, this may be an accurate reflection of life for some in Scotland's NRI communities, but this situation is used to show how the NRI remain part of the global Indian middle class, remain 'Indian' despite living in Scotland. The ease with which the characters fly to and from India and other parts of Europe from Glasgow further emphasises their transnational standing within the Indian global middle class, as does Isha's status as a student of medicine ambitious to return to India once qualified. She is one of India's 'well-qualified doctors . . . who have an increased interactivity with their homeland'[37] who have increased in number with economic liberalisation.

Additionally, take Gaurav's struggle with ill-gotten wealth. Gaurav's song, 'Main Bewafa, Main Bekadar', describes the turmoil he feels over accepting 100 million rupees for breaking Isha's heart. It begins as he admits to Taj that he has sold his soul for money. The backdrop to the song blends recognisable tourist locations (Edinburgh Castle, the Scott Monument, Calton Hill) with locations rarely seen in a Bollywood film, including the streets of Glasgow City's Centre (the sign for the Buchanan Street Metro Station appears in the foreground) and a range of railway stations and bus and train interiors. Unattractive high-rise flats even appear in the background as Guarav drives his scooter through an under-pass. This peculiar blending of locations stresses the beauty of the typical tourist locations but also something of the everyday life of the NRI, who may well encounter Glasgow's more uninspiring vistas whilst on its public transport systems. Thus, whilst the film retains the appeal to the tourist's gaze of *KKHH* and *Kandukondain Kandukondain*, *Pyaar Ishq aur Mohabbat* also appeals to an NRI audience by acknowledging their everyday experience of life in a country like Scotland. The locations used question whether a diasporic life is tantamount to the selling of one's soul for money, even if the film ultimately resolves that this is not the case, as long as filial duty is upheld.

The song ends with Guarav (who eventually renounces his wealth for love) standing in the centre of a football goal in the unremarkable Broadwood Stadium in Cumbernauld. Guarav is shot at an off-kilter angle within the frame and net of the football goal, illustrating how he has been trapped by the foreign culture of Scotland, here suggested through the national game. To recent arrival Guarav, the land of opportunity has turned into a prison of loneliness (a fact emphasised by his solitude on empty buses and trains), as he has temporarily forgotten his Indian values in the pursuit of wealth. Guarav is completely out of place in this culture and, without his Indian heritage, all alone. In general, then, NRI audiences are directly addressed by the film, which stresses their need to remain within the realm of the Indian global middle class in spite of their geographical separation from the motherland. Thus Dwyer's argument that *DDLJ* reinforces 'the belief that Indianness is not so much a question of citizenship as of sharing family values'[38] can also be applied here.

Even though *Pyaar Ishq aur Mohabbat* was shot entirely on location in diasporic countries, the message it promotes still speaks clearly from the centre as the Bollywood film industry attempts to construct 'the identities of those who do not necessarily see India as the centre of their psycho-political imaginaries'.[39] In *Pyaar Ishq aur Mohabbat* NRIs are Indian, not British-Indian or Scottish-Indian. The film uses Scottish locations to illustrate that although the Indian diaspora is economically capable of crossing international borders a subsequent mingling of cultures is not advised. Its appeal to the diasporic market is evident, but this is part of a larger appeal to the global audience of the Indian middle class, whose values it upholds by raising 'love' (a shorthand for these values) over money.

Bollywood films shot in Scotland illuminate a great deal about the current state of filmmaking in Scotland and India. Both *KKHH* and *Kandukondain Kandukondain* illustrate how Scotland's tourist destinations are being put up for sale, whilst *Pyaar Ishq aur Mohabbat* demonstrates how Bollywood takes advantage of international location shooting to target the lucrative diaspora whilst retaining its appeal to the Indian market. The question I will address in the final part of this chapter is exactly how the Scottish NRI is depicted differently in the only recent Scottish film to tackle the subject, *Nina's Heavenly Delights*.

Nina's Heavenly Delights (2006)

Nina's Heavenly Delights was the first feature film directed by Pratibha Parmar, who is most well known for her documentaries, including *Warrior Marks* (1993) about female genital mutilation in Africa. *Nina's Heavenly Delights*, by contrast, is more light-hearted fare. A Kali Films production made for £1.2m, the film follows Nina Shah (Shelley Conn), a young Scottish woman of Indian parents who left her home in Glasgow on the day of her arranged marriage to Sanjay (Raji James), the son of her parents' friend Raj (Art Malik). Nina returns from her chosen exile in London to attend her father's funeral. She discovers that her father had lost half of the family restaurant, the New Taj, on a bet. Determined to return the New Taj to its former glory she takes her father's place in the Best of the West curry competition. With the help of her new business partner and lesbian lover, Lisa (Laura Fraser), she wins the televised competition. In the course of events her brother Kary (Atta Yaqub) reveals his secret marriage to Caucasian Scot, Janice (Kathleen McDermott), her younger sister Priya (Zoe Henretty) declares her love of traditional Scottish dancing and her mother, Suman (Veena Sood), lifts the veil on her longstanding chaste love for Raj.

A straightforward compare and contrast of *Nina's Heavenly Delights* and *Pyaar Ishq aur Mohabbat* would be entirely unfair to both films. They are products of different film industries with different target audiences and cannot be compared like for like. Whilst *Pyaar Ishq aur Mohabbat* belongs to the Bollywood film industry, and primarily targets middle-class Indian audiences (both in India and worldwide), *Nina's Heavenly Delights* is a British film whose predecessors and contemporaries include *My Beautiful Laundrette*, *Bhaji on the Beach*, *East is East*, *Bend it Like Beckham* and *Bride and Prejudice*. Although it references Bollywood cinema, *Nina's Heavenly Delights'* aesthetic is actually closer to British cinema's brand of narrative realism in a popular genre format. Its song and dance sequences are dieget- ically integrated, rather than the self-conscious spectacles of a Bollywood film, its narrative is linear rather than episodic and aims towards romantic resolution in a very mainstream manner. This, despite the fact that it is that rarest of breeds, a homosexual love story with a happy ending.

That said, there are some similarities in their depiction of Scotland's NRI. Like *Pyaar Ishq aur Mohabbat*, *Nina's Heavenly Delights* also begins with the arrival of its protagonist in Scotland. This time, however, Nina arrives from London, not India, and is picked up from Glasgow International Airport rather than Prestwick. Indeed, she is met by her out, gay, cross-dressing male friend Bobbi (Ronny Jhutti) rather than a poten- tial male partner, as Isha was in *Pyaar Ishq aur Mohabbat*. Yet this touch- ing down in Scotland serves the same purposes. As Bobbi and Nina leave the airport, the sign declaring 'BAA Glasgow International Airport' is prominently visible on the building. The camera even tilts upwards to locate the sign as Bobbi's van leaves the shot. Although arguably akin to previous British films about travellers from England arriving in Scotland (as discussed in Chapter 2), this purposeful establishing of location again illustrates something of the reality of NRI arrival in Scotland and, like *Pyaar Ishq aur Mohabbat*, stresses the internationally connected nature of the diaspora. This is emphasised later in the film by the arrival of the Best of the West curry competition's host, Murli (Kulvinder Ghir), from India, along with the crew (from Mogul Productions Mumbai) of the fictional Bollywood film shooting *Love in a Wet Climate* on location. Once again, the diaspora and the homeland are shown to be easily connected.

The aspirational tone of *Pyaar Ishq aur Mohabbat* also recurs in *Nina's Heavenly Delights*. Although the fantastical stately home of Bhardwaj Hall is replaced by the more likely (if stereotypical) world of family run curry houses and cash-and-carry's, the diaspora is still figured in terms of its ability to succeed. This is most apparent in the Best of the West curry competition on which the fate of the New Taj rests. The major difference is that financial success is obtained through partnership with an indigenous Scot, Nina's business partner and lover, Lisa. Here another difference with *Pyaar Ishq aur Mohabbat* becomes apparent. Again *Nina's Heavenly Delights* focuses on an NRI community that almost exists in isolation from the rest of Glasgow's citizens. This effect is created through the repeated use of aerial shots of the city over which 'Korma Radio' addresses Glasgow's NRI population (discussing amongst other things, delayed flights from Mumbai). There are also any number of shots of empty city streets through which drives Bobbi's colourfully decorated van (painted by Pakistani master truck artist Ghulam Sarwar whilst on a visit to Scotland). Finally, the characters are depicted in various practically deserted locations (city streets, kitchens, the cash-and-carry, the distinctive footbridge in Glasgow Green etc), all of which creates a sense of an NRI life lived in isolation, just as in *Pyaar Ishq aur Mohabbat*. However, in *Nina's Heavenly Delights* there are many more non-Indian characters, including such recognisable Scottish faces as the comedienne Elaine C. Smith as Auntie Mamie and Kathleen McDermott from *Morvern Callar* (2002) as Janice. NRI characters are thus more fully integrated into Glaswegian society (Nina and Lisa are in love, Kary and Janice are married, Suman and Auntie Mamie are colleagues, Bobbi's boyfriend is a Caucasian Scottish plumber etc) than the 'mini-India' group of *Pyaar Ishq aur Mohabbat*. In this way *Nina's Heavenly Delights* constructs a fantasy Glasgow in which all cross- or intercultural desires are not only permitted, but also provide the recipe for financial success.

This recipe for success is most clearly evident in the final Bollywood-styled dance sequence, which takes place after the narrative has resolved and just before the credits. The sequence contains the mixture of traditional Tartanry (Priya and her friends' Scottish dance outfits) alongside traditional Indian dress that we see in *Pyaar Ishq aur Mohabbat's* Bhardwaj Hall scene. However, this time it is not a case of postcolonial role reversal but a display of integration as NRI characters 'cross dress' (as it were) in Tartanry, just as Scots do in saris. Although this sequence ends with a metacinematic nod to art cinema (Parmar cites European art cinema as a major inspiration)[40] as the dance in front of traditional Highland scenery is revealed to be taking place in a studio set in front of a green screen, it nonetheless contains the key to unlocking *Nina's Heavenly Delights'* play with Bollywood and British cinema, and with British and NRI identities, both of which are blended together through their global/local mingling in Glasgow.

Masala Identities

Nina's Heavenly Delights' advertising and promotional materials make a point of its indebtedness to Bollywood cinema. Verve Pictures' website refers to the film as: 'Bollywood spectacle . . . blended with romance and laughter',[41] and the production notes, as 'Scottish humour meets Bollywood spectacle'.[42] Yet the film's aesthetic is not that of Bollywood. Rather, the film is filled with many of the trappings often associated with Bollywood in the West. As Rajinder Kumar Dudrah notes in *Bollywood* (2006), in the early noughties 'the camp kitsch and fun aspects of Bollywood'[43] were appropriated, commodified and often trivialised by mainstream British popular culture, which deployed these signifiers of Bollywood in some-what simplistic ways. Whilst it would be harsh to lump *Nina's Heavenly Delights* in with this bandwagon movement, there is an element of truth in viewing the film in this way. However, with more positive ramifications for *Nina's Heavenly Delights*, when discussing the increasing number of films that examine the NRI, from *Bhaji on the Beach* to *Bride and Prejudice*, Dudrah points out that

> The use of Bollywood film aesthetics as part of diasporic film-making practices in the UK and US are being developed to represent fluid images of, and to depict eclectic narratives about, its characters, not least its South Asian protagonists. The Bollywood referents are also being adapted and translated as part of a fusion of different cinematic traditions and styles of film-making that are able to draw on and make a number of social commentaries.[44]

It is in this sense that I view *Nina's Heavenly Delights'* references to Bollywood. Most apparent of these is the scene in which Suman watches the classic Bollywood film *Mughal-e-Azam* (1960) and in Anarkali's (Madhubala) song of forbidden love, 'Pyar Kiya To Darna Kya', comes to accept her daughter's homosexuality as being similar to her own hidden desires for Raj. The subtitled lyrics state:

> In this world you only love once.
> You live with this pain of love.
> You die with this pain of love.
> What is there to be afraid of when you are in love?
> To love does not mean that you have stolen anything.

The song swells to become an accompaniment to the action as we cut to Lisa and Nina beginning to undress each other in Nina's bedroom. The film's Bollywood references also include various other songs from Bollywood films and three dance sequences, albeit all diegetically motivated and never quite becoming the foregrounded spectacle of a Bollywood film. These dances revolve around the cross-dressing Bobbi, proprietor of Bobbi's Bollywood Bowl, a DVD rental store, who is pictured at one point dancing to a Bollywood song track for some local children of different racial origins. These moments in the film illustrate *Nina's Heavenly Delights'* willingness to 'draw on' 'Bollywood referents in the manner Dudrah describes, in order to make its 'social commentaries', especially the fourth and final dance sequence, an homage to Bollywood films shooting in Scotland. In this instance, the blending of these different cinemas and their traditions reflects the film's exploration of blended identities, in line with debates surrounding the limitations and possibilities of considering identity as hybrid in postcolonial contexts found in the works of writers like Homi Bhabha.[45] In *Nina's Heavenly Delights* these identities are less Indian-Scottish than they are NRI-Scottish, the film's joining of NRI Nina and Scottish Lisa as lesbian lovers functioning as an allegory for the 'forbidden' intermingling of these identities.

Geoffrey Macnab points out in his *Sight and Sound* review that *Nina's Heavenly Delights* gives a strong sense of a fairytale, especially in the recurring appearance of the ghost of Nina's father.[46] Its examination of homosexual life in Glasgow is also rather fairytale-like, mostly addressing the issues in a context involving family members and close friends in and around the New Taj. There is not much in the way of interaction with the rest of the Glasgow community, where a less friendly reception might be received in some quarters by openly gay lovers, especially in an interracial couple. Despite this appeal to fairytale (and the youthful target audience suggested by its PG certificate), accusations could also be levelled at the films clichéd depiction of a particularly timid lesbian desire blossoming in a restaurant kitchen over bubbling pots and pans. Moreover, *Nina's Heavenly Delights* is very consciously politically correct, including three young, interracial couples (gay male, lesbian and heterosexual) along with its respect for both love *and* arranged marriage in the complex story of Suman and Raj, their love being consummated only after Suman's husband has died and Suman has fulfilled her obligation as a wife. This happy hybrid community paints Glasgow NRI-Scottish by absenting all 'others' from the lives of those that we do see.

Yet, we could also consider this fairytale utopia more positively, as a way of facilitating an examination, or reimagining, of new, tolerant forms of identity in a global diaspora, of which Scotland is only one outpost. In this respect, *Nina's Heavenly Delights* provides the solution to Gayatri Gopinath's observation in *Impossible Desires* (2005) that films like *Bend it Like Beckham*, by studiously avoiding lesbian desire, 'efface the ways in which insurgent queer female sexualities trouble, disrupt and refigure 'home' space from within'.[47] After all, it is precisely this process that is enacted by Nina's return to her family home in Glasgow, culminating in the final 'coming out' scenes in which various family members reveal their secret identities – that Priya is a Scottish dancer, Kary has secretly married Janice, Suman is in love with Raj and, eventually, that Nina is a lesbian. As I discuss further in Chapter 9, this is not such an unusual device for imagining new identities, as a somewhat similar utopian community is constructed in Edinburgh in *Women Talking Dirty* (1999) so as to provide a space in which to explore platonic female friendship.

Local History, Global Flavour

Nina's story illustrates how closely personal histories are tied to their diasporic context. As Nina and Lisa's friendship initially blossoms a fragment of Nina's childhood past is revealed by Lisa's unlikely uncovering of some childish graffiti ('Nina 4 Lorna. True Love'), hidden under peeling flock wallpaper in the New Taj. Lisa, her suspicion of Nina's lesbianism confirmed, teases her:

> Lorna Mullen! I remember Lorna. Captain of the school hockey team, big blue eyes, tall, legs right up to her oxters.[48] I'm shocked! I wouldn't have thought she was your type!

In this way, NRI Nina is intrinsically tied to a Scottish past, as a schoolgirl attending the same school as Lisa. Yet this local history is also connected to a larger, global context. On her arrival in Scotland, Nina walks out of the airport with Bobbi past a 'Welcome to Scotland' sign only to depart in Bobbi's brightly decorated van, a mode of transport more associated with the Indian subcontinent than Scotland. Whilst Nina has arrived from London, Lisa's father Joe has disappeared to Benidorm, and the Korma radio presenter discusses flights from Mumbai in the same broadcast as he tells the local community that Mrs Khan's lost cat has been spotted in Dundee. However, it is in the film's cooking sequences, and their deliberate appeal to the senses, that these global and local diasporic links are made most evident.

Before any images are seen, the film begins with the sound of food cooking. Thus, before any visual information is provided, an aural sensation is called upon. The credits are then interspersed with images of Nina as a young girl being taught to cook by her father. There are close ups of Nina's child's hands as she counts out chillis and her father's adult hands as he cuts and arranges ingredients. These are interspersed with the titles, across which warm yellow, orange and red swirling patterns play, reminiscent of cartoon expressions of steam and aroma rising from cooked food. We then cut to close-ups of food sizzling and sauce gently bubbling in a pan. As Nina tastes the finished food with her eyes closed her father tells her:

Taste it. Taste it in your heart. No matter what the recipe says . . . always follow your heart. Best chicken chakuti this side of Maryhill! One day . . . you're going to be the best cook in Glasgow.

The close-ups, along with Nina's father's emphasis on the body 'taste it in your heart', suggest a form of haptic cinema akin to that theorised by Laura U. Marks in *The Skin of the Film* (2000). For Marks, in intercultural cinema such practices as the persistent emphasis on food cooking 'call upon memories of the senses in order to represent the experiences of people living in the diaspora.'[49] Rather than an ethnographic fetishization, or exoticization of ethnic foods and culinary traditions, for Marks such representations create haptic images that can potentially keep alive cultural memories in the bodies of diasporic populations (through the evocation of smells and tastes or activities like cooking). In this instance the appeal to the senses in an attempt to recover memory in a diasporic context functions to situate Nina within a local, personally remembered history of her NRI childhood in Scotland.

When Nina teaches Lisa how to prepare a curry, informing her that 'it's all about chemistry', we are again shown close-ups of the mixing and grinding of spices and the chopping of raw vegetables. An extended close-up of a frying pan is used, with a series of temporal ellipses as the food cooks. As the ingredients are added, words of steam written in copperplate appear magically from the food and float dreamily up with the aromas: 'ginger', 'tumeric', 'garam masala', 'garlic', 'cumin', 'coriander'. A similar effect is achieved later in the film when Nina's father's handwritten recipes dissolve into close-ups of vegetables being chopped and food prepared in pans on the stove. The act of cooking keeps alive Nina's memory of her father, which we see both in her actions and her recitation of his words of advice, in both cases as though she were recalling words physically inscribed within her. Cooking, then, is a way for Nina to recreate her father's presence from her childhood, and the film's images an expression of this physical, sensory memory. This is not a memory of a homeland like India, however, but of a diasporic NRI childhood in Maryhill, Glasgow.

From Mumbai to Maryhill, in *Nina's Heavenly Delights*, for Nina's generation of NRIs in Scotland, identity is Scottish-NRI, a local/global hybrid. This is the major difference between *Pyaar Ishq aur Mohabbat* and *Nina's Heavenly Delights*. Although both films examine the position of Scotland's NRIs in relation to a larger, global context, in *Nina's Heavenly Delights* there is an emphasis on personal memories occurring in the diaspora that are informing of Scottish-NRI identities. Significantly, *Nina's Heavenly Delights* ends with Nina and Lisa in the New Taj as it

Figure 3.1 New Taj/New Scotland: Nina (Shelley Conn) and Lisa (Laura Fraser) cook up some *masala* identities in *Nina's Heavenly Delights* (2006)

reopens under their management. This conclusion mirrors the ending of *American Cousins* (2003), another aspirational story of diaspora that I discuss in Chapter 7.

When Lisa and Nina cook together, the local and the global meet. Nina and Lisa's first kiss also takes place in the kitchen. Lesbianism thus acts as a metaphor for Scottish-NRI identity, and Scotland's local interaction with the world illustrates a similar East–West chemistry, the *masala* (blended, or mixed) identity of the Scottish-NRI. It is noticeable that Nina's father, although omnipresent as a ghost, is dead, and that Lisa's father has disappeared to Benidorm for golf and sex. Lesbianism, then, suggests the need to construct a new form of memory that is not connected to the father/nation (be it Scotland or India), for Nina, a literal and symbolic 'New Taj'. Noticeably, when discussing her fears of coming out, Nina states, 'If I say it, there's no going back', lesbianism in this instance illustrating both homosexuality and the breaking away from tradition, the Scottish-NRI divorcing itself from its past (something one goes 'back' to) in favour of a 'forbidden', hybrid present. It is no coincidence, either, that the meal they prepare is Nina's mother's wedding banquet, or that Nina wears her father's chef's coat and works from his recipe book, with his ghost even appearing to stir the food during the televised cookery competition. Their televised coming out scene, then, replays Nina's familial history but also transforms it in a new diasporic context where a generation of global/local orphans reinvent their own traditions.

This informing Scottish location is evidently Glasgow, from the moment Nina's father proclaims the food the 'best chicken chakuti this side of Maryhill' and Nina 'the best cook in Glasgow'. This concrete sense of place is reinforced by the use of recognisable locations like the brightly lit Barrowland Ballroom concert venue and the distinctive Scottish Executive and Conference Centre (SECC) building on the Pacific Quay by the Clyde. If we were to follow Bashir Maan's argument in *The New Scots* (1992) we might be tempted to argue that this location works so well because Scotland, for Maan a more welcoming place to Asians in the last century than England,[50] enabled the conditions for a Scottish-NRI hybrid identity to flourish. Although this might be to take things slightly too far, this is an aspirational fairytale for PG viewers after all, it is perhaps enough to note that *Nina's Heavenly Delights* does not use Glasgow as a film set in quite the same way as either *KKHH* and *Kandukondain Kandukondain* or even *Pyaar Ishq aur Mohabbat*. Instead, a film set in Scotland, it grounds its *masala* NRI-Scottish identity precisely in its informing diasporic context.

Notes

1. I use 'Bollywood' to refer to popular Indian cinema. Although *Kandukondain Kandukondain* is a Tamil film (and the term Bollywood usually refers to Hindi films produced in Bombay) in the Scottish context, this term is generally understood to include all popular Indian cinema.
2. For example: Allan Hunter, 'Declaration of Independence', *Screen International*, 1221 (1999), p. 12; Allan Hunter, 'Scotland Takes the High Road', *Screen International*, 1281 (2000), p. 11; Allan Hunter, 'Glasgow Smiles', *Screen International*, 1354 (2002), p. 10; Allan Hunter 'Scotland the Brave, *Screen International*, 1442 (2004), pp. 16–17.
3. Juliette Garside, 'Poverty, crime, drug addiction, violence . . . why is cinema so obsessed with Scotland's dark side?' *Sunday Herald*, 2 June 2002. http://www.sundayherald.com/25137 (01/02/06).
4. Scottish Executive, *Scottish Screen* (Edinburgh: Stationary Office), 2002, p. 10.
5. Krysia Rosanska, 'Krysia Goes to Bollywood', *Roughcuts*, July 2000, p. 10.
6. J. Geetha, 'Bollywood Ending', *Sight and Sound*, 13: 6 (2003), pp. 31–2.
7. For instance, http://www.scotlandthemovie.com/ (03/08/08).
8. Angelique Chrisafis, 'Tourism on Standby for Bollywood Boom', *Guardian*, 6 May 2002, p. 3. http://film.guardian.co.uk/bollywood/story/0,11871,710675,00.html (03/08/08).

9. Friends of Scotland, 'Bollywood Holyrood' http://www.friendsofscotland. gov.uk/culture/asia.html (03/08/08).
10. Scottish Executive, *Scottish Screen*, p. 51.
11. Scottish Executive, PACT (Producers Alliance for Cinema and Television) in Scotland, Scottish Enterprise, Highlands and Islands Enterprise and Scottish Screen, *Audit of the Screen Industries in Scotland*, 2003, p. 99.
12. Vijay Mishra, *Bollywood Cinema* (London: Routledge, 2002), p. 235.
13. Rhys Blakely, 'UK Treaty Offers Tax Break to Woo Bollywood Movies on to British Soil', *The Times*, 17 May 2008, p. 60.
14. Emma Cowing, 'Bollywood Focuses on Scotland for Film Locations', *The Scotsman*, 19 July 2000: 5, p. 5.
15. Geetha, 'Bollywood Ending', p. 31.
16. Scottish Executive, *Audit of the Screen Industries in Scotland*, p. 100.
17. Mishra, *Bollywood Cinema*, p. 235.
18. Bella Jaisinghani, 'Shooting With a Business Angle', *The Financial Express*, 13 June 2004. http://www.financialexpress.com/ (01/02/06).
19. Chrisafis, 'Tourism on Standby for Bollywood Boom', p. 3.
20. Blakely, 'UK Treaty Offers Tax Break to Woo Bollywood Movies on to British Soil', p. 60.
21. Ibid.
22. Ravinder Kaur, 'Viewing the West through Bollywood', *Contemporary South Asia* 1: 2 (2002), pp. 199–209, p. 205.
23. Ibid.
24. Ibid., p. 209, n. 17.
25. Mishra, *Bollywood Cinema*, p. 249.
26. Rachel Dwyer, *All You Want is Money, All You Need is Love* (London: Cassell, 2000), p. 79.
27. Ibid., p. 91.
28. Kaur, 'Viewing the West through Bollywood', p. 205.
29. Dwyer, *All You Want is Money*, p. 100.
30. Raminder Kaur, 'Cruising on the *Vilayeti* Bandwagon', in Raminder Kaur and Ajay J. Sinha (eds.) *Bollyworld* (New Delhi: Sage, 2005), pp. 309–29.
31. Raminder Kaur and Ajay J. Sinha, 'Bollyworld', in Kaur and Sinha (eds) *Bollyworld*, pp. 11–34, p. 27.
32. Andrew Wills, 'Locating Bollywood', in Julian Stringer (ed.), *Movie Blockbusters* (London: Routledge, 2003). pp. 255–68, p. 258.
33. Tejaswini Ganti, *Bollywood* (London: Routledge, 2004), p. 86.
34. Wills, 'Locating Bollywood', p. 265.
35. Mishra, *Bollywood Cinema*, p. 260.
36. 'Bollywood Holyrood'.
37. Kaur, 'Viewing the West through Bollywood', p. 205.
38. Dwyer, *All You Want is Money*, p. 141.
39. Kaur, 'Cruising on the *Vilayeti* Bandwagon', in Kaur and Sinha (eds), *Bollyworld*, pp. 309–29, p. 316.

40. *Nina's Heavenly Delights* Press Pack: http://www.vervepics.com/docs/nhdnotes.pdf (03/08/08).
41. Verve Pictures website: http://www.vervepics.com/ninasheavenlydelights.shtml (03/08/08).
42. *Nina's Heavenly Delights* Press Pack.
43. Rajinder Kumar Dudrah, *Bollywood* (New Delhi: Sage Publications, 2006), pp. 117–40, p. 118.
44. Ibid., p. 164.
45. Homi Bhabha, *The Location of Culture* (London: Routledge, 1994).
46. Geoffrey Macnab, Nina's Heavenly Delights, *Sight and Sound*, 16: 10 (2006), p. 74.
47. Gayatri Gopinath, *Impossible Desires* (Durham, NC, and London: Duke University Press, 2005), p. 129.
48. A Scots word meaning 'armpits'.
49. Laura U. Marks, *The Skin of the Film* (Durham, NC, and London: Duke University Press, 2000), p. xi.
50. Bashir Maan, *The New Scots* (Edinburgh: John Donald, 1992), p. 203.

CHAPTER 4

(Loch Ness) Monster Movie: A Return to Primal Scotland

This chapter examines the Loch Ness monster movie, an incarnation of the monster genre completely ignored in academic discussions of Scotland and cinema. It begins with a brief examination of the history of Nessie, including the media coverage that accompanied the monster's first reported sightings in the twentieth century, its relationship with tourism and the ways in which the early British Nessie movie *The Secret of the Loch* (1934) used the monster to examine the relationship between England and Scotland. This theme is pursued throughout the rest of the chapter, for the majority of which I focus on *Loch Ness* (1996), examining its contested status in terms of the national identity this US/UK coproduction offers to international viewers.

With so many movies set in Scotland produced from London, Nessie movies demonstrate the often unresolvable difficulties surrounding our understanding of autoethnographic cinematic representations of Scotland. Instead, through comparison with other globally peripheral films like *Crocodile Dundee* (1986) and contemporary US monster movies *Jurassic Park* (1993), *Anaconda* (1997) and *Lake Placid* (1999), *Loch Ness* is positioned in a broader, global context. Its deliberate appeal to international markets is highlighted, bringing discussion back to the monster's relationship with tourism, a theme which leads into the concluding discussion of *The Water Horse* (2007).

Nessie: The Monster and Modernity

According to legend, Nessie is a prehistoric aquatic monster who lives in Scotland, a nation that has for several centuries been considered 'far flung' in relation to the old imperial European civilisations. Steuart Campbell notes that for centuries 'there was a widespread Highland belief that a water horse or kelpie inhabited not only Loch Ness but nearly every lake in Scotland.'[1] The most commonly recounted myth of Nessie's existence is that of St Columba, who supposedly encountered the monster in the sixth century. On a mission to convert Scotland's Picts, St Columba reputedly banished the monster back to the depths with powerful words, presumably (we must infer) as he did any existing pre-Christian beliefs. This particular recounting of St Columba's encounter with the monster illustrates precisely Nessie's typical use as prehistoric Other against which the 'civilised' defines itself.

It was in the nineteenth century that Nessie was transformed from mythological beastie to dinosaur, at a time when, Campbell notes, 'folklore . . . modernised itself by adapting to the findings of science'.[2] In this particular case Nessie was rationalised into a dinosaur in the wake of exhibits depicting prehistoric monsters at the Great Exhibition of London in 1851. The Great Exhibition was a showcase of British scientific ingenuity and colonial treasures; the monster as we know it today has its origins in the British Empire and the scientific classification and display of the 'primitive' (from around the world) by the modern state. Moreover, Nessie's redefinition from folk monster to relic of the primordial past occurred at a time when various European countries actively constructed the national traditions needed to define national status.[3] Thus, the idea of an anachronistic dinosaur in a loch came to define Scotland as a nation, meshing with the already existing British myth of Scotland as wilderness (the myth of Tartanry), that emerged after the Highland clearances.

Nessie's celebrity status sprang up in the 1930s due to newspaper, photographic and cinematic coverage of the monster. As Benedict Anderson argued in *Imagined Communities* (1983), identity in the modern nation is constructed through a sense of imagined belonging. This is instigated by such technological inventions as the printing press (which facilitated the mass circulation of newspapers), railway, telephone, radio, cinema and so on. These technological advances create the belief that people exist as part of a much larger community, specifically a nation, than is otherwise experienced on a daily basis. It was through these same technologies that Loch Ness's monster came to represent Scotland, and to put Loch Ness on the map for British tourists.

The international identification of Loch Ness with the now world famous kelpie began on 2 May 1933 with a short article in the *Inverness Courier* entitled 'Strange Spectacle on Loch Ness'. The article reported a sighting of the monster by a 'well known business man who lives near Inverness', and his wife, 'a University graduate'. They were the MacKays of Drumnadrochit, who were 'motoring along the north shore of the loch' at the time of the sighting.[4] The exact reason for their visit to the loch is not given, but the article's mention of their social status (a married couple, business man and university graduate) and their physical condition, 'motoring', places them within the middle classes. In its very inception, then, Nessie's appeal was to the tourist's gaze, or at the very least, a certain demographic likely to enjoy the pleasures of tourism.

Reported sightings of the monster in the 1930s are often attributed to the Depression, and the press's need for light, engaging stories. Yet there is more to it than this. Scotland has been a recognised tourist destination for several centuries, with greater access for visitors being facilitated by the railway in the nineteenth century and the motor car and aeroplane in the twentieth and twenty-first. During the 1920s and 1930s the promise of automobile freedom and touristic leisure time in the countryside began to appeal to middle-class car owners. As John Urry observes, during the interwar years the 'increasingly domesticated middle classes, comfortably and safely located in their Morris Minor's: "began to tour England and take photographs in greater numbers than ever before."'[5] This practice, John and Margaret Gold note, in *Imagining Scotland* (1995), was also prevalent in Scotland.[6] It is significant, then, that the 'spectacle' of the monster first appears in Scotland around this time, to a motoring middle-class couple. As is often noted, the increase in sightings of Nessie in the 1930s coincided with the completion of a new road along the north shore, giving motorists a tourist's view of the loch. Thus, the coincidence of the numerous reported sightings of the 1930s with the Depression signals that, whether intentional or not, they would have appealed to would-be motoring tourists, thereby potentially increasing the circulation of money in Scotland.

Photographic snaps of Nessie were also taken in 1933, but the most famous, Colonel Robert K. Wilson's 'surgeon's photo', was taken in 1934 and published in *The Daily Mail*. Not only was it the most remarkably clear picture of anything purporting to be Nessie, but also, Wilson – a gynaecologist from London driving to Inverness whilst on holiday in Scotland with a friend[7] – was the perfect guarantee of the veracity of the 'spectacle' of Loch Ness. He was both a respectable member of the professional classes and a tourist. Thus, owing to the monster's appeal to the British middle classes, a Scottish newspaper's tiny column about a sighting of the monster led to 'national' (as in, British) coverage in *The Daily Mail*. In the wake of these sightings the first British film about the monster was made in 1934: *The Secret of the Loch*. This film depicted the discovery of Scotland's monster as an event that both confirmed pre-existing views of Scotland as England's wild pre-modern other and simultaneously disavowed Scotland's supposedly pre-modern status to bring Scotland and England together as a unified imagined community (Britain), solidifying the Union through the media circus surrounding Scotland's new, accessible tourist attraction.

The Secret of the Loch (1934)

The Secret of the Loch (1934), was made by London based Wyndham Productions, at Associated Talking Pictures (A.T.P) Studios, Ealing. As contemporary reviewers noted, deliberately cashing in on the recent media attention surrounding sightings of Nessie,[8] the film focuses on a young reporter, Jimmy Anderson (Frederick Peisley) who travels to Scotland to report on sightings of Nessie. There he encounters several other journalists from London. The local laird, Professor Heggie (Seymour Hicks) prepares a dive to prove the existence of Nessie. In the meantime Jimmy falls for Heggie's granddaughter, Angela (Nancy O'Neal). In the final sequences Nessie appears underwater and menaces the dive. When the monster resurfaces it is photographed by the waiting journalists.

The film begins with a title carrying an extract from *The Daily Mail*, which reads,

> Whether people believe in the existence of a Loch Ness '<u>MONSTER</u>' or not. Highlanders are convinced that the watery depths harbour some fantastic and abnormal creature.

This is followed by a shot of a pile of newspapers with headlines reporting sightings of Nessie. Although this opening draws the well-worn distinction between civilisation (including the metropolitan audience who are addressed by the humorous title) and superstitious Highlanders, it also establishes the film's playful examination of the way in which Nessie is reported in the press. *The Secret of the Loch* is extremely self-conscious about its status as a film about a mythical monster. From the very beginning we are aware that we are watching a film about the creation of the myth. Thus, in spite of its deployment of expected Kailyard locations – the local pub at Foyers, the laird's castle at Craig Gorm and repeated scenic shots of the loch – the way Scotland is depicted in this film does not provide a straightforward, 'negative', colonising view of Scotland as wilderness. After all, despite the opening jibe at the expense of the backward Highlanders, they will ultimately be proved right. Even so, although Scotland is represented in a self-conscious way as a place where myths are generated, it still functions as the defining other of England. The subtle difference is the film's play with Scotland's geographical proximity to the metropolitan centre, which is seen to have been brought much closer by the technological innovations of modernity – specifically the newspaper, railway and telephone – that have apparently unified the modern state of Britain in its paradoxical appreciation of (the media spectacle of) the premodern monster.

Initially there is a comic acknowledgement that the local Scots do not appreciate the view taken by the *Daily Sun* (a London-based newspaper) that sightings of the monster are evidence of a Scottish 'mass hallucination'. Yet despite this initial acknowledgement of national difference, London – as the central presence of the newspaper in the opening sequence shows – remains the driving force of the narrative, and the guarantor of truth. It is to the National Museum of Science that Heggie goes to prove the existence of the monster. No matter what the locals in the Kailyard think, the overall veracity of Nessie's existence is something that only Heggie's distinguished peers in the scientific community can provide. Typically, the truth surrounding events in Scotland is decided elsewhere by the British middle classes (Heggie included) rather than the local Scots. Indeed, these London-based scientists do not require an eyewitness experience of the monster, but rather to see photographic proof, which is ultimately provided by the London newspapers.

The Secret of the Loch considers Scotland to be a part of Britain because of the technological advances of modernity that have linked the wilderness to the metropolis. Not surprisingly it is the railroad, symbol of modernity and facilitator of imagined communities, which carries Anderson to Scotland. Moreover, there is a running gag throughout the film concerning the telephone in the local pub which, although it bears an 'out of order' sign, actually does work. It is the reporter for the *Daily Post* who continually re hangs the sign, tricking his competitors so he can be the first to ring in the scoop. Thus, modern technology is shown to link Scotland and the English metropolis, and the film playfully toys with audience preconceptions to the contrary.

The fact that the London-based newspapers all send their reporters to Scotland further illustrates that the imagined community to which the monster signifies 'Scotland' consists of a British readership. Thus, whilst Scotland is seen as a rejuvenative wilderness (for the English tourist at least), in line with the romantic myth of Tartanry, it is also a land where myths are created that have the potential to unify Britain. Scotland is at once England's peripheral other and yet, paradoxically, central to the state. The English reporter Anderson will both witness the monster in the loch and write the story for the London-based *Daily Sun*. This newspaper will circulate throughout Britain and deliver the scientific proof (the photograph of Nessie) that Scotland's Highlanders – backward as they are depicted in this film – are not prone to mass hallucinations after all. This is the paradox that structures a great many Nessie films. Proving the monster's existence scientifically ensures that Scotland retains its image as a pre-modern wilderness where monsters exist, but simultaneously incorporates this primitive land within the imagined community of the modern state of Britain.

In addition to emphasising the union of the two nations through technology, *The Secret of the Loch* contains an English–Scottish romance typical of any number of British films set in Scotland. While Heggie is in London, the young reporter Anderson is introduced. Anderson's trajectory from London to Scotland follows that of many other English visitors to the rejuvenative wilderness of cinematic Scotland. Visits to Scotland by English protagonists often represent the unity that exists between the two nations through a romantic union between the English stranger and a native Scot.[9] This is again the case in *The Secret of the Loch*. Anderson falls for Heggie's granddaughter, Angela, their union being defined by their communal belonging to the British middle classes. Not only is Angela's voice devoid of any trace of a Scottish accent (in contrast to the rest of the assembled locals), but so too are she and Anderson rendered as a typical middle-class tourist couple when – immediately after Anderson shows Angela an amusing postcard of Nessie playing the bagpipes – they go for a countryside drive in her open-top motorcar. Here the middle-class Scottish woman and English man stand out against the Kailyard locals, representing the union of the British middle classes that supposedly spans the national divide. Hence, although Scotland is depicted as a romantic wilderness in line with the myth of Tartanry, this wilderness is clearly identified as a middle-class, British (touristic) domain. Furthermore, even though he discusses the link between the monster and his Scottish ancestry, and ever takes on a member of the London Zoological Society in an argument when the Englishman patronisingly dubs Loch Ness a 'pond', Heggie's class and educational background, which he shares with the other scientists, sublates his Scottish identity. His identity, like that of Anderson and Angela, is British middle class.

Thus, rather than a metropolitan view that unproblematically positions Scotland as England's other, *The Secret of the Loch* incorporates Scotland (and its monster) within the imagined community of Britain. This is the paradox at the heart of the British view of Nessie. The monster's existence proves that Scotland still functions as the metropolis's defining primitive other. However, modern technology now provides the intrepid metropolitan with access to the monster. Technology at once brings Scotland and England closer together geographically and simultaneously provides the (scientific) proof that they are still centuries apart. Admittedly this photographic evidence, proof that modernity has the power to see into the darkest recesses of any wilderness, continues the positioning of Scotland as the metropolis's primitive other. Yet in *The Secret of the Loch* Scotland

and its monster are clearly part of an imagined community encompassing all of Britain.

Mirroring the narrative's discourse on modern Britain, the use of modern technology to penetrate the wilderness is also integral to the cinematic 'spectacle' of Nessie. The final scenes include two underwater sequences in which divers make the perilous voyage into the loch. These sequences literally demonstrate the ability of modernity to render visible the primal depths, reconfirming through cinematic spectacle the narrative's examination of modernity's penetration of the wilds of Scotland. In the first sequence, Jack Campbell – a diver from Plymouth, who also arrives on the train – is eaten by Nessie. The second diver, Anderson himself, narrowly survives an encounter with a fearsome 'giant' iguana! Modern diving equipment makes possible this venture into the wild, yet modernity's prowess is also considered rather dangerous, rendering the divers vulnerable to the monster.

This ambivalent discourse on the monster and modernity is typical of the monster movie genre. The diver's vulnerability suggests that modernity is constantly in peril from the return of the monstrous repressed. Indeed, this is made evident from the beginning of the film when Heggie puts the monster's appearance down to blasting operations in the area which have inadvertently reawakened a dinosaur egg. However, in *The Secret of the Loch* this generic discourse on imperilled modernity (and its ultimate survival of its encounter with the monster) is used to demonstrate two things simultaneously. Firstly, the spectacle of technology (in this case cinema) and its ability to render visible the unknown. Secondly, the corresponding accessibility of remote areas of Britain facilitated by modernity, in particular the 'closeness' (by road, rail, or even cinema screen) of the primitive 'spectacle' of Scotland to England.

This celebration of the ability of modernity to 'capture' the pre-modern on film is emphasised when reporters by the side of the loch photograph the monster. Modernity posits a prehistoric other in the monster and goes looking for it. The monster must exist to validate modernity's development beyond its pre-modern past. Yet the monster that we see in the film is obviously a fake. After all, with modernity able to see into the wild, there can be no more pre-modern. Monsters simply cannot exist. As modernity by definition can never capture on film the pre-modern Other that would justify its existence, so it fabricates it instead. Hence, the spectacle of Nessie, the monster in the Scottish wilderness, as seen in cinema. Scotland, then, remains effectively colonised by its representation in the film, but this colonisation functions within a broader construction of the imagined community of Britain.

Nessie in the nineties

Since the 1930s several British Nessie movies have appeared, including the Adam Faith vehicle *What a Whopper* (1961) and the amateur Scottish animation film, Iain Rintoul's *The Loch Ness Monster Movie* (1983). There were also several US films, including *The Loch Ness Horror* (1981), *The Evil Beneath Loch Ness* (2001) and the Herzog inspired mockumentary, *Incident at Loch Ness* (2004), which must, sadly, be omitted from this discussion of British representations of the monster. Although Rintoul's work is more complex in certain respects, *What a Whopper* engages with the same issue of British 'national' identity in relation to the monster as can be seen in *The Secret of the Loch*. Indeed, *Loch Ness*, my example from the 1990s, continues this trend, illustrating the difficulties associated with arguments for autoethnography in relation to films set in Scotland.

Whilst depicting Scottish stereotypes in a knowing manner, the nature of *Loch Ness*'s 'auto'-ethnographic status is contested because of the film's origins in London. Although it would be difficult to claim that *Loch Ness* is strictly speaking an *auto*ethnographic film (this is very much a British, rather than a Scottish production) its deployment of recognisable mythical images associated with Scotland in a knowing manner is done to maximise profits through sales at home and abroad. In fact, its ironic framing of stereotypical images of Scotland is actually aimed at Scottish, British and international audiences in general. These broader audiences, I argue, will recognise this irony not because they are Scottish, but because they are familiar with a tradition of films about Scotland (be they British, Scottish or US productions or coproductions) that includes *Brigadoon* (1954), *The Maggie* (1954), *Whisky Galore!* (1949), *Local Hero* (1983), *Highlander* (1986) and *Loch Ness* (1996). *Loch Ness* is part of a broader global phenomenon of films produced in peripheral filmmaking nations that repackage stereotypical images of themselves to offer international viewers a virtual, fantastic, tourist's experience of their own pre-modern past. Therefore, although the 'auto' that speaks in this autoethnographic film is British rather than Scottish, when viewed in a global context it offers a more positive depiction of Scotland than previous critical positions might allow.

Loch Ness (1996)

Loch Ness follows US professor of zoology, John Dempsey (Ted Danson), as he travels from Los Angeles to Scotland. Dempsey's career and life are on the skids and he is sent to Loch Ness as punishment for too many wasted research trips looking for Sasquatch (Big Foot) and the Yeti (Abominable Snowman). Dempsey is to use the latest scientific equipment to sweep the loch and disprove the existence of the monster. On arrival in Scotland, Dempsey boards at The Moffat Arms and falls for the charms of its landlady, Laura (Joely Richardson), and her young daughter, Isabel (Kirsty Graham). He begins to believe in the monster's existence and, with help from Isabel, finally encounters a family of Nessies. About to use his photographic evidence to reveal Nessie to the world, Dempsey has a change of heart, keeps the loch's secret, quits his job and moves in with Laura and Isabel. His newfound nuclear family is mirrored in the film's final image of the monster family swimming in the loch.

Loch Ness was a £6.5m Working Title and PolyGram Filmed Entertainment (PFE) production.[10] Working Title is a London-based firm most famous for the breakthrough British hit *Four Weddings and a Funeral* (1994). Even so, the national identity of *Loch Ness* is often disputed, being variously listed as a UK production, a US/UK coproduction and a Hollywood film.[11] For the British Film Institute, using a primarily financial measurement, *Loch Ness* is considered a US film with UK creative input,[12] what might be termed a runaway Hollywood production, a US-financed film made abroad. This confusion may be partly due to PolyGram's status as a European company based in the USA whose African-born CEO, Michael Kuhn was a Cambridge educated lawyer before moving to Los Angeles.[13] The film's narrative may also confuse matters as it deliberately appeals to the mainstream US market. In fact, whilst produced by a British company and directed by Englishman John Henderson, *Loch Ness* was the first screenplay written by American John Fusco, who visited Scotland as a student.[14] Adding to the confusion is the presence of Hollywood star Ted Danson in the leading role, some initial sequences set in the US and the proudly flagged involvement of Jim Henson's Creature Shop.

Yet *Loch Ness*'s contested identity is also a symptom of a larger trend within British and international films in general for internationally funded coproductions based in one country that auto-exoticise in order to appeal to international markets, particularly that of the USA. The subsequent development of Working Title casts more light on this strategy.

In 1994, thanks to a considered release and marketing strategy on the part of PolyGram,[15] *Four Weddings and a Funeral* was by far the highest grossing British film in the USA, making $53 million at the box office. Its closest rival, *Sirens*, made only $8 million.[16] It would go on to make $240 million worldwide from its initial $4 million budget.[17] Although *Four Weddings* and *Loch Ness* were in development at the same time, Working

Title assumed that *Loch Ness* would be the bigger hit,[18] presumably because of its generic '*Local Hero*–ness'. The surprise was that what British producers thought US audiences would go for turned out to be a different type of auto-exoticism, the romantic lives of British middle-class thirty-somethings in *Four Weddings*. Since then, Working Title's targeting of the US market has continued. In 1998 PFE was sold by its parent company, Phillips, to Seagram. In 1999 Working Title signed a deal with Universal Pictures, also owned by Seagram. Universal now secure US distribution of many of Working Title's films, enabling them to continue producing medium and larger budget films in the knowledge that they can target the lucrative US market. These have included *Bridget Jones's Diary* (2001), *Johnny English* (2003), *Love Actually* (2003) and *Elizabeth: The Golden Age* (2007).

Loch Ness, then, is perhaps best considered an international coproduction in financial terms, but one that articulates a British perspective on the monster for international consumption. The politics of possible US (or more accurately, Hollywood) outsourcing aside, for the purposes of this chapter, what is interesting is that in aiming at the US market, as Mike Wayne notes, 'an absolute prerequisite for financial viability' on the part of PolyGram,[19] *Loch Ness* appears to construct an ambiguous sense of British national identity which is particularly telling in its depiction of Scotland.

'Going Home' Again

A key reference point for understanding *Loch Ness* is Bill Forsyth's *Local Hero* (1983). *Local Hero* engaged with a tradition of films that represent the arrival of an American stranger in Scotland. Although Forsyth denied any link between his film and its predecessor, *The Maggie* (1954),[20] *Local Hero*'s meditation on the contrasts between modern life in the USA and an apparently unspoilt pre-modern life in Scotland is extremely similar to both *The Maggie* and *Brigadoon*. As various critics have noted, there are parallels between the film's plot – in which Scottish locals conform (or rather, perform) to type in order to increase the price a US oil firm is willing to pay for their village – and the same strategy as it is deployed in the film's repackaging of Scotland's Kailyard for international consumption.[21] Although *Local Hero*'s status as a Scottish film is not entirely straightforward, in contrast to *Loch Ness* it can be considered more authentically autoethnographic in its deployment of the well-worn theme of an American visitor to a small Scottish community as a strategy through which to sell a film that many would consider Scottish. This same approach is visible in *Loch Ness*, an international coproduction produced by a British company that adopts Scotland's monster as its own, yet *Loch Ness* appropriates the dual address of the autoethnographic film to slightly different effect.

On first viewing, *Loch Ness* initially appears to be a similarly autoethnographic expression of Scotland to *Local Hero*. It auto-exoticises in a number of ways, most obviously by centring on the myth of Nessie, and using attractive tourist locations to depict Scotland. The contrast between the soulless city and the rejuvenative wilderness seen in both *Brigadoon* and *Local Hero* is charted through Dempsey's development from failed professor in Los Angeles to a family man in Scotland, and the Scotland which Dempsey encounters at the Moffat Arms is clearly the Kailyard, full of locals he describes as 'tight fisted weanies in kilts' whose 'national pastime' is overcharging the US tourist.

As we might expect, a double address ironically frames the deployment of the usual mythical imagery. With an obvious nod to *Local Hero*, on arrival Dempsey is met by an endearingly enthusiastic and gauky young Scotsman, Adrian (James Frain). Frain does a humorous impersonation of Peter Capaldi's Oldsen, the sidekick of Mac, (Peter Riegert) the American visitor in *Local Hero*. Indeed, this is an in-joke about an in-joke, as Capaldi seemed to be impersonating John Gordon Sinclair's acting style in Forsyth's earlier film, *Gregory's Girl* (1981). Sinclair even briefly appeared in *Local Hero* to mock this mockery! The most obvious knowing deployment of irony in relation to Scottish myths occurs on Dempsey's arrival when he is taken to a hotel full of tourists where each room is 'done out in a different tartan', and a ceilidh is in full swing. This touristic aspect of Scotland is quickly rejected by Dempsey for its inauthenticity. Although his 'authentic' experience ultimately turns out to be the Kailyard, the credibility of the tartan experience of touristic Scotland is mocked, as the hotel is full of 'Cryptozoologists' ('Nessie hunters') who are unable to tell reality from myth. Thus there is an obvious invitation for the audience, like Dempsey, to reject the clichés of invented tartans and ceilidhs for the tourists.

Yet there is more to this ironic framing than just autoethnography, not simply because the 'auto' in this instance is British. On the one hand, it is tempting to conclude that *Loch Ness* reappropriates the Kailyard myth to sell its British image of Scotland abroad. In this case, in spite of its ironic framing, the Kailyard effectively reverts to a metropolitan myth used to distance Scotland from England, as discussed in *Scotch Reels*. On the other hand, we might argue that international audiences in general are sophisticated enough to realise that the Kailyard is being deployed in an ironic

manner. After all, *Local Hero* is understandable to, and has been assimi-
lated by, international audiences, who do not necessarily consider it to
offer a true-to-life depiction of Scotland.

At this point, then, the interminable discussion of whether such images
are 'negative' or 'positive', English (British) or Scottish, 'auto'- or autoethnographic, becomes unprofitable. Ian Goode, critiquing the limitations
of critical positions that emphasise a national (Scottish) perspective, has
shown of *Local Hero*'s attempts to 'unfix and merge identities' that its
depiction of US protagonists encountering Scotland almost suggests a
diasporic reading of the film (as I suggested of both *Brigadoon* and *Rob Roy*
(1995) in the Introduction). In *Loch Ness*, at the very least its representation of Scotland through a US visitor's eyes ensures that, for international
audiences, 'the film can be assessed productively, from a location that
looks from the outside in, as well as the inside out'.[22] Accordingly, an
alternative approach is needed to help draw out the broader reasons for
Loch Ness's ironic use of existing stereotypes rather than the argument
from autoethnography.

Ness-talgia

In 1994, Graeme Turner described how, in films like *Crocodile Dundee*
(1986), Australia is typically sold as a tourist destination through images of
a tropical outback wilderness and a focus on the pioneering lives of its
European settlers. Turner described how *Crocodile Dundee* deployed this
discourse to appeal to international markets, thereby providing American
viewers with a fantasy of their own frontier past. As Turner notes,
Crocodile Dundee entails the usual difficulties associated with this auto-
exoticising. On the one hand it is an ' 'ironically knowing' con'[23] through
which Australian cinema competes in global markets by selling American
dreams of a lost frontier past back to US audiences. On the other, there is
a danger that these images bolster US opinions of Australia as a backward
nation. This is exactly the same issue that plagues *Loch Ness*, with the
added difficulty of the film's international funding and its British (English)
production base.

In 2002, Koichi Iwabuchi drew on Turner's argument to make a more
general point about the international consumption of another culture's
past, defining it as 'capitalist nostalgia'.[24] Whilst discussing Japan's repositioning of itself in relation to an economically resurgent Asia, Iwabuchi
examines how capitalist nostalgia is no longer necessarily linked to the
national past. By appropriating transnational images of another culture's
past, a 'borrowed nostalgia'[25] is now possible, in which one culture's

present (often reconstructed as primitive) comes to represent another culture's past. We might consider this argument particularly applicable to a film like *Brigadoon*, in which two US tourists with backpacks and rifles, New Yorkers on a grouse shooting holiday in the Highlands, walk into an enchanted pre-modern Scottish village where time stopped in 1754 (exactly 200 years before the film's release). Whilst Jeff Douglas (Van Johnson) cracks wise about the impending American War of Independence, Tommy Albright (Gene Kelly) falls in love and forsakes modern life to live in Brigadoon forever. Douglas and Albright resemble the many US tourists (and indeed, with backpacks and rifles, military servicemen), to descend on Europe during, and in the wake of World War II, looking, perhaps, for an origin – an identity that stretches back before the founding of the US in the War of Independence – searching for their own Brigadoon.

In such films, representations of cultural difference are deployed to establish an 'advanced/backward' dichotomy between the cultures observing and observed. In this way Australia can stand in for the US's recent past in *Crocodile Dundee*,[26] as can Scotland in *Brigadoon* or *Rob Roy*. In *Loch Ness*, however, this potentially colonising practice is repackaged and sold back to the centre. *Loch Ness* uses its ironically framed Kailyard Scotland to offer American audiences a chance to visit, along with Dempsey, their pre-modern past, in Scotland. Included in the package, however, is a reconsideration of the centre-periphery hierarchy found in the contemporary US monster movie when it is reconsidered from a peripherally outsourced (British) perspective.

British Monster – US Monster

In its framing of Nessie as a British, as opposed to Scottish, monster, *Loch Ness* belongs to the same tradition as *The Secret of the Loch*. Once photographic evidence is obtained it is to the Natural History Museum in London that Dempsey travels to prove that the monster exists. London is depicted as the bustling metropolis, in stark contrast to Kailyard Scotland, through establishing shots of recognisable tourist locations, such as the River Thames, Big Ben, the Houses of Parliament and Trafalgar Square. As the camera pans across these locations a BBC van appears prominently in shot on two occasions, the second time parked outside the museum to record the proceedings. Once again through its 'national' media it is the British state that will be united by the existence of Nessie, even though this entails reconfirming the pre-modern status of Scotland. However, despite its recycling of its predecessors' approach to the monster, *Loch*

Ness is actually far less concerned with depicting relations between Scotland and England. Most obviously, the visitor to Scotland is an American, as opposed to the Englishmen of *The Secret of the Loch*. Indeed, whilst Dempsey's findings will be made public by the British Broadcasting Corporation, this time they will actually reach an (imagined) global community. This particular media circus has been arranged by Dempsey's boss, Professor Bob Mercer (Harris Yulin), to inform the world of the American university's discovery. In contrast to *The Secret of the Loch*, then, *Loch Ness* envisages Britain as at the heart of a global audience, and like *Crocodile Dundee*, aims to present Scotland as a tourist's fantasy of a pre-modern land that can stand in for an imagined USA of the past.

For this reason a recognisable cinematic version of Scotland is created throughout the film. Dempsey's plane lands at a small rural landing strip as opposed to a major urban area, the Kailyard is out in force, there are repeated shots of the scenic loch (albeit an amalgam of Loch Torridon and Loch Ness), immaculately preserved period buses from the 1950s still service this fantasy Scotland, and Nessie's family live in an underground cave beneath Eilean Donan Castle. As was the case in the 1930s, then, Nessie's primary function remains that of tourist attraction. Moreover, the film's ironic framing of these tired mythical images of Scotland, although undoubtedly consumed by local audiences (be they Scottish or British) in a knowing fashion, is also a way of referencing the tradition of films about Scotland – which includes *Brigadoon* and *Local Hero* – with which international audiences will be familiar. In fact, the two levels of address provided by this ironic framing function in a manner typical of post-classical Hollywood films in general, which deploy what Noel Carroll describes as a 'two-tiered' address.[27] This dual address appeals at a surface level to the casual viewer (who, in this case, has probably simply taken their family to see the latest children's film) and also to a more engaged, cinematically informed viewer, who is addressed through knowing references to previous films about Scotland. As these films are international currency, this secondary, engaged audience does not have to be Scottish to be (autoethnographically) in on the joke, *they simply have to have seen films about Scotland*. Rather than a global/local (autoethnographic) address, then, *Loch Ness* uses Scotland's cinematic past to facilitate the creation of a global (entertained)/global (informed) address.

In this respect the uninformed and informed audiences are addressed rather like tourists who – like Dempsey in the hotel full of cryptozoologists – may or not be aware that what they consume is a myth that the locals (in this case, the British filmmakers) are complicit in selling them. As, generally speaking, most tourists will be aware that the existence of a prehistoric monster in a Scottish loch is pretty unlikely, the film invites a willing suspension of disbelief typical of the tourist. Indeed, whether the viewer is informed or uninformed should make no difference as to the pleasure to be had in consuming the myth.

Loch Ness, then, a British film with US finance, provides audiences with a virtual legacy of Scotland's past on which to ground its latest offering. Scotland is packaged for international audiences as a borrowed, virtual past, appealing to 'capitalist nostalgia' by depicting a Kailyard fantasyland in which to experience a virtual version of pre-modern existence. The findings of the Hydra Report in 1997 should come as no surprise, then, as tourism was bound to rise in the wake of films like Loch Ness which offer a touristic view of Scotland (the latest cinematic version of the 'Strange Spectacle on Loch Ness') for consumption by international audiences.

Monstrous Childhood

To consolidate its nostalgic effect, Loch Ness links the monster movie's exploration of the need for modernity to capture the monster on film to the theme of childhood innocence. It equates its reconstructed pre-modern Scotland not with an elegiac 'lost' national past, as in the Scotch Reels critique, but with the individual viewer's past, a time of imaginary belief before entrance into the rational strictures of modern, adult society.

When Dempsey's predecessor, Dr Abernathy takes a picture of the monster at the start of the film, he slips, hits his head and dies. Dempsey replaces him, but despite all his scientific equipment he is only able to see the monster with Isabel's help. When he does photograph Nessie, the monster's underground cave begins to collapse around him. Modern science, then, cannot capture the pre-modern. Only a childlike belief makes the continued existence of the pre-modern possible. Thus, Isabel – who is blessed with a supernatural insight, or 'St Columba's gift' as the local's call it – responds to Dempsey's statement, 'I have to see it before I can believe it', with, 'No Dr Dempsey, you've got to believe it before you can see it.' Having learned his lesson, when Dempsey addresses the scientific community in London, he first evokes his own childhood dreams of being able to prove the existence of such a monster. He then provides Isabel's drawing of the monster as his proof, instead of the actual photograph of Nessie, science being rejected in favour of a 'primitive', childlike belief in the pre-modern past.

This lack of scientific proof enables Scotland to continue to exist as a pre-modern wilderness, uncorrupted by 'McNessie burger' tourist culture. For this reason Dempsey gives the photographs of Nessie to the Water

Bailiff after his impassioned speeches against the consequences of scientific advancement, such as 'acid rain', 'pollution' and 'warming air'. Instead, as in *The Secret of the Loch*, the existence of the pre-modern is rendered as a spectacle that can only be constructed by cinema. It is no coincidence that when the Water Bailiff criticises Dempsey's attempts to sound the loch scientifically he refers to his sonar equipment in a manner that likens it to the means of cinematic production, as 'lights', 'lenses' and 'computers'. Hence, the spectacle of scientific advancement offered by the CGI is seen in the monster family swimming away at the end. This family clearly reflects the film's target audience. Like Dempsey, the family audience has spent the last 100 minutes enjoying a virtual pre-modern past, constructed (ironically) by cinema, a modern technological innovation. Through this spectacle, scientific advancement in filmmaking is paradoxically rendered as another way of maintaining belief in the impossible pre-modern. However, this time the cinematic spectacle serves not to maintain a sense of British identity in which the whole is paradoxically divided – the civilised and the pre-modern, the English and the Scottish – as in *The Secret of the Loch*, but to reflect a more globalised centre/periphery (as in, US funds/British film) arrangement.

Jurassic Hero

Loch Ness also illustrates how the centre and the periphery of global filmmaking adopt different modes of address when exploring their interrelationship in the monster movie. Films like *Crocodile Dundee* and *Loch Ness* are produced by peripheral filmmaking nations (albeit often with US financial assistance) who offer international audiences a brief holiday in their supposedly pre-modern local cultures. However, in contrast to the US monster movies *Jurassic Park* (1993), *Anaconda* (1997) and *Lake Placid* (1999), these guided tours include some form of engagement with the local population that undermines globally accepted stereotypes about these peripheral nations.

Typically, US monster movies of the 1990s are concerned with the relationship between the monster and modernity and in discovering a pre-modern primal scene in which to situate their fish-out-of-water protagonists. *Jurassic Park* and *Anaconda* are all set at the global periphery, *Jurassic Park* on a remote Pacific island, *Anaconda* in the Brazilian rainforest, and whilst *Lake Placid* is set in the US, the forests and lakes of Maine are treated as though they are a remote wilderness, complete with giant Asian crocodile. They all take place in supposedly wild terrain on the outskirts of civilised society. Indeed, to emphasise their retreat to the wilderness *Anaconda* and *Lake Placid* in particular begin with establishing shots of their respective natural environments combined with point-of-view shots from the unseen aquatic monsters. The globally peripheral landscapes are thus established as the domain of these primitive creatures, dangerous territories which the US visitor must enter cautiously.

The US films all have at least one renowned expert (palaeontologist, zoologist or anthropologist) as a major character. By focusing on scientific experts confronting monsters, the US movies use the genre's 'man versus nature' theme to explore the global dominance of the US knowledge economy.[28] The protagonists in the majority of these films are, in Peter F Drucker's terms, 'knowledge workers'.[29] In *Jurassic Park*, Alan Grant (Sam Neill) and Ellie Sattler (Laura Dern) are professors, a palaeontologist and paleobotanist, looking for their next research grant. In *Anaconda*, anthropologist Professor Steven Cale (Eric Stoltz) is searching for the lost tribe of the Shirishama Indians, the fabled 'people of the mists', with documentary crew in tow. Finally, in *Lake Placid*, palaeontologist Kelly Scott (Bridget Fonda) is sent to Maine to examine evidence that a giant reptile may be loose in the lake.

All these films, then, explore the limits of mankind's control over nature, and, at the close, the monsters usually remain in charge of their domains. The scientific experts demonstrate the continued ingenuity of the knowledge society as they all survive to document the monster's existence. By contrast, however, whilst in the US films the representatives of the knowledge economy are threatened by monstrous wildlife, in *Loch Ness* Nessie is the one threatened by the arrival of the centre's knowledge worker, Dempsey. In the US films the knowledge workers are forcibly reduced to a pre-modern state by the monstrous environment. In *Loch Ness* the enduring charm of the pre-modern is emphasised for the positive effect it has on the visitor. As in *Crocodile Dundee*, in *Loch Ness* the US visitor must learn to accommodate himself to the local culture. This comes in Dempsey's ability to finally see (that is, believe in) the monster. In the US monster movies by contrast, it is simply a case of the US visitors triumphally overcoming their situation by themselves.

Admittedly, all the surviving characters of the US movies are 'rejuvenated' by their respective film's conclusion, ensuring that the representatives of the knowledge society comes away with a newfound belief in the traditional values of which their career-oriented lives have deprived them. Yet although Dempsey's trajectory in *Loch Ness* is basically the same as that of his contemporaries, the US movies portray this rejuvenation as an action that happens between US visitors to the periphery, thereby retaining the splendid isolation of the centre. By contrast, in *Loch Ness*, Laura

and Isabel serve as local guides for Dempsey, and through them he comes
to understand his place within the community. Indeed, his interaction
with this virtual fantasy of a pre-modern society remasculinises him into
an ideological position long imposed upon the rest of the world by
Hollywood films. Therefore, Dempsey's incorporation into the Kailyard
potentially unites a *globally imagined community* in its (capitalist) nostalgia
for the pre-modern as *Loch Ness* uses its romantic narrative to suggest the
rejuvenative power for both parties of the international relationship
between centre and periphery. In this case, tourism – both physical and
cinematic – is the particular service industry which *Loch Ness* promotes, in
contrast to the US films' celebration of a knowledge economy resourceful
enough to triumph over any monstrous resurgence of the primitive pre-
modern. Thus, this British-produced film capitalises on capitalist nostalgia to entice the international tourist into a paradoxical world in which the
very medium of their experience is the unacknowledged though known
representative of the modernity that is counterposed with the pre-modern
(monstrous) world.

In its integrated interaction between centre and periphery, *Loch Ness*,
despite its disputed identity, is still ultimately autoethnographic. Further
evidence of this is found in a related context in which Diane Negra notes
how certain US romances of the 1990s use European locations to offer
sanctuary to romantically dysfunctional US women fleeing a contemporary American society increasingly traumatised by insecurity in the home
and workplace. These films offer a touristic immersion in the European
location precisely like that of *Loch Ness*. Negra states,

> The desire to identify with indigenous populations and feel a sense of inclusion
> within local culture is a key feature of the recent tourist romances which assume that
> the national/cultural location visited is more 'real' than the (inevitably American)
> culture the protagonists leave behind.[30]

What Negra does not mention is that two of the films she focuses on,
Four Weddings and a Funeral and *Notting Hill* (1999), are, like *Loch Ness*,
Working Title productions. Although we could argue that the company,
though based in Britain, is an example of the increasing outsourcing of
Hollywood productions, the fantasy tourism on offer, at least in these
films, can also be considered an autoethnographic expression constructed
at the periphery (albeit using US funds) to be sold back to the centre.
These films, then, demonstrate how the relationship between Hollywood
and British firms like Working Title – which Mike Wayne describes as
'neo-colonial' – does at least provide a loophole through which the periphery can back chat, surreptitiously, to the centre of economic power.[31] The

European sanctuary on offer in many Working Title films, including *Loch Ness*, can thus be seen as projections of what a British production company thinks US audiences may believe to be deficient about life in contemporary US society (a little like a proprietor of a tourist shop second guessing his or her clientele's preconceptions when stocking up on souvenirs), rather than necessarily being considered direct expressions of US beliefs. *Loch Ness*'s representation of the Kailyard, then, creates an image of a life that Britain perceives the USA to think that it has lost.

The Water Horse (2007)

As I write, *The Water Horse* is enjoying a prolonged theatrical release, so I end with a brief discussion of this most recent Nessie movie whose relationship to tourism expands upon this discussion of *Loch Ness*. *The Water Horse* is the story of a young boy, Angus MacMorrow (Alex Etel), growing up in a small village by the side of Loch Ness during World War II. Angus finds an egg which hatches into a Water Horse. He names it Crusoe and takes care of it until large enough to be released into the loch. Events are complicated by the presence of a troop of British soldiers who are billeted in Angus's house and charged with defending the loch from Nazi U-boats (a historical precedent closer to Loch Ewe than Loch Ness). Crusoe, mistaken for a submarine by military technology, is forced to escape the barrage of the British guns and swims away into the sea. Angus completes his coming of age in the process, finally accepting the death of his father during the war.

Like *Loch Ness*, *The Water Horse* is not easy to position in terms of a specific national cinema. The origins of the film lie in Scotland, in producer Douglas Rae of Ecosse Films who spent ten years raising the money for the production. Ecosse are based in London and were responsible for Scottish set films *Mrs Brown* (1997), *Wilderness* (2006) and the BBC television series *Monarch of the Glen* (2000–5). Yet *The Water Horse* exists somewhere between a UK/US coproduction, and a US film made in New Zealand with some location shooting in Scotland. Its Scottish credentials include the appearance of veteran Scottish actor Brian Cox as the grown up Angus spinning his yarn about the kelpie (in flashback) to young US backpackers in the present, and establishing shots of Eilean Donan Castle and Ardkinglas House (Loch Fyne, Argyll), as stand-ins for Loch Ness. However, in total, only two of the twelve weeks of shooting took place in Scotland, the other ten in New Zealand. Moreover, the film was directed by American Jay Russell, the script was adapted by American Robert Nelson Jacobs on the bequest of Harvey Weinstein (when the film was

Figure 4.1 CGI Tourist Attraction: The latest Nessie spectacle in
The Water Horse (2007)

initially with Miramax[32]) and it was finally financed to the tune of $50 million by US money, with the first company to take a risk being Walden Media (who had previously produced *The Chronicles of Narnia* (2005)) and later Revolution Studios. Moreover, *The Water Horse* was produced in New Zealand, with the monster created by Weta Digital, the same special effects team who worked on *The Lord of the Rings* trilogy, *King Kong* (2005) and *The Chronicles of Narnia: Prince Caspian* (2008).

In spite of its ambiguous identity, much of the British press coverage surrounding *The Water Horse* focused on the tourist revenue it would bring into Scotland. In April 2007, Visit Scotland announced, from New York's annual Tartan Week celebrations, that they would be working in partnership with Sony Pictures Entertainment to promote the film.[33] Similarly, in January 2008, to mark the film's release in UK cinemas, *The Sunday Times* ran a feature focusing on the 'floods of tourists' the film was likely to bring to Scotland.[34] The BBC, for its part, stressed the rise in interest in Scotland as a film location caused by the film, as well as the increase of income into the area it prompted (estimated at over £200,000 around promotional events) and the likely rise in tourism to follow.[35]

In its relationship to tourism *The Water Horse* has much in common with *Loch Ness*. The most telling alteration to the original story from Dick King-Smith's children's novel of the same name is the setting of the film during the Second World War. In contrast to the film, the novel ends in 1933 with both mention of the road built along the north shore of the loch and (as a direct consequence) a mock-up of a newspaper clipping (like that in *The Inverness Courier*) telling of a reported sighting of the monster by Mr and Mrs Mackay as they were driving along the new road.[36] In the book, then, tourists are considered a potential threat to the survival of the pre-modern monster. The film on the other hand, reveals its intended links to the tourist trade in its shifting of this threat from tourists to the military. In this way, *The Water Horse*, described by one reviewer as a 'tourist brochure' of the Scottish landscape,[37] is designed for consumption by an international tourist gaze in the post-Cold War era.

The narrative is framed as a yarn spun to US backpackers, prompted by their viewing of a copy of the 'surgeon's photo' of Nessie on a local pub wall. In contrast to the book, the film posits the military, or rather the global spread of militarised modernity that the film traces back to World War II, as the major threat to the remaining patch of globally peripheral wilderness in which Crusoe frolics and to which US tourists flock. This is illustrated most clearly in the image of the submarine net that stretches across the entire loch, blocking Crusoe's escape to the sea. This artificial boundary between militarised modernity and the wilderness is triumphally breached by Crusoe as he finally leaps to freedom in the sea. The decision to make this threat as much a consequence of the British military's presence on the loch as any threat from German U-boats (which are entirely absent from the film) renders the story more universally applicable than a Britain versus Germany plot might have done. Thus, again as in *Loch Ness*, it is the monster as mythical beast that reassures the international viewer that there is a boundary between civilised (militarised) modernity and wilderness. Paradoxically, however, the monster's very survival vindicates the totalising spread of modernity represented by the military.

The major difference between *The Water Horse* and *Loch Ness* is that the CGI monster appears much sooner, after less than fifteen minutes, and plays a central role in the creation of spectacle throughout the film. This is undoubtedly due to the advances in technology that have taken place between the two films, *The Water Horse* providing its youthful target audience with the spectacle of underwater fairground-like rides, as Angus is transported on Crusoe's back both across the loch and through a magical underwater kingdom that includes sunken ships and an ancient stone circle. This foregrounding of the spectacular places the film on a par with previous Weta Digital productions like *The Lord of the Rings*, and perhaps resonates with the knowing association of the audience (adults at least) of the setting for the story with the spectacular scenery of touristic New Zealand. Thus, the spectacle of the monster illustrates, once again, the paradoxically divided yet whole, civilised/pre-modern identity established in *The Secret of the Loch*. However, rather more like *Loch Ness*, this centre/periphery relationship reflects a global arena in which the spread of CGI technology to the global periphery (New Zealand) demonstrates its role in constructing globally appealing images of the 'wilderness' that simultaneously affirm and deny the existence of the pre-modern periphery for the international tourist gaze.

In both its setting and its technological spectacle, then, *The Water Horse* participates in the selling of both countries as tourist destinations. New Zealand has long-established links with Scotland, and indeed, the two have often been compared; the large Scottish diaspora of earlier centuries left its mark in the naming of cities – for instance, Dunedin, from the Scots Gaelic for Edinburgh. In both its setting and its technological spectacle, *The Water Horse* participates in the selling of both countries as tourist destinations, serving to link these two small, peripheral countries in the process of repackaging and re-exporting the Nessie myth for global audiences and for mutual tourist benefit. Emerging from a global periphery, then, films like *Loch Ness* and *The Water Horse* are set in Scotland, but deliberately shift their focus from national concerns towards a more internationally appealing touristic narrative.

This practice is demonstrated once again by director John Henderson's *Mee-Shee The Water Giant* (2005), a UK/US/German production also aimed at family audiences. Like Henderson's *Loch Ness*, which depicts the closeness of the Scottish population and Nessie's family, and, indeed, the equation of Crusoe in *The Water Horse* with Angus (whose father has been killed in the war, and whose childhood bears the scar of militarised modernity), *Mee-Shee* links its family of monsters with the Native American population of Canada, suggesting both their closeness to nature, and their pre-modern status. In all these instances – be it Scotland, New Zealand standing in for Scotland, or Canada – the global periphery is selling the spectacle of its monsters back to the world. They are offering a brief holiday from 'civilised' life in a constructed fantasy of the pre-modern wilderness that paradoxically confirms its own non-existence in an era in which the global spread of modernity is evidenced in the production of Hollywood's CGI blockbusters precisely in countries like Scotland, New Zealand and Canada.

Notes

1. Steuart Campbell, *The Loch Ness Monster* (Edinburgh: Birlinn, 2002), p. 1.
2. Ibid. p. 2.

3. John Urry, 'Globalising the Tourist Gaze', Department of Sociology, Lancaster University: http://www.atlas-euro.org/pages/pdf/WUbarcelona/WU%20 txt%20Juan-Urry-globalising-the-tourist-gaze.pdf (23/03/09).

4. Anon., 'Strange Spectacle on Loch Ness: What is it?', *The Inverness Courier*, 2 May 1933.

5. Urry draws on John Taylor's *A Dream of England* (Manchester: Manchester University Press, 1994), in John Urry, 'Globalising the Tourist Gaze', p. 4.

6. John R. Gold and Margaret M. Gold, *Imagining Scotland* (Aldershot: Scolar Press, 1995), p. 130.

7. Urry, 'Globalising the Tourist Gaze', p. 26.

8. Anon., 'The Secret of the Loch', *Kinematograph Weekly*, 1416: 208 (1934), p. 20.

9. David Martin-Jones, 'Sexual Healing: Representations of the English in Post-devolutionary Scotland', *Screen*, 46: 2 (2005), pp. 227–34.

10. Oscar Moore, 'Loch Ness', *Screen International*, 981 (1994), p. 19.

11. *Sight and Sound* lists Loch Ness a UK production in Liese Spencer, 'Loch Ness', *Sight and Sound* 6: 2 (1996), pp. 47-8, p. 47. *Empire* magazine lists it as a UK/US co-production, See Bob McCabe, 'Loch Ness', *Empire* 81 (1996), p. 40. The Internet Movie Database (IMDB) also lists it as a UK/US copro-duction: http://www.imdb.com/title/tt0113682/ Colin McArthur refers to it as a Hollywood film, Colin McArthur, *Brigadoon, Braveheart and the Scots* (London: I. B. Tauris, 2003), p. 131.

12. Eddie Dyja (ed.), *BFI Film and Television Handbook 1996* (London: BFI, 1995), p. 28.

13. Michael Kuhn, *One Hundred Films and a Funeral* (London: Thorogood, 2002), p. 15.

14. Alan Jones, 'In Search of Loch Ness', *Cinefantastique*, 28: 2 (1996), pp. 44–5, p. 44.

15. Kuhn, *One Hundred Films and a Funeral*, pp. 57–68.

16. Sarah Street, *Transatlantic Crossings* (London: Continuum, 2002), p. 202.

17. Kuhn, *One Hundred Films and a Funeral*, p. 68.

18. Alan Jones, 'In Search of Loch Ness', p. 45.

19. Mike Wayne, *The Politics of Contemporary European Cinema* (Bristol: Intellect, 2002), p. 43.

20. John Brown, 'A Suitable Job for a Scot', *Sight and Sound*, 52: 3 (1983), pp. 157–62, p. 159–60.

21. John Caughie, 'Support whose Local Hero?', *Cencrastus*, 14 (1983), pp. 44–6. Jonathan Murray, 'Straw or Wicker?' in Jonathan Murray, Lesley Stephenson, Stephen Harper and Benjamin Franks (eds), Constructing *The Wicker Man* (Dumfries: Crichton University Press, 2005), pp. 11–36, p. 28.

22. Ian Goode, 'Meditating the rural' in Robert Fish (ed.), *Cinematic Countrysides* (Manchester: Manchester University Press, 2007), pp. 109–16, pp. 122–3.

23. Graeme Turner, *Making it National* (St Leonards, NSW: Allen & Unwin, 1994), p. 117

24. Koichi Iwabuchi, 'Nostalgia for a (Different) Asian Modernity', *Positions*, 10: 3 (2002), pp. 547–73, p. 549.
25. Ibid.
26. Ibid.
27. Nöel Carroll, *Interpreting the Moving Image* (Cambridge: Cambridge University Press, 1998), p. 244.
28. Peter F. Drucker, *The Age of Discontinuity* (London: Heinemann, 1968), pp. 247–68.
29. Ibid. p. 248.
30. Diane Negra, 'Romance and/as Tourism', Elizabeth Ezra and Terry Rowden, *Transnational Cinema the* Film *Reader* (London: Routledge, 2006), pp. 169–80, p. 170.
31. Mike Wayne, 'Working Title Mark II' *International Journal of Media and Cultural Politics*, 2:1 (2006) pp. 59–73, p. 60.
32. Paul Fischer, 'Jay Russell The Water Horse: Legend of the Deep Interview', *Girl.com.au* http://www.girl.com.au/jay-russell-the-water-horse-legend-of-the-deep-interview.htm (17/07/08).
33. Media Centre, 'VisitScotland announces partnership on Water Horse movie', Visit Scotland website: http://www.visitscotland.org/news_item.htm?newsID=44688 (23/01/08).
34. Allan Brown, 'Nessie's Ready for her Close Up', *The Sunday Times: Ecosse Supplement*, 20/01/08, p. 3.
35. Steven McKenzie, 'Monster Interest in Loch Filming', BBC News website, 09/07/08: http://news.bbc.co.uk/1/hi/scotland/highlands_and_islands/7493532.stm (13/07/08)
36. Dick King-Smith, *The Water Horse* (London: Puffin, [1990] 2008), pp. 92–4.
37. Jane Lamacraft, 'The Water Horse', *Sight and Sound*, 18: 2 (2008), p. 88.

CHAPTER 5

Horror Film: History Hydes in the Highlands

This chapter engages with horror films, with a particular emphasis on two werewolf movies, *Dog Soldiers* (2002) and *Wild Country* (2005). It begins with an introduction to the relationship between Scotland and the horror film. *Dog Soldiers* is then analysed with a dedicated focus on its depiction of English and Scottish masculinities, its engagement with a British tradition of war movies, the myth of Tartanry and the allegorical connotations that surround werewolves in horror movies. The ambivalence demonstrated in its treatment of Scotland as a location further illustrates the complexities raised by British films set in Scotland that aim at broader, often international markets. *Dog Soldiers* is contrasted with the low-budget, indigenous Scottish production *Wild Country*, which focuses on the local concerns of its teenage protagonists. In both films, conventions of the horror genre enable very different types of engagement with existing myths of Scotland and Scottishness.

Crime in the City, Horror in the Highlands

The horror films usually associated with Scotland are the body snatcher films set in Edinburgh. These films are often inspired by true stories of grave robbing, an illegal activity mainly pursued for the treasures found in the grave, but which, during the early decades of the nineteenth century, was also done to procure bodies for dissection in Edinburgh's medical college. In the infamous case of William Burke and William Hare, grave robbing was replaced by murder, causing a public scandal involving Dr Robert Knox of the medical college that eventually shook up the legal constraints surrounding the provision of cadavers for medical research. This history of the Edinburgh-based grave robber films – *The Body Snatcher* (1945), *The Greed of William Hart* (1948), *The Flesh and the Fiends* (1959), *Burke and Hare* (1971), *The Doctor and the Devils* (1985) – has been discussed by Duncan Petrie in *Screening Scotland* (2000). Petrie notes in particular the influence of Scottish writer Robert Louis Stevenson on this tradition, Stevenson's short story *The Body Snatcher* (1884) being the inspiration for the 1945 Hollywood film of that name, starring Boris Karloff and Bela Lugosi.

Although the tradition of the urban horror film continues in a film currently in production, *The Meat Trade* (2009) – which is a contemporary story of body snatchers in Edinburgh based on a story by Irvine Welsh – since the 1990s this focus has been matched by a growth in films that depict 'horrific' happenings in the Highlands and Islands. Here the rejuvenative Highlands and Islands of the myth of Tartanry are refigured as a darker, more sinister space on Scotland's outskirts. This is most apparent in the humorous play with a fictional island's isolation from both the mainland and its 'civilised' historical development in *The Wicker Man* (1973), a cult favourite in which a self-righteous, virgin, Christian policeman, Sergeant Howie (Edward Woodward), travels to Summerisle in search of a missing girl. Once there, however, he is duped by the islanders at every turn, until his ultimate death as a human sacrifice, burnt alive so that the islander's pagan gods will bless their harvest. The wilds of Scotland are thus considered a potentially treacherous location where a more 'primitive' attitude to life and death persists and duplicity and double-cross are deadly commonplaces against which the unwitting outsider must guard. This view is reiterated in the spate of horror films made in the 2000s and set in Scotland's remoter parts. Whilst the 'cannibalism' in the werewolf movie evokes the popular legend of Sawney Bean, the purported Ayrshire head of a cannibal clan, in these horror films it is again the literature of Robert Louis Stevenson that is of importance. Rather than *The Body Snatcher*, however, this time *The Strange Case of Dr Jekyll and Mr Hyde* (1886) is most instructive.

Writing on British literature in *Out of History* (1996), Cairns Craig revised the position he had himself established in his contribution to Colin McArthur's collection of essays, *Scotch Reels*, pointing out the positive power of myths like Tartanry. Craig approaches the work of nineteenth-century writers like Sir Walter Scott as attempts to remythologise the past that had been excluded from an official, predominantly English history of Britain. For Craig, this 'official' version of history had left the nation of Scotland 'out of history'. He argued that Tartanry had attempted to counter this erasure of Scottish history by remythologising the roots of an independent Scottish identity.

> What cannot be integrated into the progressive view of human development projected by the historical consciousness has not, thereby, been wiped from the map of our lives; and in that residual Scottishness which cannot be integrated with the ideology of progressive English history, Scottish consciousness finds a means, however terrible and self-mutilating, of imagining forces that history will not subdue.[1]

Craig discusses Robert Louis Stevenson's *Dr Jekyll and Mr Hyde*[2] to demonstrate the destructive potential apparent when that which is excluded from a progressive history returns. In this case, the horrific, murderous presence of Mr Hyde emerges with the potential to destroy the progressive, grand narrative of English history symbolised by Dr Jekyll. Hyde represents the 'terrible and self-mutilating' force that the official history of a unified Britain cannot subdue. The two characters epitomise the two movements of history that Craig sees in conflict over the identity of Scotland. On the one hand the linear, progressive history of an English-led 'Britain' (Dr Jekyll) and, on the other, the necessarily cyclical, repetitive history of Scotland (Mr Hyde). It is this latter, monstrous history that perpetually re-emerges in literary 'imaginings' to haunt its apparently more 'civilised' double.

Rather than a nostalgic escape from official history, then, Tartanry can be seen as an attempt to counter the linear history of a unified Britain. Accordingly, popular films that employ the symbols of Tartanry previously identified in *Scotch Reels* may actually have more positive potential than was initially considered. In *Dog Soldiers* in particular, this return to prominence of the repressed in a monstrous form is depicted in the attack of a family of Scottish werewolves, close-knit and bloodthirsty. Thus, whilst on the one hand the film can be said to represent an Anglocentric desire to retain the old myths and use them to help reaffirm a traditional sense of British national identity (a *Scotch Reels* reading of the film as Tartanry) on the other, it offers the image of Scottish history reemerging (an *Out of History* inflected reading). The presence of the werewolf is especially important in this latter process as it enables the film to playfully rewrite the monstrous return of a previously repressed Scottish national history.

Dog Soldiers (2002)

Dog Soldiers follows a patrol of British soldiers, five English and one Scottish. They are airlifted into the Scottish Highlands on a routine exercise where they have to outmanoeuvre a special operations patrol. The situation rapidly deteriorates, however, when they discover that the special operations troops, with the exception of Captain Ryan (Liam Cunningham) have all been eaten by werewolves. They are themselves only saved from the lycanthropes by the timely appearance of a young woman called Megan (Emma Cleasby) in a Land Rover. Megan takes them to an isolated farmhouse where they are gradually picked off by the creatures. At the end of the film, with Megan revealed as a werewolf and the house as that of the werewolf family that surrounds them, the squad Sergeant, Wells (Sean Pertwee) blows up the house. The only survivor, Scotsman Joe Cooper (Kevin McKidd) emerges from the cellar and leaves through the front door, the only part of the house still standing.

On initial viewing, *Dog Soldiers* appears to fall in line with the negative implications of the myth of Tartanry identified by *Scotch Reels*. The opening, under the caption, 'Scotland', establishes location in a wooded exterior. A young couple (significantly, English tourists) are camping by the side of a loch. The young man is wearing a tartan patterned shirt. Harking back to a time of Romantic myth, and suggesting also the fighting spirit of the clans, the young woman presents her boyfriend with a solid silver paperweight in the shape of a sword, saying: 'No knight should be without his sword.' The couple represent the English enjoyment of the Highlands as a tourist location that emerged, along with the myth of Tartanry, after the militarily enforced Highland clearances. To these people, the warrior tradition of the clans, the paperweight and tartan shirt illustrate, have become consumable symbols of a lost Scottish past.

Tartanry is further in evidence with the arrival of the soldiers, who are helicoptered into the same area under the slightly different caption, 'The Highlands of Scotland'. Their arrival is accompanied by several clichéd images of the 'tartan monster'[3] we expect to find on the 'postcards, whisky bottle labels, shortbread tins [and] tea cloths'[4] of High Street Tartanry. They fly over snow-topped mountains, dense woodlands and scenic lochs, before disembarking, like so many visitors to cinematic Scotland before them, to be greeted by the sight of a long red-haired Highland cow.

The location of the Highlands as an uncivilised, uninhabited wilderness is repeatedly stressed, and not only through the werewolves' devouring of the young couple. The soldiers grumble about being unable to watch the England versus Germany football match on the television. Their radios are rendered useless, the isolated farmhouse is without a telephone and the werewolves disable Megan's Land Rover. By this point they are entirely cut off from civilisation. The discovery of a Claymore broadsword in the farmhouse is the icing on the tartan cake. Its juxtaposition with the ineffective machine guns and automatic pistols of the British soldiers emphasises the ancient, uncivilised status of this pre-modern land.

In fact, Scotland appears to be a land divorced not only from civilisation, but also from history itself. The film is set in a place that is identified as at once a region, 'The Highlands of Scotland', and yet also a nation, 'Scotland'. This illustrates perfectly the conflation that takes place under the mythical construction of national identity of Tartanry. The cleared ('lost') Highlands, after the defeat of the Jacobite uprising standing in for all life in contemporary Scotland. This symbolic location is established as a mythical land before time in which the only inhabitants are bloodthirsty beasts. That the werewolves are in actual fact a Scottish family does not detract from this image of an uninhabited wilderness, as to become a were-wolf in this film a person wounded by a lycanthrope first dies and is reborn. Thus, with the exception of Cooper, he of the British army, there are no Scottish people in this place, only mythical beasts whom the British army's special operations have come to hunt as though, Cooper notes, on 'safari'. For this reason, in the opening of *Dog Soldiers*, Scotland is ren-dered as an English vision of Tartanry, a cleared wilderness playground for English hunters and holidaymakers.

What use, then, can a film so apparently imbued with the spirit of Tartanry be for our understanding of contemporary representations of Scotland, especially as it was mostly filmed on location in Luxembourg? To answer this question, the role of the werewolf in this popular genre film must be explored in more depth.

Tartan Monster, Tartan Monstrous

Over the last century the appearance of werewolves in films from around the world has been interpreted by critics in a variety of ways. These range from: lycanthropy as an 'upper class disease'[5] (*The Werewolf of London* (1935)), the teenage werewolf as symbol of the struggle of nonconformists in fifties America (*I Was a Teenage Werewolf* (1957)),[6] the curse of the werewolf as the 'debilitating effects of sexuality'[7] on the British profes-sional in the early 1960s (*The Curse of the Werewolf* (1961)), the werewolf as manifestation of the American WASP id in the aftermath of Vietnam and Watergate (*The Howling* (1981), *An American Werewolf in London* (1981))[8] or, indeed, the werewolf as ancient American history returning to counter the modern development of said WASP id (*Wolfen* (1981)).[9] The one common factor to most werewolf movies, however, is their conflation of lycanthropic transformation with masculinity. It was not until *The Howling* and *Wolf* (1994) that the female werewolf began to emerge. Yet even here her presence is marginalised, as both female protagonists remain human for the majority of the film and only transform at the very end.

Since the late nineties, however, lycanthropic tendencies have begun to be attributed to several strong female leads. For instance, *An American Werewolf in Paris* (1997) sees Julie Delpy's Serafine playing a much larger role in the narrative as a female werewolf working on a serum to suppress her lycanthropic cycle. Three years later, *Ginger Snaps* (2000) positions a female werewolf as major protagonist and links her transformation during the full moon with the onset of menstruation. The examination of the female werewolf, also currently a growing movement in literature, and, to a lesser degree on television (for example, Kelley Armstrong's novel *Bitten* (2001) and season four of *Buffy The Vampire Slayer* (2000)), is also evident in *Dog Soldiers*.

This gradual emergence of the female werewolf, and her journey from periphery to centre stage, is due to the changing representation of women in the later decades of the twentieth century. Extending an argument often made about female (frequently lesbian) vampires in cinema, their changing representations can be said to negotiate the increased prominence of women in society since the women's liberation movement, feminism and gay rights activism of the 1960s and 1970s onwards.[10] That the recent trend for female werewolf movies should emerge well over twenty years after these vampire movies, however, suggests that another, more current social movement is also reflected here.

Dog Soldiers establishes that its werewolves are a family, functioning under the guidance of a paternal, Alpha male. However, when Megan lets them into the farmhouse she explicitly links her own imminent transformation with her menstrual cycle. Doubling over and holding her stomach as though experiencing a cramp she declares, 'Its that time of the month'. Admittedly, this idea of the lunar cycle linking the werewolf to the menstrual cycle is not new. As early as 1973, Walter Evans makes the connection between the 'werewolf's bloody attacks'[11] and the menstrual cycle. Similarly, Barbara Creed, expanding on Evans' work, argues that the werewolf is a feminised monster due to its ability to 'give birth to itself in either animal or human form'[12] on a monthly basis. This correlation is, she argues elsewhere, due to ancient tradition that links the cycle of the moon and the woman's menstrual cycle.[13] Thus, although it is a relatively new phenomena to see the link between the werewolf and the menstrual cycle rendered so explicitly, there is a long tradition of figuring the return of the repressed[14] as a monstrous feminine.

However, this new representation of the werewolf is not simply a negative reaction to the perceived threat of a predatory female sexuality. After all, if it were, then why would the entire werewolf family be coded as 'feminine' in this way, Alpha male and all? Rather, by viewing *Dog Soldiers* in light of a number of British films emerging at that time and similarly concerned with groups of men in peril, a different reading is possible. Many British films of the 1990s and early 2000s, including *Brassed Off* (1996), *The Full Monty* (1997) and *Billy Elliott* (2000), explored possible solutions for endangered communities (but, more specifically, an endangered traditional masculinity), caught by the economic shift from an industrial- to a services-based economy. This same concern for the 'hands-on' male under threat from an external, feminising force, can be seen in *Dog Soldiers*. The monstrous force that is the werewolf clan can be understood as an illustration of the way the services economy, which emerged across the developed world in the 1980s and 1990s, has been culturally coded as feminine. It is for this reason, I argue, that the female werewolf has come to the fore since the late 1990s: as a monstrous symbol of this new 'feminine' economy. This can be seen in *Dog Soldiers*, a film which avoids the direct reference of the other films to changing masculinities in a post-industrial context, departing instead for the wilds of Scotland.

The beer and football ethos of the squad expresses perfectly the resurgence of 'new laddism' in British films of the 1990s that was observed by Claire Monk to be the result of a 'perceived crisis in male economic power and gender privilege', itself evidence of 'the apparent ascendancy of women in the post-industrial workplace'.[15] The threat of this post-industrial monstrous femininity is seen in the film as a creeping, insidious foe that would assimilate, or if not, devour all men that it encounters. Megan, who lures the soldiers to the farmhouse, is prefigured by Cooper's comment what he most fears is 'spiders . . . and women . . . and, err . . . spider-women'. Megan is the manifestation of these fears, the arachnid who literally lures the soldiers into her parlour, and also the monstrous – part-hairy animal, part human – spider/wolf-woman. The werewolves, similarly, are seven-foot tall phallic usurpers of masculine power, symbols of Private Witherspoon's (Spoon) greatest fear, castration. For the majority of the film the soldiers are trapped in the farmhouse interior, a domestic setting usually coded as feminine, and emphasised as such by a concentration of events in the kitchen and bedroom. The attack of the werewolves on the men in this location manifests an image of contemporary anxiety that masculinity will be domesticated and finally overrun by the monstrous femininity of the services economy. It is for this reason that the final breaching of the squad's defences is treacherously perpetrated from within by the menstruating Megan. Thus, much as Dana B. Polen, Harlan Kennedy and Mark Jancovich[16] have theorised the monster in horror films as representative of an internal threat to the nation, *Dog Soldiers* suggests that the greatest present threat to traditional, industrial masculinity (read, 'British' identity) is the feminising force of the services industry.

However, what is interesting about *Dog Soldiers* is that it deploys the myth of Tartanry in order to combat this feminine threat. It replays, somewhat in the manner of a Freudian primal scene (a fictionalised historical origin that, once understood, provides a cure for traumas suffered in the present), the post-1746 Highland clearances, and the incorporation of the Highland clansman into the British army. The replaying of this originary moment of the creation of 'British' masculinity functions as a false origin, an imagined Freudian Wolf-Man (!)[17] if you will, from which a singular history supposedly emanates. Through the figure of the Scotsman, Cooper, the one member of the patrol to survive the night, *Dog Soldiers* attempts to suture over contemporary anxieties concerning masculinity and national identity in general. In Cooper we see the continued potency of traditional British masculinity, at exactly the point at which this reality has been challenged economically by the emergence of a 'feminine', post-industrial economy.

Tommy Cooper

Initially the film's vision of the masculinity able to counter the feminising forces of the services industry seems straightforward. Cooper, the last man standing is the only Scotsman in the squad. His triumph in the Highlands of Scotland – and indeed, his good showing in Wales during the selection process for special operations – suggests that the Scotsman *essentially* embodies an ancient, Celtic masculine strength. It would appear that this is the return of the repressed that emerges from the peripheries of Britain to offer future salvation from the feminising services industry that has already swamped England.

However, closer analysis shows that the film uses Cooper to suggest that it is the British masculinity that exists as a product of the *civilising* of this ancient Celtic masculinity that offers salvation. For this reason the primal scene replayed in the film is that of events in the Highlands circa 1745–6, the period setting immortalised by the myth of Tartanry. It was, after all, as a consequence of the failure of the Jacobite uprising that the Highland warrior was incorporated into the British army, exactly the civilising process that the film advocates to save contemporary masculinity. Cooper's survival illustrates that for masculinity to save itself in this new, potentially feminising context, it must retain its ancient Celtic roots but temper them with the English rationalism of the Enlightenment project. The ideal masculine figure in *Dog Soldiers*, then, is the British soldier, a Scottish body with an English head on its shoulders.

This becomes clearer if we fill in a little of the history. In the years immediately following the defeat of the Jacobite forces at Culloden in 1746, several restrictions were placed upon the Highland clans. These were to preempt future uprisings and to assimilate this area of Scotland into Britain. They included the Disarming Act of 1746, which removed the Highlander's right to own arms or to wear the traditional dress of the Highland clans. These symbols of Highland pride, however, were still legally endorsed by the English crown, but only for those who joined the British army. The Highland warrior was thus 'civilised' into the military equivalent of the economic position of the Lowland middle classes. As Craig notes, these token symbols were used to 'create a sense of regimental honour and individuality, but they were not allowed to challenge the existing values of modern Scotland'[18] (that is those of the English and the Lowland middle classes).[19] During the American and Napoleanic wars that followed, various Scottish regiments of the British army excelled themselves against the supposedly common enemies of the British Empire. It was, in part at least, the distinguishing feats of these regiments that once more legitimised the wearing of the kilt.

Whilst the Highland clearances themselves did not take place immediately after the defeat at Culloden, as Pittock notes they have dovetailed, in myth, with 1746. Through this dovetailing the sense of a nation defeated militarily was compounded by the sense of a lost way of life. Scotland was now also a nation defeated economically as the myriad small farms of the Highlands were depopulated and the land given over to intensive sheep farming and tourist hunting retreats. This mythical dovetailing is also present in *Dog Soldiers*, the replaying of the incorporation of the Scotsman into the British army occurring at the same moment that the Scottish farmhouse – which has stood for centuries – is destroyed (or rather, forcibly cleared) by the English Sergeant, Wells.

By replaying these events *Dog Soldiers* suggests that the historical 'civilising' of Scotland contains the seeds of a solution to the contemporary crisis of British masculinity. When the farmhouse is destroyed, Cooper is left in the basement with Captain Ryan, the last remaining werewolf. As Ryan attempts to kill Cooper, Cooper finds the hikers' silver sword paperweight and uses it to kill Ryan. As he slays Ryan he utters the words synonymous with the English World Cup victory over Germany of 1966, 'They think it's all over, it is now.' With these words, Cooper shows that he has been fully incorporated into the beer and football ethos expressed by the new lads of his squad of British troops. These are not words that one would expect to hear from many Scotsmen, although one might from someone claiming to be British. Thus the film posits a solution to the problem of the feminising force of the services industry in the composite form of an ancient, Celtic masculinity in its civilised form, the British soldier.

Dog Soldiers' replaying of the post–Culloden incorporation of the Scottish Highland clans into the Union is further bolstered by its

Figure 5.1 An English head on Scottish soldiers? Cooper (Kevin McKidd) is the last man standing in the monstrous Highlands. *Dog Soldiers* (2002)

conflation of imperial heritage nostalgia (self-consciously evoked through the film's *Zulu* (1964) styled scenario) with the English football team's endeavour in Europe. This emphasises the role masculinity can still play both as military defender of the British (imperial) nation, and as a part of the services economy. Rather like music in *Brassed Off*, stripping in *The Full Monty* and dancing in *Billy Elliott*, football functions in *Dog Soldiers* as an illustration of one way in which English (through the anglicising of Cooper, read British) masculinity has a role to play in the growing entertainment industry. The slight difference is that this masculinity functions as a performer on the world stage, as a world cup qualifier is played away from home against Germany. The film paints an anglocentric picture of a unified nation (Britain) still capable of its past imperial strength, whilst deliberately erasing the difference between the nations through Cooper's incorporation into an English history of footballing success. Similarly, Spoon equates the predicament the soldiers find themselves in and the battle at Rourke's Drift depicted in the film *Zulu* in terms that at once acknowledge and then erase the fact that the troops involved there were a Welsh regiment. He says,

> Y'know what this reminds me of? Rourke's Drift. A hundred men of Harlech making a desperate stand against ten thousand Zulu warriors. Outnumbered,

surrounded, staring death in the face, not flinching for a moment. Balls of British steel.

Spoon, then, expresses the belief that an industrial, 'steely' British (but not Welsh, or even Scottish) masculinity still exists in 2002, and that its role remains that of defender of the imperial 'nation' abroad. Similarly, through football the film allows the possibility of a new role for English/British masculinity, even within the new 'foreign field' of the feminine services industry.

When viewed in this way, *Dog Soldiers* appears to create the illusion of the unbroken continuation of an anglocentric view of British history. It deliberately evokes a time of imperial unity by replaying the moment of incorporation of the Highlands of Scotland into the economic and military union that was to make the British Empire great. This primal scene creates a Freudian Wolf Man in Cooper – part wild, ancient, Scottish masculinity, part civilised English rationality – that suggests a continuity between the masculinity that existed at the dawn of the industrial revolution which would eventually fuel the British Empire and that of the present. Thus, contemporary anxieties over the diminishing role played by traditional masculinity in the emergent post-industrial, feminine, services economy are reassured by an image that suggests the continuation (primarily through football and the military) of a traditionally defined, active masculinity that is a direct result of the economic and military successes of the imperial past. This is finally illustrated in the tabloid newspaper shown over the end credits, where Cooper's 'Werewolves Ate My Platoon' story shares the front page with the headline, 'England 5 Germany 1: Team Bounce Back Abroad.'

(There is no. . .) Out of History

However, another interpretation of the film is possible. In contrast to the pro-British stance I have so far outlined the film can also be read as an allegory for the potential return of Scottish national identity. Again, here, it is the interpretation of the role of the werewolves that is crucial. This reading sees the werewolves not as the monstrous feminine that is the post-industrial milieu; rather, they symbolise the monstrous Mr Hyde that is Scottish history. This repressed history here reemerges to derail the grand narrative of progressive, English-led, official British history. In a manner that correlates with the arguments put forward by Craig, *Dog Soldiers* demonstrates the 'heightened self-consciousness of the Scottish imaginary'. Primarily this is an effect created through the film's self-consciousness – a trait typical of the post *Scream* (1996) horror film – and the possibilities this offers for reading against the grain of its otherwise unionist narrative. As these contrary interpretations demonstrate, the Highlands functions as a backdrop (a film set resonant with mythical associations) against which the struggle for ownership of Tartanry is played out.

Dog Soldiers unapologetically foregrounds its intertextual borrowings. The most prominent of these are taken from *Zulu* and *Aliens* (1986) and strongly suggest that the film can be watched reflexively. For instance, as Spoon's speech evokes the schoolboy machismo of *Zulu*, the refrain of 'Men of Harlech' is heard, plaintively whining in the background. It stops abruptly, however, as Spoon finishes speaking, and Joe replies, incredulously, 'You're bloody loving this, aren't ya?' Hence the film knowingly acknowledges its place within a heritage tradition whilst simultaneously debasing this very tradition through the use of irreverent comedy. Here, any reverence for imperial tradition is abolished by the incongruity it establishes between music and dialogue.

In fact, from its first scene the film foregrounds the fantastical nature of what is represented in the Highlands of Scotland, its self-referentiality bringing its discussion of myth making to the foreground. The opening sequence establishes that the male English hiker is a writer. His immediate death at the hands of the werewolves creates the impression that the story has been immediately wrestled from the hands of this, now dead, English author. Hence, from its beginning the film plays out the struggle for meaning between the English mythmakers and the mythical beasts they create. The devouring of the hikers similarly questions the complacency of the English perception of the Highlands as an unpopulated, scenic tourist destination. It is as though the population previously thought evicted from the area by the clearances has returned in a monstrous form to reclaim its heritage.

We can now see the werewolves as functioning much more in the manner of Mr Hyde as theorised by Craig. Through them, Scottish consciousness finding 'a means, however terrible and self-mutilating, of imagining forces that history will not subdue'. The cyclical nature of their perpetual reemergence, therefore, and its conflation with femininity, can be seen to symbolise the return of the repressed that is the excluded history of Scotland. Historically it fed off the British army in order to finally reimpose itself against the constrictions placed on it by the linear narrative of masculine, British history. That this cyclical return of the repressed is coded as feminine illustrates the problems the British heartland now has dealing with its own identity, after the devolution of the peripheries against which it traditionally established its own masculine potency.

Moreover, through its repeated references to childhood and fairy tales, the film suggests the potential of myth to establish an alternative origin for a new Scottish identity. References include, the squad's discussion of the legend of the Beast of Bodmin Moor, their campfire spooky-storytelling session and the mention of the fairy tales 'Goldilocks and the Three Bears', 'The Three Little Pigs', and 'Little Red Riding Hood'. It is as though there is a folk history available in these uncivilised woodlands, the recounting of which has the power to un-ground the singular history of 'civilised' progression. To this end, members of the squad are at times rendered childlike. This is most clearly seen in the wounded Wells', 'up the wooden hill' as he is led upstairs, his playground teasing of Cooper over his tension with Megan ('I like your new girlfriend, Coop') and his and Cooper's Narnia-esque escape from the werewolves through the bedroom wardrobe.

Similarly, the film challenges the Enlightenment rationalism of the troops' belief system when Megan argues that they are not fighting any normal foe.

> Think about it Cooper. Up until today you believed there was a line between myth and reality. It may have been a very fine line sometimes, but at least it was a line. Those things out there, they're real. And if they're real, what else is real? You know what lives in the shadows now.

Megan's comments suggest that the film is using the Highlands as a location precisely because it is there that imagination holds sway over reason. This enables a reconsideration, through myth, of just exactly what other history, or indeed, histories, could be living in the 'shadows' of the officially recognised version.

The haunting presence of the werewolf family that inhabit the farmhouse adds to this interpretation. The ancient Celtic family have lived in the glen for centuries. If the Claymore in the trunk is anything to go by, they have presumably been living an underground, guerrilla-type existence since before the disarming act of 1746. They represent the lost history of Scotland, of the period following the rebellion and the clearances up to the present, a history that, through its repression as part of an Anglocentric British narrative of progression, has turned monstrous. In this respect they are very similar to the wolves in *Wolfen*, the representatives of the ancient Native American civilisation that was all but wiped out by American history but still haunts its wilder parts.

Megan's presence similarly acts as a focus for this reading. As a recently graduated zoologist, Megan, in the Enlightenment tradition, would study the behaviour of the animal Other. For this reason, despite her initial disappointment at finding that the soldiers are unable to save her, she attempts to help them. However, at a specific point in the narrative her loyalty shifts, and she sides with the werewolves. Megan attempts to get the soldiers to understand that the people they hope to destroy are still human, despite the negative representation they may have been fed – through English myths like that of Sawney Bean and his family – that the Scottish are all wild, uncivilised cannibals.

MEGAN: They're good people, they're kind people.
COOPER: More's the pity.
MEGAN: Why?
COOPER: Because we're going to have to kill them all.
WELLS: Too right mate. (*Smashes the family photo with a hammer.*)

With the smashing of the photo of the human side of the Scottish family, there is a lingering close-up of Megan's face as she realises that the survival of the British troops will be dependent upon entirely destroying (clearing) not only the family's way of life but also the representation of their history. Up until this point she had pinned her hopes on the British narrative of progress to lift her out of her status as werewolf under a Scottish tradition turned monstrous through repression. Instead, Wells's smashing of the photo shows her that, along with the destruction of their way of life by the British soldiers, the myth of Tartanry will destroy any civilised representation of this human side of the Scottish.

This is why Megan eventually crosses over to the side of the animal Other, as she realises that there is no way she can escape the pull of the resurgent mythical history that the soldiers wish to obliterate. She says, 'When I found you last night I truly believed you were the best chance I had of getting out. But now we have no chance. There is no out, there never was.' Megan finally realises that 'there never was' an 'out' of history. The civilising process brought by the incorporation of the Highlands into British history after 1746 could never succeed in altogether destroying Scottish history; it could only drive it underground into myth and fantasy. From there it would perpetually return in its most 'terrible and self-mutilating, of imagining forces'. As she says of the werewolves when they enter the house, 'they were always here, I just unlocked the door'. Through the figure of the werewolf, then, the wild, hairy 'homo celticus'[20] stereotype so often applied to representations of Scotland is cleverly deconstructed.

(Coming) Out of History

The film's use of the iconography of the closet has further significance for this interpretation, and indeed, recurs in the chapter that follows on the costume drama. At two points the trapped soldiers discover several 'skeletons in the cupboard'. In the upstairs bedroom, Wells and Cooper hide in the wardrobe where they realise that the werewolves have been storing the bodies of their victims. Later, when Cooper hides in the cellar at the end of the film he finds himself in a meat locker of human corpses. These images are at once suggestive of two points. Firstly, rather like Stevenson's Mr Hyde, there is a strong homosexual connotation attributed to the monsters who are excluded from history.[21] They are, quite literally, the closeted Other upon which English history bases its legitimacy, much as the progressive lineage of heterosexuality does with homosexuality. Secondly, however, these images of the closet also suggest the subversive power of this excluded history to reemerge and 'queer' the progression of legitimate history. There always remains the possibility that should this closeted force 'out' itself it will no longer be out of history. This suggestion is made from the film's first moments, in the humorous audio match of the sound of the young woman hiker's trouser zip as it is undone by her boyfriend across the cut to the tent zip being undone by the werewolves. Here, the usual gruesome fate of sexually active characters in the horror genre is linked to the action of a wild force that would challenge and destroy the lineage of heterosexual legitimacy, much as Scottish history does British legitimacy.

Finally, Cooper's backward glance as he leaves the ruined farmhouse is also helpful. Cooper is filmed from inside the shell of the house, framed by the doorway as he walks away, his left arm folded across his chest holding his wounded right arm. This is a reference to John Wayne's Ethan walking away from the Edwards's homestead at the end of *The Searchers* (1956). Although the suggestion is initially one of looking back on a lost nation that falls very much in line with previous representations of the myth of Tartanry,[22] this could also be read as the film pointing out that we have just watched a narrative which – a little like *The Searchers* – examines the difference between the civilised and the uncivilised. However, rather than returning the family to the civilised position of the homesteaders, as *The Searchers* does, here the house is destroyed by the supposedly civilising force of the British army. With this now inverted reference in mind, the film seems less an attempt to recreate the primal scene of Tartanry and more an illustration of the damage that such an event caused to Scottish history. Just as the film's previous evocation of the glories of empire in its allusion to *Zulu* was playfully debunked through the comic timing between music and dialogue, the entire narrative of continued unification is questioned by the final intertextual reference. We end, not with a backward glance representing the loss of a Scottish past, but rather with the final image of Cooper, the Scottish soldier, walking away from his 'civilised' past in the British Empire.

Descent into the Wilderness, or *Wild Country*?

It is possible to position the monstrous return of the Scottish history seen in *Dog Soldiers* in the context of contemporaneous British films. For instance, *Darklands* (1996), written and directed by Welshman Julian Richards and made for £1 million, is a Welsh updating of *The Wicker Man* that allegorically addresses the issue of Welsh national independence. *Darklands* follows Frazer Truick (Craig Fairbrass) a newspaper reporter who discovers that a resurgent Welsh nationalist party (perhaps a fictional equivalent of Plaid Cymru) is founded on an ancient druidic cult that practices ritualistic human sacrifice at times of national turmoil. Inevitably, Truick becomes their sacrifice to alleviate the pressures of economic downturn caused by the decline in the nation's manufacturing industries. As Steve Blandford notes in *Film, Drama and The Break-Up of Britain* (2007), although *Darklands* remains a 'minority-interest cult film', emerging in 1997 'it displayed both political and aesthetic independence and suggested a broadening of the scope of what was possible in a developing local culture'.[23] The horror film, then, is a very capable medium for allegorically engaging with the resurgence of national independence in the Celtic peripheries around the time of devolution.

Elsewhere I have made the case that *Dog Soldiers* can be read as a commentary on devolution (whether altogether conscious in intent or not) in that its examination of the monstrous return of Scottish history emerged when the union of Scotland and England was beginning the process of political devolution in the late 1990s and early 2000s.[24] However, it is difficult to pinpoint the authorial intent that might lie behind such a specific interpretation of the film's playful exploration of myth, history and changing British identities. For instance, writer and director Neil Marshall, when discussing in interview his reasons for making a werewolf film in Scotland, does not mention the broader political context. Rather, he talks of his personal experiences of Scotland (in a manner reminiscent of so many English tourists before him), and of the lurking menace of Scotland's repressed history in its wilder extremes. He states,

> I wanted to make a werewolf movie, a soldier movie, and a film set in Scotland. I've been to Scotland on holiday for years and was inspired by the possibility of something 'other' living in the forest.[25]

And again:

> I fell in love with the Highlands after years of going on holiday there . . . It wasn't too far from Newcastle, and it struck me as being a country full of beauty as well as underlying menace – especially on supernaturally dark, stormy days. I thought, here was the perfect atmospheric location to have something wild and ferocious running around.[26]

The fact that Marshall immediately kills off his own doppelganger (a Geordie tourist like Newcastle-born-and-bred Marshall) in the opening scene of the film illustrates how self-conscious he is about the film's life beyond the control of the deceased English author/auteur. Thus, the Scottish monsters are presumably intended to be seen to be getting their own back on the English tourists after centuries of haunting their cleared homelands, and in this sense the film's engagement with Tartanry in a Highland setting also seems intentional. After all, the Scottish setting was retained even though the film was primarily shot in Petite-Suisse, Luxembourg in 2001, when an outbreak of foot and mouth disease in sheep and cattle rendered location shooting in Scotland problematic. However, whether or not we can extend this reading to a deliberate reflection on the then contemporary reality of devolution on the part of Marshall is debateable. This is especially so considering the film was six years in pre-production,[27] beginning before political devolution became a reality, and was eventually produced on a budget of £4.5 million by Los Angeles-based Kismet Productions, The Noel Gay Motion Picture Company (London) and The Carousel Picture Company (Luxembourg). Although manufactured primarily for the UK market, where it recouped over half of its budget in box office receipts alone, it seems unlikely that this international production, unlike *Darklands*, had devolution in its sights, even if its exploration of the Highlands' submerged history resonated with events of the time.

Devolution aside, what is interesting for the context of this discussion of Scotland as a location within which horror films are made, is that since *Dog Soldiers* the majority of these films have veered away from the engagement with the location as an informing setting seen in *Dog Soldiers*. There has been a rapid shift from horror films set in Scotland to horror films that use Scotland as a film set. These include Marshall's next monster movie shot in Scotland (although set in the USA this time, and in any case, predominantly underground) *The Descent* (2005), the teen slasher film *Wilderness* (2006) (set on an island that could be, literally, anywhere), the zombie movie set in Eastern Europe, *Outpost* (2008), and even Neil Marshall's third attempt, inspired by both *Escape from New York* (1981) and *Mad Max* (1979), *Doomsday* (2008). This last is particularly interesting in that its Scottish settings and costumes are used to create a colourful, Scottish-themed, futuristic, post-apocalyptic, cannibal-holocaust theme park adventure! Thus, although *Dog Soldiers* was the catalyst for the popular appreciation of a spree of British horror films, including everything from *28 Days Later* (2002) to *Severance* (2006), thanks to the genre's potential for broad, international appeal, the role Scotland was to play in those films soon became one of backdrop, rather than integrated setting.

Wild Country (2005)

One notable exception to this trend is the low-budget Scottish werewolf movie, *Wild Country*. *Wild Country* is the story of a teenage mother, Kelly Ann (Samantha Shields), who, on the advice of the Catholic Church, gives up her daughter for adoption. Six weeks after the birth, she and four friends go on a night hike in the countryside organised by the Catholic priest, Father Steve (Peter Capaldi) and the St Aidan's Youth Club; Kelly Ann and her boyfriend Lee (Martin Compston) discover a baby, seemingly abandoned in an old ruined castle, only to discover it is a child of a werewolf couple who inhabit the ruins. After the teenagers kill the adult female werewolf, the film concludes with Kelly Ann, the only survivor of the group, transformed into a werewolf as she wet nurses the child. The final image is of a happy family peacefully roaming the countryside, werewolf mother (Kelly Ann), father and child.

Wild Country is an entirely home grown Scottish production shot on high-definition video (HD), primarily in Mugdock Country Park outside Glasgow, on a budget of around £800,000. It was written and directed by the Scot Craig Strachan, who, based in Los Angeles, has worked on both UK and US television shows and films. It was produced by Ros Borland for the Scottish production company Gabriel Films (Glasgow), which was established in 1998 to make films with a Scottish element. Together Strachan and Borland are the directors of Gabriel Films.[28] Borland also produced Strachan's earlier short film, *Hidden* (2000), and was associate producer of *Afterlife* (2003), a Scottish film about a young girl, Roberta (Paula Sage) with Down's Syndrome written by Andrea Gibb, who also wrote *Nina's Heavenly Delights* (2006). Like *Wild Country*, both *Hidden* and *Afterlife* were produced by Gabriel Films. Borland was also a coproducer on the high-profile international hit *The Last King of Scotland* (2006) for the Scottish Unit of Slate North. Interestingly, however, despite the indigenous nature of *Wild Country*, it was entirely funded by private backers, with Borland and Strachan having more luck raising funds from US than UK sources.

Wild Country joins a number of other, low-budget indigenous Scottish films that have either had a very limited theatrical release or gone straight to DVD, including *White Angel* (1994), *Urban Ghost Story* (1998), *Frozen* (2005) and *Night People* (2005). Like all these other small independent films, *Wild Country* is distributed by Guerilla Films, who – although in existence as producers and distributors since the early 1980s – have specialised in promoting low-budget British and Irish films since 1999.[29] For example, they distributed the extremely low budget (£300,000) nerdy teen comedy *GamerZ* (2005), which had en extremely limited theatrical release before going to DVD, where it performed well in the US and – like *Dog Soldiers* – looks set to be remade for the US market. Thanks to Guerilla Films, movies produced by companies like Gabriel Films, which are only likely to make the most minimal of commercial profit (if any at all), are seen by the public. The existence of Guerilla Films ensures that the tail end of the low-budget market in the UK and Ireland continues to thrive, and slightly different types of films can be made with at least the likelihood of a limited distribution deal. Thus, although *Wild Country* is a low-budget film and did not receive the same distribution or media coverage as *Dog Soldiers*, at a time when the market for DVD is far larger (in terms of scale and profit) than that of theatrical release, it is no less important for local and national audiences (especially, perhaps, for teenage audiences, one of the largest consumer demographics) than *Dog Soldiers*.

Unlike *Dog Soldiers*, which examines the transforming nature of national identities in Britain around the turn of the century, *Wild Country* focuses on characters from a very specific demographic (teenagers from a Catholic community) within a particular region; the west of Scotland, and Glasgow in particular. The title, *Wild Country*, thus refers not to the nation but to a specific area of the country. Strachan conceived of the film as an exploration of parenthood depicted through a blend of the social realism often associated with gritty films set in Scotland and the thrills of the horror genre.[30] Through the blend, this low-budget film – shot with a hand-held digital camera which makes the aesthetic appear rough around the edges – engages with a topic that is of interest to its target audience of teenagers, exploring, through the horror genre, the serious topic of teenage pregnancy and the 'call of the wild' of sexual desire that leads to parenthood.

The film's realist opening provides a protracted close-up of the face of teenager Kelly Ann as she gives birth. The minimal production values are played to their strengths as the hospital room appears washed of all colour, bare and lifeless. Kelly Ann is then depicted in the same gloomy environment, in despair, as Father Steve arrives to inform her that her baby has been adopted. The location of her family home in a Glasgow council estate adds to the sense of a reality that is experienced by many young people in the city, as does the mixed cast of professional and non-professional actors, whose accents add an element of regional authenticity to the drama. Thus, the association of Scottish films with a realist style is used to suggest that there is a 'real' concern under discussion, teen pregnancy, before the horror genre, lurking in the darkness, pounces on the audience once the film shifts into the wild countryside.

In this instance the resonance of the Scottish wilderness, when deployed as part of a horror film, has a regional, or local, flavour. As the youth club members are driven into the country by Father Steve he spins them the spooky yarn of the cannibal Sawney Bean, noting that they are entering 'Sawney Bean Country', and that legend tells of how his descendents still live in the region. When, at the film's conclusion, Kelly Ann kills the hypocritical, fornicating Father Steve and chooses to roam free with her new werewolf family, she appears to have tapped into this local past, reconnecting with the myth of wild, cannibalistic Scotland in order to break free of religious doctrine and be part of a family instead. On the one hand this conclusion could be interpreted as fairly anti-establishment, with Kelly Ann's cannibalism of Father Steve suggesting a resurgence of a primal past that rejects the teachings of organised religion in favour of a wilder expression of youthful sexual freedom. On the other, the fact that Father Steve is a philandering priest, and Kelly Ann's choice is ultimately to be part of a family (however monstrous), may suggest a more conservative reaffirmation of the status quo. In either case, the film uses the horror genre as a way of opening up discussion of these two poles of meaning, for a teen audience to whom it is of relevance.

Hyde-out Scotland

As *Wild Country* shows, although, following *The Descent*, the horror film in Scotland quickly consolidated around a fantasy 'anywhere'-Scotland, independent, locally engaged, low-budget productions that may not travel far beyond Scotland (or the UK in general) still subsist. The long-awaited sequel to *Dog Soldiers*, *Dog Soldiers: Fresh Meat* – a US/UK/Hungary coproduction also by Kismet International Pictures, being filmed in Wales

– may provide further developments. This time the squad of soldiers in the Highlands are US troops, so perhaps the story will broaden out into an international context, but presumably there will be a loss of emphasis on things Scottish. On the other hand, an alternative like that of *Wild Country* may be offered by the Glasgow-based production company, Black Camel Pictures. Whilst Black Camel specialise in low-mid budget 'anywhere' Scotland productions, like *Outpost* (£1.2m) and the forthcoming futuristic, dystopian vampire-cop movie *Blood Makes Noise* (2009) (£6m), and are in this sense moving in line with the trend towards the use of Scotland as a film set outlined above, they also advertise their desire to develop debut, micro–budget (£30,000 to £500,000) horror/thriller films in Scotland.[31] It is in this range that another film like *Wild Country*, that does engage with issues pertinent to Scottish audiences, may well emerge. What is clear, however, is that in the horror genre, filmic representations of Scotland are expanding upon previous myths associated with the Scottish wilderness in ways that appeal to different target audiences at home and abroad.

Notes

1. Cairns Craig, *Out of History* (Edinburgh: Polygon, 1996), p. 44.
2. Ibid., pp. 43–4.
3. Tom Nairn, *The Break Up of Britain* (London: Verson, 1977), p. 116 & p. 162.
4. Colin McArthur, 'Introduction', in Colin McArthur (ed.), *Scotch Reels* (London: BFI, 1982), pp. 1–6, p. 2.
5. Reed, Joseph, 'Subgenres in Horror Pictures', Barry Keith Grant, ed., *Planks of Reason* (London: The Scarecrow Press, 1984), pp. 101–12, p. 103.
6. Mark Jancovich, *Rational Fears* (Manchester: Manchester University Press, 1996).
7. Peter Hutchings, *Hammer and Beyond* (Manchester: Manchester University Press, 1993), p. 69.
8. Harlan Kennedy, 'Things that go Howl in the Id', *Film Comment*, 18: 2 (1982), pp. 37–9.
9. Kennedy, 'Things that go Howl in the Id' and Dana B. Polan, 'Eros and Syphilization', in Grant, *Planks of Reason*, pp. 201–11.
10. Bonnie Zimmerman, 'Daughters of Darkness', Grant, *Planks of Reason*, pp. 153–63, p. 155, and Andrew Tudor, *Monsters and Mad Scientists* (Oxford: Blackwell, 1989), p. 65.
11. Walter Evans, 'Monster Movies', *Journal of Popular Film* 2: 4 (1973), pp. 353–65, p. 357.
12. Barbara Creed, 'Dark Desires', in Steven Cohan and Ina Rae Hark (eds), *Screening the Male* (London: Routledge, 1993), pp. 118–33, p. 125.

13. Barbara Creed, *The Monstrous Feminine* (London: Routledge, 1993), pp. 62–6.
14. Robin Wood and Richard Lippe eds, *The American Nightmare* (Toronto: Festival of Festivals, 1979).
15. Claire Monk, 'Men in the 90s', in Robert Murphy (ed.), *British Cinema of the 90s* (London: BFI, 2000), pp. 156–66, p. 157.
16. Polen, 'Eros and Syphilization', Kennedy, 'Things that go howl in the id', Jancovich, *Rational Fears*.
17. Freud famously dubbed one of his patients the Wolf Man. This patient, Freud believed, witnessed the 'primal scene' of his parents having sex whilst a child and repressed this memory, an act which became the cause of difficulties in later life. Sigmund Freud, 'From the History of an Infantile Neurosis', in, Peter Gay (ed.), *The Freud Reader* (London: Vintage, 1995), pp. 400–26.
18. Cairns Craig, 'Myths Against History', McArthur, *Scotch Reels*, pp. 7–16, p. 10.
19. Murray Pittock, *The Invention of Scotland* (London: Routledge, 1991), p. 62.
20. Colin McArthur, 'Scotland's Story', *Framework* 26–7 (1985): pp. 64–74.
21. Elaine Showalter, *Sexual Anarchy* (London: Virago, 1990).
22. John Caughie, 'Representing Scotland', in Eddie Dick (ed.), *From Limelight to Satellite* (London: BFI & SFC, 1990), pp. 13–30, p. 25.
23. Steve Blandford, *Film, Drama and the Break-Up of Britain* (Bristol: Intellect, 2007), p. 96.
24. David Martin-Jones, 'National Symbols', *Symbolism*, 7 (2008), pp. 169–200.
25. James Korsner, 'Neil Marshall: Dog Soldiers' http://www.bbc.co.uk/films/2002/04/15/neil_marshall_dog_soldiers_interview.shtml (27/01/08).
26. Alan Jones, 'The Bark and Bite of *Dog Soldiers*', *Fangoria* 212 (2002), pp. 40–4, p. 40.
27. Sheila Roberts, 'Neil Marshall Interview: Doomsday', http://www.moviesonline.ca/movienews_12586.html (27/01/08).
28. Gabriel Films website: http://www.gabrielfilms.co.uk/ (10/02/08).
29. Guerilla Films website: http://www.guerilla-films.com/about.asp (10/02/08).
30. *Wild Country* Production Notes, available at http://www.wildcountry-thefilm.com/productionnotes.htm (10/02/08).
31. 'Black Camel Pictures – Micro-budget initiative', in *eroughcuts*, a weekly email newsletter, produced by Scottish Screen, 17 January 2008.

CHAPTER 6

Costume Drama: From Men in Kilts to Developing Diasporas

This chapter examines the most well known of all the popular genres associated with Scotland, the costume drama (sometimes referred to as the
period drama, heritage or historical film). Costume dramas with a Scottish
theme have been made throughout the twentieth century, by both British
and US production companies. Initially the debate surrounding costume
drama is introduced – in particular the contested term 'heritage cinema'
– and the role that costume dramas made and set in Scotland increasingly
play in this debate. Because of the popularity of this particular genre,
however, and as there is already so much written about the well-known
films set in Scotland (including those focused on men, like *Rob Roy* (1995)
and *Braveheart* (1995)), I examine an example featuring a female protagonist, *The Governess* (1998).

In *The Governess*, the wilderness of Scotland is represented as a fantasy-
land, but its mythical resonance as a place somehow 'before history' actually facilitates the construction of a diasporic history, or 'heritage', that
stands apart from concerns of British or Scottish identity. Thus, the
setting of Scotland is integral to the film's deployment of its feminist
reworking of history (a process typical of the contemporary costume
drama), in this case to explore a diasporic Jewish identity that does not
belong to the same historical traditions as those normally encountered in
the wilds of cinematic Scotland.

English Heritage/Scottish Heritage

Several books provide focused explorations of the costume drama in
British cinema, the most influential being Sue Harper's *Picturing the Past*
(1994) and Pam Cook's *Fashioning the Nation* (1996). In terms of Scottish
subject matter, in *Screening Scotland* (2000), Duncan Petrie has charted
the history of costume films set in eighteenth-century Scotland – derived
in part from the legacy of the Romantic literature of Sir Walter Scott and
Robert Louis Stevenson – noting in particular those films which focus on
the Jacobite rebellions of 1715 and 1745. Thus there have been numerous

(British and US) *Rob Roy* adaptations since the early years of silent cinema, along with adaptations of *Kidnapped, Young Lochinvar, Heart of Midlothian*, and *The Master of Ballantrae*, in addition to two productions of the story of Bonnie Prince Charlie (1923 and 1944), various adaptations of *Macbeth* and so on.[1]

However, since the 1990s, it is increasingly women who have become the focus of costume dramas set in Scotland, in films such as *Mary Reilly* (1996), *Mrs Brown* (1997), *The Governess* (1998), *The House of Mirth* (2000) – filmed in Scotland, although set in New York – *The Queen* (2006) and *Death Defying Acts* (2007). This trend falls in line with the international popularity of costume dramas with strong female protagonists, including *Howards End* (1992), *The Piano* (1993), *Sense and Sensibility* (1995) and *Elizabeth* (1998). The extent to which these films can be considered to be set in Scotland, or to use Scotland as a film set, requires a deeper understanding of the way the costume drama functions as a genre, necessitating that I delve first into the contested territory of 'heritage cinema'. This term derives from a critical debate that began in the press (as opposed to being an industry-defined generic label) with reference to certain British costume dramas, especially literary adaptations and historical films belonging to the 'quality' film niche market. It was the heritage cinema debate to which Petrie was responding in *Screening Scotland* by asserting that Scotland had a distinctive heritage cinema tradition based around its Jacobite past. With this background in place I will examine one example of the shift towards costume dramas set in Scotland with female protagonists, *The Governess*.

In his now seminal 'Re-presenting the National Past' (1993), Andrew Higson argued that a then emergent strand of quality costume dramas could be considered in the context of the growth of the heritage industry in Britain. Examining films such as the adaptations of E. M. Forster's novels *A Passage to India* (1984), *A Room With a View* (1985) and *Maurice* (1987), Higson observed that, although often using the past to explore issues pertinent to contemporary audiences in a manner that lent itself to a potentially progressive, liberal-humanist narrative (for instance, foregrounding homosexuality in Maurice), the spectacle of heritage (in particular, country estates, period costumes, props and décor) was ultimately deployed to an ideologically conservative end. Higson viewed the emergence of this particular movement in heritage cinema as linked to the transformation of British society in the 1980s. The heritage industry surfaced as part of a broader movement towards tourism and the services industry in general, and the spectacle of the past offered by these films provided an escape from the realities of the social turmoil facing many in Thatcherite Britain. Thus,

against a reality of 'political and economic measures, often sharply contested, that tended to encourage high unemployment, marked inequalities
of income and standards of living, and a more general social malaise among
the dispossessed that drifted periodically into social unrest',[2] in the
heritage film cycle, 'the past is displayed as visually spectacular pastiche,
inviting a nostalgic gaze that resists the ironies and social critiques so often
suggested narratively by these films'.[3] In short, Higson argued that, their
progressive narratives notwithstanding, heritage cinema offered the
'imperialist and upper class'[4] British past as a place into which audiences
could travel to escape the unpleasant realities of the present. This imagined past was being sold internationally by British cinema as a narrowly
defined image of national identity, as though as part of the heritage
industry.

Higson's work has been reconsidered by a number of critics, including
Higson himself. In the main, constructive critiques of Higson's position
have been provided by feminist critics, with a few key voices being of
relevance to this argument. One much-cited example, Claire Monk,
reconsidered Higson's argument in relation to his left-wing, anti-
Thatcherite position, observing that his conclusions do not take into
account the pleasures that heritage spectacle afford women and/or gay
viewers. Monk notes in particular that many films Higson identifies as
part of his heritage cycle are identifiable as woman's films (films made for
female audiences), whose focus on female desire enables a consideration of
contemporary gender politics in a recreated past.[5] Monk's position follows
that of Sue Harper (which actually predates Higson by some years), whose
focus on the popular Gainsborough melodramas of the 1930s and 1940s,
demonstrated how racy costume dramas set in a romanticised past – such
as *The Man in Grey* (1943), *Fanny by Gaslight* (1944), *The Wicked Lady*
(1945) and *Caravan* (1946) – enabled an exploration of 'ideas about history
and sexuality' to be expressed 'which were impossible in existing, more
"respectable" signifying systems'.[6] In other words, although Gainsborough
costume melodramas did not aim for historical accuracy or period authenticity in the same way as the heritage films identified by Higson their
fantasy recreations of the past facilitated the pleasurable exploration of the
'fears and desires' of their contemporary (and predominantly female)
audience.[7] Harper established this argument in greater contextual depth
in *Picturing the Past* (1994),[8] and other critics have developed this debate
around the role and function of the costume drama/heritage film (including Stella Bruzzi, Pamela Church Gibson, Julianne Pidduck and Belén
Vidal), several of whose works are discussed further below.[9] Whether
focusing on audience demographics or the mode of address of the costume

drama, amongst these writers there is a critical consensus that these films offer certain audiences (often predominantly female audiences) a chance to examine present-day issues and anxieties in a fictional, and at times fantastical, past.

For the purposes of this chapter, the work of Pam Cook is of great significance. Cook's position in *Dissolving Views* (1996) correlates with that of Harper. Cook also assesses the pleasures available to female audiences in costume drama, again with an emphasis on fantasy and spectacle as productive – as opposed to conservative – elements of films set in the past. Cook critiques the implicit (and potentially rather elitist) intellectual championing of realism over excessive display evident in the work of Higson,[10] who considers the heritage film to provide a degree of realism in its reconstruction of the 'historical reality' of the national past, an element usually considered absent from costume dramas.[11] Indeed, Cook follows up on this argument in *Fashioning the Nation* where she engages with Colin McArthur's argument from *Scotch Reels*, observing the 'complexity' and 'imaginative appeal' of popular genres (like the costume dramas set in Scotland), which McArthur considers regressive in their nostalgia for a lost past. She states,

> It is rarely considered that nostalgia might play a productive role in national identity, releasing the desire for social change or resistance. The recent historical epic *Rob Roy*, for example, recalls a turbulent moment in Scottish history when the clans were breaking apart. The elements of Tartanry and Kailyard dismissed by contributors to *Scotch Reels* are much in evidence: costume, music and landscape are used emotively to create a sense of the Scottish past as an arena for heroic action against social injustice . . . Rather than a refusal of nostalgia, it seems more pertinent to investigate the powerful emotional appeal of reliving the past and the part it plays in popular imaginings of community and resistance at specific historical moments.[12]

In contrast to McArthur's desire for a more realist engagement with issues pertinent to contemporary Scotland, as opposed to what he sees as the regurgitation of the myth of Tartanry, Cook argues for the positive potential of historical spectacle to enable contemporary audiences to re-imagine their current identities. Interestingly, many years later, it is McArthur (alongside Tim Edensor and Lin Anderson) who has taken up Cook's challenge by exploring the response of Scottish audiences to films like *Rob Roy* and *Braveheart*. In *Brigadoon, Braveheart and the Scots* (2003) McArthur analyses the impact of the Hollywood costume drama *Braveheart* within Scotland, the so-called '*Braveheart* effect', including its political use by the Scottish National Party (SNP) in their quest for independence from the state of Britain, as well as its impact on sports journalism and the tourist industry in Scotland.[13]

The development of the argument surrounding heritage cinema, and Scotland's role within it considered, it is pertinent to return to Petrie's argument from *Screening Scotland* concerning the possibility that many costume dramas produced in Scotland constitute a Scottish heritage cinema. To recap and expand slightly, Petrie notes the prevalence of a cinematic image of Scotland constructed around 'the romance, tropes and symbols of eighteenth-century Jacobitism'[14] and links it to the deployment of this very vision of Scotland in the 'heritage industries', as observed by David McCrone and his co-authors in *Scotland – The Brand* (1995). For Petrie, costume dramas set in Scotland demonstrate

> a full-blown celebration of myth, fantasy and overt display, rather than any concerted attempt to resurrect or engage with historical reality. Yet by revelling in the popular spectacle of inauthenticity these mythical constructions of Scotland . . . directly engage a wide range of audience pleasures, emotions and fantasies.[15]

Petrie's argument draws on both Harper and Cook and attempts to re-engage the *Scotch Reels* debate around the representation of rugged masculinity in films like *Rob Roy* and *Braveheart*, based on the feminist appreciation of the spectacle provided by the male body (as object for the female spectator's gaze) in the costume film. Petrie positions this argument in relation to debates surrounding previous representations of Scotland, in addition to Higson's argument concerning English tradition in British heritage cinema. For Petrie, then, the fantasy, myth and spectacle derided by McArthur in *Scotch Reels* is part of the audience pleasures offered by the tradition of Scottish heritage cinema that he catalogues, which draws on the association of the Highlands of Scotland with a romantic conception of Jacobite revolt and defeat.

The question of whether contemporary costume dramas with a Scottish theme are set in Scotland or treat Scotland as a film set depends on whether the film in question is considered to be a costume drama or an example of heritage cinema. With such a popular and long-running debate, several critics have attempted to interrogate the nuances that distinguish heritage films from costume dramas. John Hill, for instance, describes the heritage cinema as a 'subspecies' of the costume drama 'in which a greater premium is not only placed upon the artistic worthiness which is derived from literature or the theatre but also the degree of historical detail or "accuracy" to which the film aspires'.[16] Understanding the heritage film in this manner means that it can be considered distinct from the spectacular construction of the past as a fantasy space in costume dramas like the post-war Gainsborough melodramas. Similarly, in *British Film* (2004), Jim Leach distinguishes between the 'specific historical period' of the heritage film, as opposed to the 'vaguely defined past, which shows little respect for history or the national heritage'[17] of the costume film. Following Monk, Pamela Church Gibson has taken this debate further, arguing that we have now entered a 'post-heritage' era in which films like *Elizabeth* (1998) have rejuvenated the spectacular (as opposed to 'authentic') reconstruction of the past of the costume drama, and, whilst self-consciously deploying the conventions of the heritage film, have become hybridised by generic elements from popular genres like the gangster film.[18] Yet, as is demonstrated most clearly in Higson's nuanced consideration of the way the heritage film *Howards End* (1992) advertises itself using imagery suggestive of romance (and in particular, the pleasures associated with the women's film) in *English Heritage, English Cinema* (2003),[19] as with any genre, definitions of heritage cinema and costume drama depend on which films you analyse, how you group them together, the manner in which you approach the films and the context/s in which you examine them.

In this respect, the position of Sheldon Hall in his contribution to the second edition of *The British Cinema Book* (2001) sets up the argument that follows. Hall argues that discussions of the heritage film undertaken so far have been narrow in their conception of which films constitute heritage cinema, and a more inclusive field of study is likely to provide a broader understanding of the genre.[20] This is because, Hall contends, the specific heritage films chosen for analysis to date have been selected because of their ability to construct a representative image of British cinema in the 1980s, 1990s or 2000s. Acknowledging the need for greater inclusivity, regardless of how 'representative' of British cinema or English/ Scottish identity a film is, for the remainder of this chapter I will focus on *The Governess*, a post-heritage hybrid of the costume drama and Gothic film, to explore how this particular movie illuminates the manner in which Scotland functions as a film set (a fantasy land of the past) in which female desires can be played out in order to construct a diasporic (as opposed to national) sense of history.

The Governess (1998)

The Governess opens in East London in the 1840s, on a Sephardic Jewish community that includes the family of Rosina Da Silva (Minnie Driver) and her younger sister Rebecca (Emma Bird). Rosina regularly passes through streets in which prostitutes ply their trade, who taunt her for being a 'Jew girl', but is unabashed by (and curious about) their greater sexual knowledge. When her father dies suddenly (mugged in the street, possibly whilst visiting a prostitute), Rosina refuses an arranged marriage with an established member of the Jewish community (a fish merchant much senior to her in years), taking, instead, the job of governess on an estate on the Isle of Skye. To obtain the position she passes herself off as a Mary Blackchurch, explaining that her dark-hued skin is the result of her mother being half Italian. Gradually Rosina/Mary obtains the trust of the estate's owner, Charles Cavendish (Tom Wilkinson), and assists him in his scientific exploration of photography. They become sexually involved, an affair which Rosina/Mary does much to initiate. When Rosina/Mary (whilst conducting in private the Jewish Passover Seder) stumbles across an essential ingredient that assists Charles in his search for an image fixative, they briefly fantasise about the future together after they register their discovery and their fame spreads. However, the return of Charles's son Henry (Jonathan Rhys Meyers), sent down from Oxford for being found with a prostitute in an opium den in Spitalfields, complicates matters. Ultimately, Charles breaks off the affair with Rosina/Mary, and takes all the credit for developing the photographic fixative. In retaliation, Rosina/Mary shows Charles's wife a photograph of her naked husband (sleeping after they had made love), reveals her Jewish identity and leaves their employment. On returning to London she finds her mother has died of cholera, but with her new-found skills in photography she rescues her family, setting up shop as a portrait photographer to a clientele of well-off Jewish families.

A Parallax production funded by the Arts Council of England and Wales, British Screen and BBC Films, which recouped its £2.8 million budget by performing far better in US theatres ($4m) than in the UK (just over £100,000), *The Governess* uses Scotland as a location shoot. The majority of the narrative takes place on the Cavendish estate on the Isle of Skye, although the filming took place in Brodick Castle on the Isle of Arran, and the estate's baronial interiors were filmed on sets in London's Pinewood Studios.[21] Yet this is a location that is specifically identified as Scotland, unlike, say, the use of several 'anonymous' locations in and around Glasgow as backdrops standing in for New York in *The House of Mirth*. Even so, *The Governess* uses Scotland more as a film set than as a setting. Although the majority of the film takes place in Scotland, events unfold in a country estate owned by an English family. The Scotland on offer consists of the estate's overgrown gardens, the brief shots of rural landscape through which Rosina/Mary passes in a carriage on her arrival and the seashore along which she frequently walks with her charge. This is not an identifiable Scotland, then, but a remote wilderness very much in the Romantic tradition and in line with the myth of Tartanry. Indeed, although the majority of the film takes place in Scotland, it is bracketed by the two episodes in London, ensuring that London is equated with 'normal' life and Scotland is figured as a strange wilderness to (and from) which Rosina/Mary travels for a brief interlude, a fantasy land (she has no encounters with locals beyond Lily the maid) in which to briefly try on a new lifestyle and identity.

Yet, as befits the emphasis on female development typical of the contemporary costume drama/heritage film (as they enable contemporary audiences to reflect on their current lives in a recreated past), after rejecting a proposal of marriage, Rosina/Mary uses her time in Scotland to develop professional skills that will enable her to care for her family on her return to London. Thus, although 'Scotland' and 'the past' become synonymous in this film (as Rosina/Mary leaves urban civilisation, like the viewer, to briefly experiment with a new identity in a Romanticised Scotland), if we consider the manner in which the costume drama functions then we should not necessarily consider this a regressive regurgitation of previous myths associated with Scotland. Rather, Scotland provides an opportunity to explore female empowerment, and is simultaneously able to meditate cinematically on the possibility of diasporic heritage. For this reason, I will examine the film's hybrid nature first (and the manner in which this complicates previous conclusions concerning mythical cinematic constructions of Scotland) before exploring how a diasporic history is constructed by this hybrid format.

Post-heritage Hybrid in Scotland

The Governess could be argued to belong to the critical category of the heritage film, given its intimate recreation of the interior of the estate house and fetishisation of costume and country house décor. However, this aspect of the film should be viewed alongside the bleak landscape, overgrown garden and cold, bare workshop interior, which are more reminiscent of the Gothic. Moreover, the expressive *mise-en-scène*, emphasis on sex (albeit in a far more explicit form than in Gainsborough melodramas) and fantasised history in the narrative of photographic development all point to the pleasures of the post-heritage costume drama. I will examine its Gothic aspect first.

In *Contemporary Scottish Fictions* (2004), Petrie demonstrates the potential that the Gothic tradition has in the Scottish context to facilitate a reimagining of the official (British) record of the past, and Scotland's position within it.[22] Although *The Governess* lacks the engagement with Calvinism of many works of the Scottish Gothic tradition, and indeed the

mystery, paranoia and fear often associated with the Gothic more generally, it does contain aspects typical of the Gothic. These include the rural
isolation of the estate, the split world of communal drawing room and
workshop to which all are forbidden entry, the divided personality of
Jewish Rosina/Protestant Mary (both of the latter reminiscent of
Stevenson's Jekyll and Hyde) and the melodramatic behaviour of the pas-
sionate young Henry. Moreover, in its narrative about the development of
photography, the film clearly displays the Gothic's 'engagement with the
anxieties generated by late Victorian scientific discourse'.[23] It is this discourse on the 'new' scientific processes of modernisation with which *The
Governess* engages in the 'imaginative' manner usually associated with the
Scottish wilderness (as seen in Chapter 5 in films like *Dog Soldiers*) to
consider a diasporic 'out of' history. The official historical record cannot
be said to hold sway in *The Governess*, since Rosina/Mary's story, which
we witness as viewers, is 'without' (both outside and erased from) the historical record. The moment at which Charles denies Rosina/Mary's role
in the discovery of the fixative that enables an historical record to be kept
through photography is a self-conscious acknowledgement (typical of the
post-heritage hybrid) of the fictionalised nature of the past on display in
The Governess. This resonance of the Scottish Gothic tradition, then, a
generic form which, more generally, demonstrated nineteenth-century
unease surrounding the constructed nature of national identity as it
encounters its Imperial Other, is used to enable a reconsideration of the
past from a diasporic (as opposed to a national) viewpoint.

This Gothic element to the film – stressing the role of the imagination
in the Scottish wilderness to expose the fractures in national identity –
combines neatly with the pleasures of the costume drama. *The Governess*'s
version of the past, whilst seemingly an 'authentic' depiction of nineteenth-century London and Scotland as befits the heritage film (complete
with references to the Royal Society of Edinburgh's role in validating scientific discoveries), simultaneously portrays a romantic, fantastic Scotland
akin to the construction of the past in the post-heritage film, or the
costume drama more generally. The spectacle laid out before the viewer is
primarily of a sexual encounter rather than a 'realistic' recreation of a past
that has – by definition – been erased from history and British (English
and Scottish) heritage. As Cook notes of Gainsborough melodramas,
through 'their particular conjunction of femininity, foreignness and masquerade' 'these flamboyant films reinscribed the feminine principle,
defined in terms of a transgressive, itinerant spirit, in history'.[24] Similarly,
The Governess – in this respect far closer to a Gainsborough film like
Caravan than a heritage film like *Howards End* – reconsiders history from

a diasporic position by deploying the 'femininity, foreignness and masquerade' of the costume drama in conjunction with the resonances of the Scottish Gothic tradition's power to reimagine the past. Demonstrating the flexibility that Harper notes as a characteristic of the costume drama's ability to 'constantly reform its definitions of national identity'[25] the film toys with the past in a manner that suggests the need for a remythologising of dominant modes of national heritage, portraying 'history' in a manner that makes it accessible as a spectacle which addresses contemporary concerns both for women and diasporic viewers.

Its post-heritage hybrid format and the possibilities that offers for reconsidering identity, allow the film to be considered more multifaceted than its otherwise typical depiction of Scotland might suggest. The arrival of Rosina/Mary in Scotland illustrates how – in its depiction of Scotland as a fantasy space on the edge of civilisation – the myth of Scotland as remote wilderness associated with Tartanry is very self-consciously combined with the pleasures and the possibilities offered by the Gothic and the costume drama. As Rosina/Mary's carriage travels through lush, green Scottish countryside, she composes a letter to her sister Rebecca describing her journey:

> Green, green and more green. Anodyne, hostile countryside. How I detest it and long for cities and chimneys. Still, the Isle of Skye. It sounds absurdly romantic, Gothic even.

This final, more upbeat statement brings a dissolve, transporting Rosina/Mary from the jolting carriage to her arrival on Skye, Rosina/Mary's arrival being typical of many films set in Scotland in genres like the road movie (Chapter 2) and the horror film (Chapter 5). Unlike many heritage films, this landscape is not framed so as to sell the location as a tourist attraction but, rather, to position Rosina/Mary's story in an empty landscape of anonymous green fields and empty seashore. It signals that Scotland will function in this film somewhat typically as a Romantic, Gothic restorative space. Whilst initially encountered as an unrelentingly dull landscape that contrasts sharply with the urban London for which homesick Rosina/Mary longs, Scotland soon becomes the land of the romantic/sexual encounter that provides a rejuvenative cure for the visitor.[26] From the *tabula rasa* of the homogenous 'green, green and more green' of the primitive wilderness, Rosina/Mary will create her own history, through her liberating affair with Charles and the knowledge it provides her with of photographic practice. Thus, although Rosina/Mary's vomiting – brought on by her arduous journey by horse-drawn coach – initially suggests her abjection within this overpowering scenery,

Figure 6.1 Historical Reconstruction: Rosina/Mary finds herself in a (Scottish) *tabula rasa*. *The Governess* (1998)

ultimately this landscape will provide her with the opportunity for self-enhancement.

Rosina/Mary's journey to Scotland positions *The Governess* in relation to a number of other contemporary costume dramas about travel to foreign parts. In *Contemporary Costume Film* (2004), Julianne Pidduck notes the costume drama's creation of the past as 'fantasy zones for the exploration of national identity, gender and sexuality'[27] through encounters with the cultural Other. Pidduck discusses in this context the tourist travel of wealthy British and US characters to a nineteenth-century Europe associated with historical and cultural roots supposedly lacking in the USA, in films such as *A Room With a View* and *The Portrait of a Lady* (1996).[28] Drawing on Pidduck's work, Sarah Neely has noted how the arrival of the English aristocracy in Scotland in *Mrs Brown* resonates with many heritage films of the 1980s in which the imperial Raj is visited by the English upper classes so that they may reconsider their identity in a 'foreign' place.[29] *The Governess* charts a slightly different type of trajectory again. This time it is a movement of a character into a landscape whose mythical resonances and association with a time before history (the Scottish cinematic wilderness) combine with the possibilities and pleasures offered by both the costume drama and the Gothic to enable the construction of a female driven, diasporic history. Rosina/Mary does not go in search of an informing past in the museums and art galleries of Europe, or seek out the 'primitive' colonial Other. Rather, she reworks her own position in British society through an encounter with the latest advances in Enlightenment rationality in a context (a supposedly empty wilderness) known for its more mythical, primitive opportunities for 'awakenings', both sexual and (reimagined) historical. In *The Governess*, then, the myth of Scotland as the restorative, eternal feminine meshes with the costume drama's emphasis on sexual liberation in a fantasy past and is simultaneously able to accommodate the reimagining of the past of the (Scottish) Gothic.

Diasporic Heritage

The majority of existing material on *The Governess* stresses the film's foregrounding of the female gaze, focusing in particular on its self-conscious exploration and subversion of the subject–object relations usually associated with gender roles in cinema. After all, the film very deliberately explores the traditional, normative positions that place men behind the camera (subjects) and women in front of it (objects of the male gaze). In this way *The Governess* uses its reconstructed past as a fantasy space in which to reconsider shifting gender roles in the present.[30] Moreover, as Jim Leach argues, by viewing *The Governess* alongside other films of the 1990s/2000s directed by women, the very existence of this film by writer–director Sandra Goldbacher illustrates the emergence of a distinctive female point of view in the British film industry in the 1990s.[31] Yet, I would argue that the film's foregrounded construction of a female point of view for its audience (through alignment of the spectator with Rosina/Mary's experiences) is only one aspect of its engagement with the possibility of creating a diasporic (in this instance, Jewish) heritage. In the context of post-heritage debates, whilst offering the pleasures of the costume drama, in its positioning of a diaporic female Jewish character at the centre of its narrative *The Governess* self-consciously constructs an 'alternative heritage' to that usually found in 1980s and 1990s heritage films that focus on the English upper classes. Here I appropriate the term 'alternative heritage' from Moya Luckett, who considers the alternative images of British heritage that can be offered by many movies not usually considered as heritage films.[32] If, for Luckett, a film like *Quadrophenia* (1979) can offer an alternative vision of British identity, a subcultural, working-class heritage very different to, say, *Howards End*, then, similarly, *The Governess* offers another alternative, a diasporic, Jewish heritage that is again very different from the version of English/British national heritage and national identity offered in Merchant-Ivory films.

This engagement with an otherwise invisible Jewish history in the heritage film is evident in a number of ways, not least in Rosina's passing of herself as Mary Blackchurch. This conceit places the spectator, who is aligned with Rosina's point of view throughout (both through the camerawork and her voiceover), in a position of greater knowledge than the English characters she encounters. As we witness a disguised Jewish woman's adventures amongst the English upper classes, the act of performance that normally constructs English history in the heritage film is rendered transparent. So too is its need to exclude all Others from its official version, as seen in Charles's decision to exclude Rosina/Mary's involvement in the scientific process from his published findings. This theme of performance, in fact, runs throughout the film, from the moment when Rosina is charged with the financial care of her family after her father's death and discusses with her sister Rebecca the possibility of taking to the stage. In a manner typical of the self-conscious post-heritage film, *The Governess* depicts Rosina and Rebecca aping Gentile gentility as she prepares for her role as Mary Blackchurch, illustrating the mannered performance that lies behind normative portrayals of the English upper classes in the heritage film. Two other moments also stand out, the first being the depiction of the Jewish community in London as a hidden or closeted space, at the start of the film, and the second, the role of Rosina's photographic portrait business on her eventual return to London.

As Vidal notes of the introduction of the viewer to Rosina's family, we are initially positioned in line with Rosina's point of view as she observes them through a green, stained glass window, providing us with an 'outsider position in English society, as we enter the unknown and "exotic" world of Jewish culture'.[33] As Vidal also observes, this scene prefigures the scenes in the workshop on Skye, in which we will again be aligned with the gaze of Rosina as she experiments with photography, performs various roles before the camera (including characters derived from biblical stories, such as Salome and Queen Esther, who passed as a gentile and, as Queen of Persia, saved the Jews from massacre) and ultimately objectifies Charles by taking his photograph. Yet the diasporic discourse that is constructed by these moments in the film is also of importance. These confined spaces of the Jewish home and the photographic workshop are safe areas in which Rosina can practice performing roles she can subsequently use in the outside world. Thus she transforms herself into Mary Blackchurch before leaving London for Skye, and again develops (!) into a photographer in the workshop before returning home once more. These spaces are the dressing rooms, or closets (in this sense akin to those of *Dog Soldiers* discussed in Chapter 5) from which Rosina is able to fashion a diasporic history.

This 'Out of History' comes out of the closet when Rosina/Mary exposes the masquerade of normative identity of the English upper classes by presenting them with a photograph of their naked patriarch, Charles, exposed in his desire for the Jewish Other. Thus, whilst Charles's objection to being positioned as an object can be considered in terms of his gender (in that he does not wish to give up his position of subject by being photographed by Mary), it also illustrates his fear of losing his position as normative subject (the English upper-class patriarch), against which the Jewish (and otherwise diasporic) Other is positioned.

The second such moment occurs when Rosina returns to London and is shown taking a portrait photograph of two young Jewish girls in her new salon. *The Governess*'s alternative heritage is here seen to be established retrospectively through Jewish director Sandra Goldbacher's film, just as the photographs (origins and virtual memories for later generations) that Rosina take of her clients with the photographic equipment and the knowledge she picks up in Scotland will come to function for the Jewish community in London. Hence the alignment of the spectator with the female point of view so often noted by scholars writing on *The Governess* is consistent with a feminist reappraisal of history typical of the heritage film, but it also functions to reinsert a forgotten diasporic history through a fictional photographic media, the cinema. This is foregrounded most clearly when Rosina/Mary tells Charles, 'You've made it possible to capture the essence of people, to fix memory, to fix people, lost people.' Here the terms are deliberately ambiguous, photography having the ability both to fix the image of people in time, and indeed, to 'fix' (as in correct) the missing memories of a 'lost people' like the Jewish diaspora. It is no coincidence that Rosina/Mary stumbles across the magic ingredient, salt water, needed to fix these images when conducting her secret Passover Seder, a ceremony that commemorates the freeing of the Jews from slavery in Ancient Egypt. Nor is it by accident that Rosina/Mary places herself in front of the camera as Salome and Esther, these biblical heroines providing her with the virtual origins, fixed in photographic form, of her diasporic heritage.

Gypsy Setting

The Governess's alignment of the spectator with the heritage cinema's usual Other, the diaspora, again aligns the film with the functioning of the costume drama. In *Fashioning the Nation*, Cook develops Harper's work on the role of the gypsy in Gainsborough melodramas, stating that, 'while clearly functioning as metaphors for exotic "otherness", as signifiers of ethnic impurity they are often given a central and positive role in English society, with interesting consequences for the films' portrayal of national identity'.[34] Indeed, noting the interplay between British and European filmmakers in the 1930s and 1940s, Cook demonstrates how Gainsborough costume dramas often dealt with a loss of identity (*Madonna of the Seven Moons* (1944) being a prime example) and an exploration of identity's hybrid nature. She states that 'costume films deal in fantasies of loss of identity. They suggest that identity itself is fluid and unstable . . . and . . . that national identity is not pure, but mixed.'[35] For her part, Rosina/Mary's identity is not solely that of a Jewish woman performing as a Christian. Her claim that her skin is dark hued because her mother is Italian may also be taken as 'truth' within the world of the film, as it resonates with Goldbacher's own ancestry (her father is an Italian Jew)[36]. That Rosina/Mary has spent time in Paris whilst a child again suggests a diasporic, rather than a settled, 'national' lifestyle. This correlates with the European Otherness of Gainsborough, from the Italian setting of *Madonna of the Seven Moons* to the sexually liberated Spanish gypsies in *Caravan*. Thus, in *The Governess*, Rosina/Mary's hybrid diasporic identity functions a little like the liminal ethnicities of gypsies and European Others in Gainsborough costume dramas, both being 'travellers who transgress boundaries of nation and property . . . [who] have little or no stake in national identity and . . . are ethnically mixed'.[37] To return to Leach's words, if *The Governess* functions like the costume drama because it constructs a 'vaguely defined past, which shows little respect for history or the national heritage', this is to its benefit, as it attempts to construct a diasporic heritage in the era of post-heritage cinema.

This investigation of the role of diaspora within national identity sets *The Governess* apart from perhaps the most well known earlier representation of Jewishness in heritage cinema, *Chariots of Fire* (1981). Hill, writing on the representation of the Jewish character Harold Abrahams (Ben Cross) in the broader context of the multicultural cast of characters in *Chariots of Fire*, notes how the film 'seeks to overcome these differences and forge an image of "national" unity out of the multiple identities which it reveals'.[38] In this instance, the Olympic team is able to bring together characters of different class (upper and middle), faith (Christian and Jewish) and national (English and Scottish) identity into a supposedly shared notion of British identity. In *The Governess*, by contrast, the identity on offer is, as Higson notes in passing, decidedly 'un-English'.[39] It is not English Jewish, or British Jewish, as is that of Abrahams, but that of the Jewish diaspora. Rosina does not become integrated into an inclusive vision of national identity (be it Scottish, English or British) but, rather, forges a new identity for herself and her family from her time in Scotland. Thus, in the end, the female photographer is engaged in making origins for a displaced people. The photo she takes is of two Jewish sisters, not a (dead) father/nation figure. Apparently in line with Judaism's tradition of recognising matrilineal descent,[40] this image matches that of Rosina and her sister Rebecca, as a new fatherless origin for her familial, diasporic identity.

Finally, the ghostly appearance of Rosina's father in her dreams and memories evokes a similar representation of a deceased patriarch in *Nina's Heavenly Delights* (2006) (see Chapter 3). Like Nina, also saddled with the legacy of her father's debts, Rosina constructs a new diasporic history for her family in place of the 'external' (to the host nation) origin previously offered by her father. Noticeably, it is immediately after expressing her wonder at the ability of photography to 'fix people' that Rosina breaks down over the loss of her father. His ghostly visitations also then cease, as though he has been laid to rest by her discovery of a new way of recording/constructing history. Like both *Nina's Heavenly Delights* and *American Cousins* (2003), *The Governess* ends with a triumphal image (in Rosina's photography studio), demonstrating her ability to establish a successful business that will function as a new point of origin for a diasporic history. This motif recurs in the opening of restaurants (Indian and Italian respectively) at the end of the other two films. At the conclusion of *The Governess*, Rosina renders explicit the diasporic identity of her commercial venture. Although not so obvious a link as an 'Indian' or 'Italian' restaurant, her studio provides a new origin for the Jewish diaspora, in the same manner as *The Governess* does for Goldbacher. Rosina states in the closing voiceover,

> I think of Scotland hardly ever at all now. My images are much admired and I am even to give a lecture at the Royal Society. They say I have captured the beauty of my father's people, and I am glad.

Thus, a post-heritage film without a literary origin, or a national (Scottish, English, British) heritage to draw upon, *The Governess* intermingles aspects of the costume drama and the Gothic in a fantasy space outside of history provided by its Scottish setting in order to reconsider diasporic Jewish identity. In this manner, the recent feminist retrospective reappraisals of history through the heritage film and costume drama, which facilitate considerations of contemporary issues relevant to female audiences, are extended to an examination of the constructed nature of history and its typical exclusion of the diaspora from its normative images. As Rosina speaks her final words she is composing a self-portrait. The film ends, however, with two portraits side by side, those of Charles Cavendish and the two Jewish girls, to express the hybrid identity of the diaspora. Out of the scientific advances of the Enlightenment, Rosina has prospered, but her heritage is a mixture of this rational tradition (pictured in the English patriarch, Cavendish) and its excluded Other: Rosina, fantasy, spectacle, feminine, Gothic, Scottish, Jewish.

Notes

1. Duncan Petrie, *Screening Scotland* (London: BFI, 2000), pp. 53–73.
2. Andrew Higson, 'Re-presenting the National Past', in Lester D. Friedman (ed.), *Fires Were Started* (London: UCL Press, 1993), pp. 109–29, p. 110.
3. Ibid., p. 109.
4. Ibid., p. 110.
5. Claire Monk, 'The Heritage Film and Gendered Spectatorship', *CloseUp*, 1 (1997), http://www.shu.ac.uk/services/lc/closeup/monk.htm (02/07/08); Claire Monk, 'Sexuality and the Heritage', *Sight and Sound*, 5: 10 (1995), pp. 32–4, p. 33; and Claire Monk, 'The British heritage-film debate revisited', in Claire Monk & Amy Sargeant (eds), *British Historical Cinema* (London: Routledge, 2002), pp. 176–98.
6. Sue Harper, 'Historical Pleasures', in Christine Gledhill (ed.), *Home is Where the Heart Is* (London: BFI, 1987), pp. 167–96, p. 167.
7. Ibid.
8. Sue Harper, *Picturing the Past* (London: BFI, 1994), p. 122.
9. Stella Bruzzi, *Undressing Cinema* (London: Routledge, 1997), pp. 35–63; Pamela Church Gibson, 'Fewer Weddings and More Funerals', in Robert Murphy (ed.), *British Cinema of the 90s* (London: BFI, 2000), pp. 115–24; Julianne Pidduck, *Contemporary Costume Film* (London: BFI, 2004); Belén Vidal, 'Playing in a Minor Key', in Mireia Aragay (ed.), *Books in Motion* (Amsterdam/New York: Rodolphi, 2005), pp. 263–85.
10. Pam Cook, 'Neither Here nor There', in Andrew Higson (ed.), *Dissolving Views* (London: Cassell, 1996), pp. 51–65.
11. Higson, *Waving the Flag*, p. 27.
12. Pam Cook, *Fashioning the Nation* (London: BFI, 1996), p. 26.
13. Colin McArthur, *Brigadoon, Braveheart and the Scots* (London: I. B. Tauris, 2003), pp. 123–36; Tim Edensor, *National Identity, Popular Culture and Everyday Life* (Oxford: Berg, 2002), pp. 139–70; Lin Anderson, *Braveheart* (Edinburgh: Luath Press Ltd, 2005).
14. Petrie, *Screening Scotland*, p. 70.
15. Ibid.
16. John Hill, *British Cinema in the 1980s* (Oxford: Clarendon Press, 1999), p. 83.
17. Jim Leach, *British Film* (Cambridge: Cambridge University Press, 2004), p. 201.

18. Monk, 'Sexuality and the Heritage', p. 33. Pamela Church Gibson, 'From Dancing Queen to Plaster Virgin', *Journal of Popular British Cinema*, 5 (2002), pp. 133–41, and Church Gibson, 'Fewer Weddings and More Funerals', pp. 115–24.
19. Andrew Higson, *English Heritage, English Cinema* (Oxford: Oxford University Press, 2003), pp. 166–9.
20. Sheldon Hall, 'The Wrong Sort of Cinema', in Robert Murphy (ed.), *The British Cinema Book*, 2nd edn (London: BFI, 2001), pp. 191–99, pp. 194–5.
21. Max Samett, 'The Making of *The Governess*', *Eyepiece*, 20: 3 (1999), p. 22.
22. Duncan Petrie, *Contemporary Scottish Fictions* (Edinburgh: Edinburgh University Press, 2004), pp. 115–38.
23. Ibid., p. 116.
24. Cook, *Fashioning the Nation*, p. 7.
25. Sue Harper, 'Bonnie Prince Charlie Revisited', in Murphy (ed.), *The British Cinema Book*, pp. 127–34, p. 127.
26. David Martin-Jones, 'Sexual Healing: Representations of the English in Post-Devolutionary Scotland', *Screen*, 26: 2 (2005), pp. 227–33.
27. Pidduck, *Contemporary Costume Film*, p. 8.
28. Ibid., pp. 82–100.
29. Sarah Neely, 'Scotland, Heritage and Devolving British Cinema', *Screen*, 46: 2 (2005), pp. 241–5, p. 244.
30. Peter Lehman and Susan Hunt, 'Passion and a Passion for Learning in *The Governess*', *Jump Cut*, 45 (2002): http://www.ejumpcut.org/archive/jc45. 2002/ lehman/governesstext.html (05/09/06); Lynette Felber, 'Capturing the Shadows of Ghosts', *Film Quarterly*, 54: 4 (2001), pp. 27–37; Vidal, 'Playing in a Minor Key', pp. 263–85.
31. Leach, *British Film*, pp. 38–9.
32. Moya Luckett, 'Image and Nation in 1990s British Cinema', in Robert Murphy (ed.), *British Cinema of the 90s*, pp. 88–99, pp. 88–9.
33. Vidal, 'Playing in a Minor Key', p. 278.
34. Cook, *Fashioning the Nation*, p. 74.
35. Ibid., p. 90.
36. *The Governess* website, Production Notes webpage: http://www.sonypictures.com/classics/governess/index.html (17/07/08).
37. Cook, *Fashioning the Nation*, p. 103.
38. Hill, *British Cinema in the 1980s*, p. 24.
39. Higson, *English Heritage, English Cinema*, p. 29.
40. Alan Unterman, *Jews: Their Religious Beliefs and Practices* (London: Routledge, 1981), p. 14; Jack Wertheimer, 'What is a Jewish Family?', Michael J. Broyde and Michael Ausubel (eds), *Marriage, Sex and Family in Jodaism* (Lanham: Rowman & Littlefield, 2005), pp. 244–61, p. 246.

CHAPTER 7

Gangster Film: Glasgow's Transnational Identities

This chapter focuses on two gangster films made and set in Glasgow in the 2000s, the British film (with a major Scottish creative input) *American Cousins* (2003) and the French/US/UK coproduction starring Chinese martial arts action superstar Jet Li, *Danny the Dog* (*a.k.a Unleashed*) (2005). These gangster films enable a discussion of immigrant, diasporic and otherwise globally dispersed identities in contemporary Scotland. The chapter begins with a discussion of the appearance in the 1990s of gangsters in films produced in Scotland, amidst the flourishing of crime as a subject within Scottish literature, television and film in the latter decades of the twentieth century. The two films are then examined.

American Cousins draws on the US gangster movie, with its long history of depicting Italian-American immigrants and diasporic communities, to examine Scottish-Italian identity in an international context. It offers a complex vision of the 'family' (in both the nuclear, and the 'mob' sense), as at once a local and a global phenomenon. *Danny the Dog*, for its part, focuses on the international flows of people, finance and culture that pass through major Scottish cities like Glasgow, flows which exist in parallel with, but nevertheless impact upon, the lives of the local inhabitants. As in *American Cousins*, a fantastical story of gangsters facilitates an exploration of the different conceptions of 'family' that exist in such an environment. In both instances, it is the mobilisation of the gangster genre that enables these films to examine a range of different identities, at once local and global, that currently coexist in Scotland.

Scottish Crime Fiction – Scottish Crime Films

In Scottish literature it is only fairly recently that crime fiction has taken centre stage as a filter through which to examine the changing face of Scottish society. Writers like Ian Rankin have thrived, his Rebus novels, which began in the 1980s (named after the protagonist, Detective Inspector John Rebus), becoming bestsellers in the 1990s, and painting a grim, dark, rainy, murderous image of contemporary Edinburgh for worldwide consumption. In television it is the long running series *Taggart*, which began in 1983, that is most well known (this time depicting a rather drab, dreary Glasgow), although more recent examples have ranged from the idyllic rural setting of *Hamish Macbeth* (1995–7), to the darker adaptation of Rankin's Rebus novels into *Rebus* (2000–7).

In *Contemporary Scottish Fictions* (2004) Duncan Petrie considers this surge in popularity for crime fiction in Scottish literature and television part of the cultural reimagining of Scotland, and Scottish identity, that took place in the latter decades of the twentieth century.[1] In particular, for Petrie crime novels and television series enable an exploration of life in Edinburgh and Glasgow because of the access which the policeman has to characters from the different walks of life that coexist in the city, and, indeed, the different places they inhabit. What Petrie does not mention is that although the detective may come into contact with organised crime, watching him explore the city is different from exploring the criminal world on its own terms. The major difference with the recent rise in films about crime set in Scotland is that this situation is reversed, and it is characters from the other side of the tracks, especially gangsters, that are spotlighted.

Aside from the little-known Burke and Hare body-snatcher films set in Edinburgh, it is in the 1990s that Scotland has become associated with films about crime, and, for that matter, gangsters. This is interesting when compared to the English capital, London, which has been depicted as an urban crime zone in cinema throughout much of the twentieth century.[2] Undoubtedly the predominance of films set in the Highlands and Islands of Scotland has traditionally led to this bias away from the urban crime story in Scotland. Yet things have now changed. On the one hand, since the renaissance in Scottish filmmaking of the 1990s a number of films have incorporated an examination of crime, often within stories appealing to teen and twenty-something audiences. These include *Shallow Grave* (1994), *Small Faces* (1996), *Trainspotting* (1996), *16 Years of Alcohol* (2003) and *The Purifiers* (2004). Such films might usefully be seen in connection with British cinema's 'mockney' rejuvenation of gangster/heist films like Guy Ritchie's *Lock, Stock and Two Smoking Barrels* (1998) and *Snatch* (2000). Yet the Scottish films also have a lot in common with the Scottish-based slacker movie *Late Night Shopping* (2001), in which crime is not an essential element, suggesting that their primary focus is the exploration of youth concerns for an international market, rather then crime *per se*. On the other hand, there have also been several films since the 1990s to directly engage with the existence of organised crime in major urban centres, including *The Big Man* (1990), *The Life of Stuff* (1997), *The Debt*

Collector (1999), *Strictly Sinatra* (2001), *American Cousins, Man Dancin'* (2003), *In a Man's World* (2004), *Danny the Dog* and *The Clan* (2009).

In their recent edited collection, *British Crime Cinema* (1999), Steve Chibnall and Robert Murphy note that British crime films are often passed over in academic debates, their focus on crime seeming somehow 'un-British' in relation to pre-conceived notions of the nation's supposed dominant values.[3] Whilst this is true, as this chapter will demonstrate, there is another sense in which certain Scottish-based gangster films are un-British, or even, perhaps, 'un-Scottish'. In both *American Cousins* and *Danny the Dog* the concept of the gangster is mobilised to examine the broader issue of the experiences and identities of diasporic, immigrant or otherwise globally dispersed 'families' in contemporary Scotland. The exploration of the different types of identities currently possible in Scotland occurs very differently in the two films. In the former it is the hyphenated identity of the Scottish-Italian diaspora (and its broader connections with the Italian diaspora worldwide) that is emphasised. In the latter, it is the more transient, global/local identity of the transnational flows of people who settle in Scotland temporarily to gain from educational or financial opportunities before moving on again. This emphasis on migration into Scotland is unusual in that it is perhaps more normal to consider Scotland as a land from which many people emigrate before settling in diasporic communities in the USA, Canada, Australia and New Zealand. Even so, as something of a more action-packed accompaniment to the outward facing road movies that depict Scots travelling to other parts of the world discussed in Chapter 2 (*Carla's Song, Morvern Callar* and *Tickets*), these gangster films examine the nature of Scottish identities in a global, rather than solely a national, context. The difference is that theirs is an inward looking focus on Scottish immigrant and diasporic experiences, which provides an exploration of different, multicultural identities through the gangster genre.

American Cousins (2003)

American Cousins begins with two New York gangsters, Gino (Danny Nucci) and Settimo (Dan Hedaya), in the Ukraine, where a deal with the Ukranian mob for unspecified merchandise ends in a shoot-out. Settimo is wounded in the arm. He and Gino contact their boss Tony (Vincent Pastore) in New Jersey, who tells them to hide out with 'family' in Glasgow, Scotland. The two Italian-American mobsters stay with their cousin Roberto (Gerald Lepkowski) and his grandfather Nonno (Russell Hunter) at the family run fish-and-chip shop and ice cream parlour, Café del Rio. They are joined by Roberto's love interest, shop girl Alice (Shirley Henderson). As the narrative progresses it transpires that the smuggled merchandise is not drugs but seedlings for vines that can produce wine in any climate. Roberto's grandfather dies, Gino and Settimo come to the aid of Roberto (who is being threatened by local debt collectors), and Roberto saves Gino and Settimo from paid assassins on their trail. The film concludes with the Café del Rio burned to the ground, but Roberto and Alice finally get together, and Gino and Settimo are joined by their boss, Tony, and his crew, on the run from trouble in New Jersey. Together, this extended family of Scottish-Italian and Italian-Americans realise Roberto's family's dream of establishing an Italian restaurant in a converted church in Glasgow, outside of which they plant a vineyard from the hardy vines smuggled by Gino and Settimo.

American Cousins was produced by Little Wing Films, a small production company established in 2000, and based in London. Yet it has a very strong Scottish dimension. It was made on a budget of £3million (the film was originally shot on 16 mm Fujicolour, then blown up to 35 mm in Copenhagen), with finance from Little Wing Films, Scottish Screen and the Glasgow Film Fund. In terms of artistic inspiration, first-time director Don Coutts is a Scotsman, born and raised on a hill farm in the Highlands of Scotland, who attempted to break into the film industry as a young man before moving into television. He developed the idea for *American Cousins* with the Scottish-Italian journalist Sergio Casci, using script development money from Scottish Screen. They had previously worked together on a short film called *St Anthony's Day Off* (1997), about a Scottish-Italian football team watching the 1994 World Cup on television. *American Cousins'* editor, Lindy Cameron, is Coutt's wife. Production designer Andy Harris has worked on numerous Scottish film productions as far back as Bill Forsyth's *Comfort and Joy* (1984) – another Glasgow-based film about ice cream, fish and chips and a powerful Italian family/mob – and the film score's composer, Donald Shaw, was one of the founders of the Gaelic band Capercaillie. In front of the camera, the leading man, Roberto, is played by Scottish actor Gerald Lepkowski, and Nonno, by veteran Scottish actor Russell Hunter. Although a British film, then, *American Cousins* has much cause to be considered 'Scottish', although it expresses a very international conception of what it means to be from this particular small nation.

On their website, Little Wing Films downplay the gangster element to the film, describing *American Cousins* as 'a fresh, romantic comedy with immense charm . . . set against the colourful backdrop of Scottish Italian life'.[4] Yet *American Cousins* is a long way from contemporary rom-coms like *Notting Hill* (1999) or *Bridget Jones's Diary* (2001). Despite Roberto's floppy hair and earnest, bumbling charm, labelling *American Cousins* a rom-com is a savvy marketing move, prompted by the wider audience a rom-com is likely to reach compared to a gangster film, even though the two genres intertwine in the film itself.

The US Gangster Tradition

American Cousins is clearly influenced by the US gangster tradition that stretches back to early silent cinema, including everything from *Little Caesar* (1931) and *Scarface* (1932) through *White Heat* (1949) to *The Godfather* (1972), *Once Upon a Time in America* (1984), *Goodfellas* (1990), and the recent HBO television series, *The Sopranos* (1999–2007). Unlike many popular genres, academic study of the US gangster film tradition also has one of the longest histories in the discipline of film studies. A very brief survey of the development of this study of the field is instructive for understanding the way in which *American Cousins* deploys conventions of the gangster film to explore the experience of the Scottish-Italian diaspora.

The seminal moment in serious study of the gangster genre is Robert Warshow's 'The Gangster as Tragic Hero' (1948). Warshow identified the cinematic gangster as 'the man of the city',[5] whose rise and fall narrative spoke of his tragedy as he negotiated the aspirational, 'obligation to succeed'[6] demanded of him by the US city. When the discipline of film studies began to spread its wings in the 1970s, two books quickly appeared dedicated to the gangster film, Colin McArthur's *Underworld USA* (1972) and Jack Shoadoian's *Dreams and Dead Ends* (1977). Both built upon and departed from Warshow's work in numerous ways, but they also continued to explore the aspirational side of the gangster film. McArthur argues that Warshow 'rightly draws attention to the gangster's compulsive drive for success and its relationship to the value pattern of 'normal' American society',[7] yet also notes the predominance of immigrants (particularly Italian-Americans) depicted in gangster films of the 1930s as organised crime prospered under the conditions created by Prohibition. For his part, Shadoian, following Warshow's idea of the gangster's tragic rise and fall, noted that the 'gangster is a paradigm of the American Dream',[8] albeit in a criminal manner that often led to a dead end, particularly during the Depression. Over twenty years later, Martha P. Nochimson pursues a similar line of enquiry in *Dying to Belong* (2007) to express far more explicitly what seems in hindsight – especially after *The Godfather: Part II* (1974) and the remake of *Scarface* (1983) – to be one of the most important conclusions drawn from the works of Warshow, McArthur and Shadoian. The US gangster film depicts aspirational characters who follow their dreams of success, and these characters (in particular in the classics from the 1930s) are often immigrants. The US gangster genre, then, is the story of the American dream, as Shadoian noted, but, for Nochimson, this story correlates precisely with the immigrant's dream of a prosperous life in the USA.[9] In *Public Enemies, Public Heroes* (1999), Jonathan Munby draws a similar conclusion regarding the portrayal of the immigrant in the classic gangster films of the 1930s, which, particularly in the context of the Depression, 'came to express the desires of the culturally and economically ghettoised'.[10]

This focus on the immigrant is evident in the use of the gangster tradition in *American Cousins*, although the immigrant's story is told differently in Scotland and the USA. This, however, should not be surprising. As the editors of *Mob Culture* (2005) note in their introduction, the tragic rise and fall narrative identified by Warshow is typical of the limited examples of the gangster film from the 1930s that he isolated – and that any number of later critics also discussed – including *Little Caesar* and *Scarface*.[11] As the various contributions to *Mob Culture* demonstrate, by contrast, there are actually a number of other, often forgotten, or hidden, histories of the genre that do not follow precisely this pattern. The same can be said of *American Cousins*, which, although a story of an immigrant's dream, does not chart his tragic rise and fall but, rather, explores the correlations between the US and the Scottish experiences of the respective Italian diasporas. This equating of the two different diasporas is seen in several sequences in the film.

An Offer You Can't Understand

The opening of *American Cousins* links the actions of the Scottish-Italian Roberto in his cafe in Glasgow with the criminal dealings of his cousins as they trade goods in the Ukraine. The two locales are identified by establishing shots accompanied by titles. Firstly there is the Café del Rio next to the old church, over which is written, 'Glasgow, Scotland'. Then an anonymous industrial wasteland of slag heaps and old factory warehouses is identified as 'Kiev, Ukraine' (although, of course, also filmed in 'Glasgow, Scotland'). The action in the two disparate international locales is then intercut, creating a stark juxtaposition between Roberto preparing an ice cream sundae for a local girl who has saved up her pennies and Gino and Settimo doing an illicit deal with vast sums of money in the Ukraine that degenerates into a shoot-out with the double-crossing Ukranian mafia. Although the relative wealth and violence of the two occupations (ice cream seller and mobster), creates a contrast between the characters, their dealings are unified by the soundtrack, the 'Catalogue Aria' (*Madamina, il catalogo è questo*) from Mozart's opera *Don Giovanni*. The opening, then, unifies the two diasporas; the actions and occupations of the characters in these different international settings are depicted as equivalent on the basis of the respective opportunities offered by their different diasporic contexts, Glasgow and New Jersey. Whilst the east coast USA is famous for providing the conditions that created the mob, Glasgow, as Joe Pieri charts in *The Scots-Italians* (2005), is more renowned for offering Italians the chance to work their way into wealth and prosperity from humble origins selling fish and chips and ice cream. In both instances, however, the characters are united in their desire to get on in life – the immigrant's aspirational dream.

This equation of the different lives of the cousins, despite their different contexts, is reemphasised much later in the film when Roberto, following the death of Nonno, shows Gino and Settimo an old home movie. He explains that his grandfather came to Scotland because there was no work in Italy at that time and he had family and friends in the diaspora. He and his cousin Louie (Gino's grandfather) tossed a coin to see who would go to the USA, and who to Scotland. This Scottish-Italian story of diasporic origin is very close to that of Capaldi's *Soft Top Hard Shoulder* and *Strictly Sinatra* (see Chapter 2), its recurrence demonstrating the impact of the Scots-Italians (or 'Tallies' as they were initially known) on everyday life and culture in Scotland in the twentieth century.[12] As was the case with Capaldi's films, the story of immigrant origins in *American Cousins* is a direct result of screenwriter Sergio Casci's family background. Casci's great-grandfather Armando left Italy for Scotland in the late nineteenth century. Casci notes, 'I kept thinking how different my life might have been if Armando, instead of coming to Glasgow and opening a café, had travelled to the States and joined the Mob.'[13] Gino's revelation on seeing the home movie ('So, if Louie would've called heads instead a tails, I'd a ended up here?') is actually Casci's own. Humorously, Roberto responds to Gino's tacit deprecation of Scotland with an irrefutable fact, saying: 'Well, you ended up here anyway.' This funny put-down undermines Gino's belief that life in the Italian-American diaspora is somehow inherently preferable to that in Scotland, and emphasises how the contrasting diasporas are products of individual circumstances.

The film's Scottish-Italian perspective is demonstrated in various other ways. Roberto turns out to be every bit as good a mobster as Gino or Settimo, especially when he dispatches two assassins using a mop and bucket. Gino, on the other hand, is not as good a fish fryer as Roberto, and, of course, Roberto gets the girl, despite Alice's initial attraction to Gino's good looks and lively personality. Most tellingly it is the US mob who end up transplanting to Scotland, as the gang violence in New Jersey becomes too hot for them. Thus, the family's life at the Café del Rio, which has been in Roberto's family since 1929, is vindicated as the most preferable of the two options, and contrary to what Gino thinks when hearing the story of the coin toss, his grandfather Louie is shown to have lost, rather than won.

This judgement is further affirmed through the narrative of the abandoned church, next to the Café del Rio, which Roberto and his father dreamed of turning into an Italian restaurant. When Roberto first shows the restaurant to Settimo, he points out a half-finished family portrait set against a backdrop of rural Italy, begun by his father. Both restaurant conversion and painting are incomplete because of Roberto's father's untimely death. Roberto says that he should have given up on the restaurant at that point, especially when he ran out of money. Instead he carried on because, he wistfully explains, 'I've always been a dreamer.' Settimo is able to sympathise with this, noting that the restaurant project was Roberto's last remaining link to his family. This evocation of the incomplete immigrant's dream, springing directly from the countryside of Roberto's Italian ancestry, illustrates the difficulties the immigrant faces in trying to thrive in a new context where the national heritage has been left behind. As Nonno tells Roberto when he lies dying in hospital, 'Just remember who you are. Our family, from a tough place. A place a man could not survive unless he had a lot of that toughness inside him. We did survive.' The Scottish-Italian diaspora, then, carries its origins with it in its grit and determination in whatever context it finds itself. With the help of Settimo (who finishes the painting), Gino, Tony and the rest of the New Jersey crew, Roberto's interrupted family heritage can be completed. It is from this comparable diasporic experience that this section of the Scottish-Italian community draws its strength, pooling its reserves of geographically displaced toughness, rather than from the host nation of Scotland, or indeed, from Italy itself.

The vines that Gino and Settimo are smuggling provide the clearest metaphor for this toughness. The illicit cargo is a Chianti vine that can grow in any climate. The vineyard that is finally depicted outside the church, on the day of the opening of Ristorante del Rio, demonstrates that the most famous of Italian wines can be grown anywhere. The proof of this is the restaurant's speciality wine, 'Rosso del Rio, Scots Chianti'. The vines function as a metaphor for the manner in which the Italian diaspora has been able to thrive, even in a cold climate like that of Glasgow. The completed

Figure 7.1 (Non-)Traditional Scottish Breakfast: The diasporic mob family takes tea
together in *American Cousins* (2003)

restaurant, with its accompanying vineyard, is finally frozen as a label on a
wine bottle, marked 'AMERICAN COUSINS 2002 GLASGOW', over
which the closing credits roll, suggesting a blend of Catholic tradition and
business enterprise with an Italian origin, now creating exportable com-
modities through hard graft on the part of diasporas inhabiting inhospitable
climates. In this the wine label matches the restaurant and photographic
studio of *Nina's Heavenly Delights* (2006) and *The Governess* (1998) respectively, as symbol of diasporic business success. Moreover, the converted
church illustrates the prosperity of the Scottish-Italian diaspora at the time
of the rejuvenation of Glasgow around the turn of the twenty-first century.
The 'family' that the converted church/restaurant solidifies being at once
the orthodox, nuclear family (Roberto and Alice, a Scottish-Italian/Scottish
hybrid) and 'the family' (the mob, or crew), the broader, international
brotherhood of the Italian diaspora.

In respect of the film's heart-warming emphasis on the Scottish-Italian
diaspora, its positive depiction of the Italian-American mob is crucial.
American Cousins not only emerges in the wake of a history of representations of violent US gangsters, ranging from *Little Caesar* to *The Sopranos*,
but also of any number of US films that portray Italian-Americans and
Italian-American gangsters in a sympathetic light. As Bondanella has
shown in *Hollywood Italians* (2004), various gangster parodies and gangster

comedies like *Married to the Mob* (1988) and *Analyze This* (1999) have enabled audiences to laugh at, and along with, gangsters and the violent conventions of the gangster genre.[14] Moreover, films like *A Bronx Tale* (1993) have depicted Italian-Americans, their families and their neighbourhoods in a way that engenders a sense of pride in their immigrant histories.[15] Finally, the *Godfather* trilogy and television shows like *The Sopranos* have aligned audiences with gangsters and their families as central characters, allowing us an insight into their psyches and encouraging us to sympathise with their aspirations. Thus, the appearance of Vincent Pastore in *American Cousins* as the big mob boss, Tony, provides an instant association with his character 'Big Pussy' from *The Sopranos*. Although a gangster, and a killer where necessary, Big Pussy is a family man at heart, and in many ways a likeable character.

American Cousins taps into this shift in attitude towards Italian-American mobsters, both in its sympathetic portrayal of the two US gangsters Gino and Settimo and of Roberto's faithful adherence to family and hard work, as his aspirational dreams are seen to coincide with those of the Italian-American mobsters. It may be a different location, but the dream of the diaspora remains the same. *American Cousins* thus provides a correlative to the ending of *Strictly Sinatra*, which also depicts the Scottish-Italian diaspora in an uneasy relationship with a Scottish mob. Unlike *Strictly Sinatra*, however, which sees its protagonists depart Glasgow for a new life in the USA, here you do not have to leave Scotland to, as the famous song says, 'make it there'. Unlike the ending to the previous film, New York is not the only alternative to Scotland; rather, you can create your own New York in Glasgow. Put another way, if you want it enough, you can 'make it anywhere'. This message is emphasised throughout *American Cousins* by the soundtrack, with numerous scenes in the cafe, as well as various other locations, accompanied by Italian pop music from the 1960s (and indeed, by Roberto's choice of the Italian Eurovision winner from 1964, Gigliola Cinquetti's *No ho l'età* as a karaoke song), creating the impression that the immigrant's life takes place in a sort of portable atmosphere of Italianness, even though it is lived in Scotland. This mood reflects the reality of life for many Scots-Italians in the twentieth century, who have lived lives that are at once Italian in language and culture in the family sphere, and Scottish in the public.[16]

Ceilidh, is it Too Late to Say I'm Sorry?

The role of the Scottish tradition of the ceilidh (social dance) is very interesting in respect of the film's focus on diaspora. At the time of the film's release, Edward Lawrenson criticised *American Cousins* for propagating 'national stereotypes' of US characters who are 'agents of brash modernity' encountering charming 'old-world' Scots.[17] As evidence, Lawrenson notes the ceilidh scene, which he believes refers to *The Maggie* (1954), although it is actually a standard scene in any number of films set in Scotland. However, on closer inspection, this ceilidh's function is slightly different from in its predecessors. Taking a brief road trip to Loch Lomond, the characters encounter a ceilidh, which Settimo describes as 'wrestling to music'. Traditionally, in films set in Scotland, from *Whisky Galore!* (1949) to *The Last Great Wilderness* (2002), a ceilidh is the place where inhibitions fall way as the alcohol and dancing break down the barriers between locals and guests visiting Scotland. The ceilidh, then, is typically a symbol of Scotland associated with Tartanry that illustrates the curative charms Scotland offers to the tourist or visiting outsider. In this instance, the tradition holds, but it is Gino and Alice, rather than Roberto and Alice, who succumb to the sweaty charms of the ceilidh, passionately kissing in the cloakroom. This symbol of Scotland, supposedly a marker of national character (at least according to the tradition of Tartanry), is here not figured as a positive context for the third-generation immigrant, Roberto. Although he had planned to propose to Alice, instead, after witnessing her embrace Gino, he gets drunk and leaves. Moreover, on his return to Glasgow, Roberto finds that his grandfather has passed away during the night. The ceilidh, then, is not a place of rejuvenation for Roberto, but an extremely unsettling context that further detaches him from his past and threatens to destroy his future happiness with Alice. When he does finally propose to Alice, it is in the partially converted church. This setting suggests that the rejuvenation that the ceilidh offers is an illusion, only available to the transitory tourist Gino. For the settled Scottish-Italian by contrast it is the church/restaurant, the site of the diasporic dream, where the marriage of Scottish-Italian and Scot can take place. This is, after all, the continuation of a diasporic identity, as opposed to a 100 per cent 'Scottish' identity (or even, the tourist's view of it). Far from affirming national stereotypes, then, the ceilidh scene – and Roberto's karaoke song in Italian, sung whilst drunk on Scottish whisky – demonstrate that the diaspora is not entirely at home in the old world offered by national traditions, but rather, must negotiate a hybrid identity in relation to it.

Not content solely to refigure such recognisable clichés of cinematic Scotland, *American Cousins* also renegotiates stereotypes of Italianness usually found in British cinema. The mild and charming Roberto conforms to previously established stereotypes of Italian masculinity in

British cinema that, as Elisabetta Girelli has shown in relation to films like *Hell Drivers* (1957), are characterised by an 'un-British masculinity', lacking ferocity and competitiveness and marked instead by 'gentleness and sensitivity'.[18] However, in *American Cousins* Roberto is not considered 'deficient' in relation to previously established notions of active, British masculinity but, rather, to exist somewhere in between British and Italian stereotypes of masculinity, precisely as a Scots-Italian. Emerging during a very different time in the history of British cinema (when a gentler, more sensitive British masculinity has been popularised since the 1990s by actors like Hugh Grant and Colin Firth in such films as *Notting Hill* and *Bridget Jones's Diary*), Roberto's persona is particularly well attuned to the context of the globalised services economy, specifically because his diasporic identity conceals the hard realities of the Italian immigrant's struggle ('our family, from a tough place') beneath the gentler aspect of late twentieth-century British masculinity. Thus, like his Italian-American gangster cousins, when called upon to be ferocious Roberto is capable of disarming two Uzi carrying hit men and, indeed, torching his own restaurant to save everyone from the Ukranian mob. This is the same Roberto, however, who, after witnessing Gino kissing Alice at the ceilidh, expresses his feelings by singing *No ho l'età*, which translated means, 'I'm not old enough (to love you)', before fleeing the scene. Thus, at the end of the film, the 'hard and soft' or perhaps, 'gangster/rom-com' masculinity of Roberto ensures that he wins the love of his girl over his seemingly more dynamic cousin, Gino. He is a stark contrast, then, to the ill-fated 'soft' masculinity portrayed by Herbert Lom as the immigrant Gino, struggling to survive in the 'hard' masculine, post-war, industrial world of British cinema of the 1950s, in *Hell Drivers*.

In contrast to Lawrenson's position, then, I argue that in *American Cousins* it is not a case of wily local tradition holding at bay the globalising forces of US capitalism in true Kailyard style. Rather, the aspirations of Italian-American mobsters are equated with Roberto's Scottish-Italian diasporic experience, creating one big, international immigrant family that exists in parallel to previous cinematic negotiations of the relationship between Scotland and the USA.

Danny the Dog (2005)

Danny the Dog is a gangster film-cum-martial arts action movie/family melodrama. A Chinese boy, Danny (Jet Li) has been brought up as an attack dog by gangster boss Bart (Bob Hoskins), who murdered his mother. Now an adult, Danny is feared across Glasgow. When Bart arrives to collect his protection money, local businessmen know that failure to pay will lead to the (literal) unleashing of Danny's ferocious street fighting skills. On the strength of Danny's reputation and spectacular acrobatics, Bart maintains his empire and the status afforded by his illegal protection racket. Danny, for his part, behaves as an obedient dog, inhabiting Bart's cellar, seemingly ignorant of his past as a human being. However, when a wealthy local jewellery retailer attempts to assassinate Bart, Danny is inadvertently freed. Wandering the city, he is adopted by Sam (Morgan Freeman), a blind piano tuner, and his step-daughter, Victoria (Kerry Condon), a US citizen studying music in Glasgow. Victoria and Sam take to Danny and begin civilising him, adopting him into their makeshift, multicultural family. In the final, extended action showdown, Danny is forced to choose between the culturally civilising family unit offered by Victoria (who, like Danny's mother, is also a student of the piano) and Sam, and the invasively violent 'family' of Bart's mob, who attack their family home.

Although officially an international coproduction, *Danny the Dog* was primarily produced by the French company Europa Corp from a story by the famous director, writer and producer Luc Besson. Besson made his name directing a string of international hits, including *Subway* (1985), *The Big Blue* (1988), *Nikita* (1990), *Leon* (aka *The Professional* (1994)) and *The Fifth Element* (1997). Besson is also the founder and chairman of Europa Corp, which was established in 1999 and has been responsible for numerous films that were commercially successful in Europe and the USA. Besson and Li worked together previously on the Europa Corp production *Kiss of the Dragon* (2001), a Jet Li vehicle set in Paris for which Besson wrote the screenplay. *Danny the Dog* was directed by Frenchman Louis Leterrier, who also worked as artistic director on the action films *The Transporter* (2002) and directed its sequel *Transporter 2* (2005) for Europa Corp.

Danny the Dog was originally to be set in London, but locations manager David Broder (who had done recces of the city and other parts of Scotland for previous films like *Enigma* (2001)) suggested Glasgow instead. Subsequently the film was shot on location in Glasgow. In contrast to the low-budget *American Cousins*, the budget for *Danny the Dog* was in excess of £20million, although only about twenty per cent of that was spent in the UK. The Glasgow Film Office subsidised the production to the tune of around £37,000, enabling the hiring of local facilities and services. In addition, around twenty-five locals were also employed as part of the crew, including a production manager and a locations manager.[19] The dominance of Europa Corp in this production ensures that, unlike *American*

Cousins, with its gentle take on gangster violence mingled with romantic-comedy, *Danny the Dog* is a self-consciously overblown gangster film, melodrama and action movie similar to Besson's earlier films *Nikita* and *Leon*, whilst Li's street-fighting inflected martial arts displays positions it in relation to other Europa Corp productions, including the *Transporter* movies and the free-running film, *Banlieue 13* (2004).

The Long Glasgow Friday

The fact that Glasgow was used as a stand-in for London may not surprise audiences familiar with previous British gangster films. The spectacular stunts of Li aside, the presence of Bob Hoskins as gangster boss Bart triggers immediate associations with the London-based cult classic *The Long Good Friday* (1980). Director Leterrier notes in interview that it was Hoskins's performance as Harold Shand in *The Long Good Friday* that inspired his casting as Bart in *Danny the Dog*. Leterrier even goes so far as to claim that *Danny the Dog* is *The Long Good Friday* twenty years on.[20] *The Long Good Friday* is an allegorical gangster thriller that examines attempts to redevelop London's docklands with the aid of US investment.[21] As John Hill argues in his contribution to *British Crime Cinema*, Hoskins's character in *The Long Good Friday*, Harold Shand, prefigured both the entrepreneurial vigour of the self-made man who would flourish in the 'enterprise culture' of 1980s Britain, and the 'social and moral conservatism' and nationalistic patriotism of the Thatcherite era.[22] For its part, *Danny the Dog* uses its gangster narrative to explore the two very different, but coexisting, sides to society that were prefigured in *The Long Good Friday*, and which consolidated in the hiatus between the two films. Depicting Glasgow as a city with two faces, *Danny the Dog* examines the different lives lived by its local and its global inhabitants. Thus, the incongruity of Hoskins's cockney accent in Glasgow is not altogether out-of-place, as this is a Glasgow inhabited by numerous different national identities.

To anyone familiar with the city, there is no doubt that *Danny the Dog* takes place in Glasgow. One of the very first shots is of the distinctive neon sign for the Barrowland Ballroom concert venue. Moreover, Morgan Freeman's character Sam mentions the name of the city (referring to the local Broomhill Spar as 'the best supermarket in Glasgow'), and several of Glasgow's more distinctive locations feature prominently. Although the majority of the action scenes were shot in studios in France, the atmosphere of the film is created by the use of locations like the Charles Rennie Mackintosh-designed Glasgow School of Art, the huge Victorian greenhouses of the Great Western Road Botanic Gardens, the scenic beauty of

Kelvingrove Park and Museum, the distinctive Georgian architecture of Carlton Place and so on. Yet, in addition to these rather conventional attempts to establish location, the city is constructed as one of intersecting but radically disparate flows of people and finance. Most obviously, the film contrasts the 'underworld' existence of Bart's violent gangster empire with the refined culture and familial security offered by the middle-class lifestyle of Sam and Victoria. This contrast is demonstrated in the transformation of Danny, as he moves from the life of a dog kept in a dark basement by Bart to a valued family member of Sam and Victoria's homely tenement flat, even helping with the shopping and cooking. In fact, this duality appears on numerous occasions in the film and speaks of the wealth inequalities that, as Saskia Sassen has shown, are a characteristic of globalisation.[23] The coexisting haves and have-nots of contemporary society in *The Long Good Friday* and the Glasgow of *Danny the Dog* in fact demonstrate precisely the social and economic divisions of neoliberalism.

On several occasions the two sides of Glasgow society, which are seen to coexist peaceably most of the time, spill over into one another. In an initial montage establishing the routine of extortion through which Bart makes his living he is seen paying visits to various local businesses and unleashing Danny on those who refuse to pay. Bart's car pulls up in a dimly lit alley. He and his cohorts enter a dingy looking doorway and are seen emerging on the other side into the brightly lit, shiny and extremely expensive surroundings of the Argyll Arcade in Glasgow's city centre. This is a plush arcade containing only jewellers' shops. Their purposeful and fluid movement between these spaces suggests that the economic divisions they reflect (the unequally divided wealth sectors of globalisation) are in some ways linked to the violence of the gangsters. Indeed, there is more than one instance in which the violence by which Bart makes his living spills out of the darkness and into the light of the high street. When Bart is confronted by the jeweller Raffles (Vincent Regan) Danny's fight with Raffles's henchmen bursts out of his backroom and into the showroom where wealthy customers look on in surprise. As a result of this spectacle, Bart will be invited to display Danny for the illegal entertainment of the wealthy in a street fighters' dungeon arena, a fantastical setting reminiscent of a computer game scenario.

This practice of demonstrating the wealth inequalities that exist side by side in a major urban space is not peculiar to Glasgow. It was also apparent in Li's previous film for Europa Corp, *Kiss of the Dragon*, in which he physically negotiates such contrasting abutting spaces as the luxurious tourist restaurant atop a boat on the Seine and the cramped kitchens below deck, a luxury hotel and its subterranean laundry and so on. Yet, although the theme of wealth and social divisions in the city's intersecting spaces which is explored in *Danny the Dog* may have originally been intended for a London-based narrative, it is actually as pertinent to Glasgow at the time the film was made.

Of all of Scotland's major cities, Glasgow is by far the largest, and contains the most dramatic wealth inequalities. In a survey conducted in 2002 by the Child Poverty Action Group, of the ten most deprived areas of the UK, the top three for poverty and social deprivation were in Glasgow.[24] One of the three, Maryhill, joins directly onto the extremely wealthy west end, creating by contrast precisely the juxtaposition of financial wealth and opposing lack seen in the movement between distinct locations of *Danny the Dog*. Moreover, in 2008 a World Health Organisation report noted that in the Glasgow suburb of Calton, average life expectancy was fifty-four (less than in India), whereas a few miles away in Lenzie it was eighty-two.[25] Even so, it is the global dimension to the film's juxtaposition of wealth (the manner in which it is figured as a coexistence of local and global flows of people and money inhabiting the same city space) that is important for this discussion. Rather than exploring wealth inequalities within different sections of the indigenous Scottish population (by focusing, for instance, on class without any related examination of ethnicity, diaspora or immigration), *Danny the Dog* considers the wealth inequalities now typical of many major cities under the conditions created by globalisation.

It is this global dimension that singles out *Danny the Dog* from its most apparent predecessor, *The Big Man* (1990), and that illustrates the shift in emphasis in contemporary cinema produced in Scotland from a national context, to an exploration of the nation (or rather, its largest city) in a global arena. Based on a novel by William McIlvanney (author of the Glasgow-set Laidlaw crime novels), *The Big Man* also uses a fighter to explore social and wealth inequalities, a disenfranchised ex-miner, Dan Scoular (Liam Neeson), who turns to illegal bare-knuckle boxing for local gangster Matt Mason (Ian Bannen). Contrasting Scoular's post-industrial wasteland of a hometown, Thornbank, with Mason's luxurious home in the upmarket Glasgow suburb of Bearsden, *The Big Man* examines the wealth inequalities of Glasgow after a decade of Thatcherite rule. However the film has been negatively critiqued in the past,[26] *The Big Man* is interesting in that it, like *Danny the Dog*, attempts to use a popular genre format to approach the issue of wealth and social inequality in Glasgow. Moreover, the differences between the two films, made over a decade apart, point towards a shift in the social construction of Scottish society in the interim. Whilst *The Big Man* was concerned with national wealth inequalities (be they interpreted as (stereotypically) Scottish or British) in terms of class though, *Danny the Dog* focuses on the global dimension to these same wealth inequalities as they exist in a city traversed by global flows of people and trade.

The film's discussion of these global wealth divisions is flagged up very early on when Bart describes a dream to his henchmen:

> I had a dream last night. I was sitting under those, erm, umbrellas that they make out of palm leaves, y'know? And these beautiful, golden-skinned girls dressed in just, like, little grass skirts and the skin that they was born in. And they came over, one after the other, and they brought me a drink in a coconut. And as they served me the drink they brushed their tits across my face . . . That was the end of the best bits. After the girls the whole thing turned to shit. This giant mumpet [sic] turned up with a machine gun and started blasting away until there was nothing but blood and guts and bits of body everywhere . . . A real nightmare.

Here the global dimension of the film's vision of Glasgow is apparent. Bart's dream is a colonial fantasy in which he is a sexual and social over-lord of the native people who inhabit a stereotypically 'primitive' context. Mirroring his enslavement of Danny (who is sitting beside him at this time), the dream exposes the violence against a subaltern people upon which a lifestyle of luxury and leisure is built. This subtext of colonialism explains the most striking image constructed in this otherwise fantastical film, that of a Caucasian man in a white suit who has enslaved a Chinese man since childhood and now treats him like a dog. Tellingly, a little later in the film Bart returns to the topic of the dream and interprets it as a subconscious desire for retirement, which he believes may be possible if Danny is transformed into a prize fighter. However, this interpretation is immediately undercut when Raffles's henchmen appear and riddle his car with machine-gun fire, allowing Danny to escape Bart's control and dis-cover himself anew with Sam and Victoria. Here the 'mumpet' with the machine gun turns out to be Raffles, the spectre of (violent) competition that accompanies the luxurious lifestyle of the neoliberal entrepreneur in the context of globalisation.

Transnational Family

Under the tutelage of Sam and Victoria, Danny is taught the basics of human civilisation, including praying before dining, eating at a table using cutlery, shopping, cooking and laughing. He is given a paid job (piano tuner's assistant) by Sam, and taught to appreciate culture through the musical tuition provided by Victoria. In many respects, this could be any story of a bourgeois family 'civilising' a primitive. However, this is a rather carefully constructed multicultural family, which lends a specific interpretation to their actions. Sam is an African-American male father figure, Victoria a Caucasian-American (albeit played by an Irish actress) and Danny is a Chinese male. Sam and Victoria are characteristically American: they eat the traditional peanut butter and jelly sandwich internationally known to represent all things North American, and Sam's avuncular persona makes him almost an 'Uncle Sam' to Danny. They are only in Glasgow temporarily whilst Victoria attends music college. They are not national citizens, and Sam openly discusses their return to the USA with Danny in the hope that he will accompany them when they go. As it turns out, Danny was also a transient visitor to the country before being captured by Bart, as his mother was a student at the same music college. This multi-ethnic, multicultural 'family' unit, then, is representative of the global middle classes, the internationally mobile elite who are able to take advantage of the best opportunities for education and training wherever they are in the world before returning to their homelands to continue to prosper. This is made clear when Danny, after receiving his first ever pay packet from Sam, rushes to buy presents for his new family. At the local Spar supermarket he purchases the comical 'Jimmy Hats' so typical of the Scottish tourist trade. 'Jimmy Hats' are tartan patterned hats with ginger-haired wigs attached, designed to look comical at the best of times, and even more so on faces of different ethnic origin to the ginger-haired Caucasian Celt stereotype usually associated with tartan regalia. These tourist joke hats illustrate perfectly the temporary nature of Danny's new family's residence in Glasgow. For the global elite who have come to Scotland to take advantage of its world-class educational opportunities, Scottishness (or even, Scottish identity) is something that can be put on temporarily and then removed. For them, Scottishness is rather like a Jimmy Hat, a (life)style to be adopted for a short time in the knowledge that it also renders the wearer slightly comical, thereby emphasising the incongruity of their presence in another culture.

Contrasting this inclusive, homely, multicultural 'family' of the global elite, is its negative image, the enslaving, violent neoliberalism of Bart with its competing jewellery salesmen-cum-hit men, and its seedy undertow of exploitative street-fighting dungeons for the entertainment of the rich. Noticeably, it is just after buying the Jimmy Hats for Sam and Victoria that Danny is recaptured by Bart, as though his desire to join the global elite is interrupted once more by Bart's violent world of entrepreneurial capitalism. Ultimately, Danny is positioned inbetween the two versions of the global 'family' and forced to choose between the two forms of 'training'

Figure 7.2 We are (transnational) family: The internationally mobile global elite hit Glasgow for *Danny the Dog* (2005)

they offer. In the final action sequences Danny protects his preferred adopted family against the invasive forces of Bart and his paid assassins. As Danny attempts to kill Bart, he throws him against the CDs of classical music and the books that adorn the family home. Should he kill Bart (as Bart goads him to) he will have failed his training and will not be able to join the global elite – he will simply have smashed up their cultural world instead. In the end he does not kill Bart, and passes the test with the help of Sam. A position as part of the global, cultural elite is available to everyone, then, it seems, if you have the right training in how to obtain it.

Existing alongside these two versions of global capitalism (the cultural versus the entrepreneurially, even violently neoliberal) worlds are the few Scottish locals seen in the film. On the one hand, the Scottish lady, Maddy (Carole Ann Wilson), who runs the Broomhill Spar is a friend to Sam and his family. On the other, the violent young Scot, Lefty (Dylan Brown), is a henchman of Bart. Here the locals, swept up by the forces of globalisation, also have the ability to choose which side to be on. Thus, *Danny the Dog* rebrands Glasgow as a city of wealth inequalities traversed by global and local flows of people and finance, and in so doing, mirrors its own existence as a primarily French production shooting on location in Glasgow, with a US, Scottish, English, Irish and Chinese cast. As a result, its engagement with Scottishness remains focused on Glasgow's global, rather than Scotland's national, identity.

Diasporic Memory Man

Finally, the star persona of Jet Li functions to further this vision of Glasgow as a node in a network of global flows. Previously, in Chinese films like the *Once Upon a Time in China* series of the 1990s, Li's star persona developed around his ability to mediate between Eastern and Western cultures in the run-up to the handover of Hong Kong to China in 1997 after its previous status as a British protectorate.[27] Here his immense physical abilities resonate with the cultural flexibility and adaptability required of his context. In many of the films made in other contexts in which Li has since starred, these skills of flexibility and adaptability have enabled him to prosper in locations like the USA, France and, of course, Scotland. In these films, Li becomes a representative figure of the Chinese diaspora, however fantastically this is rendered. In *Lethal Weapon 4* (1998) Li plays a ruthless Chinese assassin embroiled in the trading of Chinese immigrants as slave labour into the USA. In *Romeo Must Die* (2000) he is an honourable cop from a dishonourable family who escapes from a Hong Kong prison to avenge his brother's death in California and assist hard working families whose homes are under threat from ruthless crime syndicates. In *Kiss of the Dragon* he plays a Chinese police inspector who travels to Paris to assist in the arrest of a Chinese heroin smuggler, and in *War* (2007), he plays a Chinese-American FBI agent who goes deep undercover after his family is murdered, battling triads and yakuzas in San Francisco. In all these films, Li is figured as a visitor, newly arrived immigrant or established member of a diaspora, and in each case his adaptability speaks of the immigrant's, or the global citizen's, need to be flexible in order to succeed in a new context.

Danny the Dog is no different. When Danny recovers his childhood memory in order to regain his identity it is not an informing national history that he remembers. He does not recover his childhood years in China, but rather, the moment of his mother's murder by gangsters in Glasgow where she was studying music, just prior to his unlawful adoption by Bart. His identity, then, once regained, a little like that of Roberto in *American Cousins* and Nina in *Nina's Heavenly Delights* (2006) (Chapter 3), is a transnational or diasporic (local) identity based upon an uprooted past, that was in this case violently interrupted by criminal forces suggestive of unchecked neoliberalism. He does not belong to China, Scotland, Britain or the USA. Therefore, once Danny regains his memory he is able to choose between his two families in favour of the globally mobile, transnational elite represented by Sam and Victoria on the strength of their shared cultural heritage, their common interest in Western classical music, as opposed to their greed for international capital.

Notes

1. Duncan Petrie, *Contemporary Scottish Fictions* (Edinburgh: Edinburgh University Press, 2004), pp. 139–61.
2. Steve Chibnall and Robert Murphy (eds), *British Crime Cinema* (London: Routledge, 1999).
3. Steve Chibnall and Robert Murphy, 'Parole Overdue', in Chibnall and Murphy (eds), *British Crime Cinema*, pp. 1–15, p. 2.
4. Little Wing Films website, *American Cousins* webpage: http://www.lwf.info/lwf_gotflash.htm (10/03/08).
5. Robert Warshow, *The Immediate Experience* (Cambridge, MA: Harvard University Press, 2001), p. 101.
6. Ibid., p. 103.
7. Colin McArthur, *Underworld USA* (London: Secker & Warburg, 1972), p. 66.
8. Jack Shadoian, *Dreams and Dead Ends* (Oxford: Oxford University Press, 2003), p. 3.
9. Martha P. Nochimson, *Dying to Belong* (Oxford: Blackwell, 2007), pp. 2–27.
10. Jonathan Munby, *Public Enemies, Public Heroes* (Chicago, IL: University of Chicago Press, 1999), p. 4.
11. Lee Grieveson, Esther Sonnet and Peter Stanfield (eds), *Mob Culture* (Oxford: Berg, 2005), pp. 1–10.
12. Joe Pieri, *The Scots-Italians* (Edinburgh: Mercat Press, 2005), p. 14 and p. 138.
13. *American Cousins* website, Sergio Casci webpage: http://www.american-cousins.com/ (10/03/08).
14. Peter Bondanella, *Hollywood Italians* (New York: Continuum, 2004), pp. 282–95.
15. Ibid. p. 190.
16. Pieri, *The Scots-Italians*, p. 4 and p. 10
17. Edward Lawrenson, 'American Cousins', *Sight and Sound*, 14: 1 (2004), pp. 36–7, p. 37.
18. Elisabetta Girelli, 'Transnational Maleness', *Cinema Journal*, 44: 4 (2005), pp. 44–56, p. 49.
19. Figures received by email from Jennifer Reynolds, Market Intelligence and Information Officer at the Glasgow Film Office, 01/04/08.
20. Interview on *Danny the Dog* DVD extras.
21. David Martin-Jones, *Deleuze, Cinema and National Identity* (Edinburgh: Edinburgh University Press, 2006), p. 92.
22. John Hill, 'Allegorising the Nation', in, Chibnall and Murphy (eds), *British Crime Cinema*, pp. 160–71, p. 167.
23. Saskia Sassen, *The Global City* (Princeton: Princeton University Press, 1991), p. 9.
24. Anon., 'UK's "Most Deprived" Areas Named', BBC News website: http://news.bbc.co.uk/1/hi/uk/1826411.stm (05/04/08).

25. Damien Henderson, 'Postcode Deprivation', *The Herald*, 29 August 2008, p. 15.
26. John Caughie, 'Representing Scotland', in Eddie Dick (ed.), *From Limelight to Satellite* (London: BFI/SFC, 1990), pp. 13–30, p. 17; Petrie, *Screening Scotland*, pp. 151–3.
27. Tony Williams, 'Under "Western Eyes"', *Cinema Journal*, 40: 1 (2000), pp. 3–24.

CHAPTER 8

Social Realist Melodrama: Middle-class Minorities and Floundering Fathers

This chapter examines two films that draw upon the social realist tradition, *Ae Fond Kiss* (2004) and *On a Clear Day* (2005). Initially it outlines the way social realism is defined in studies of cinema, and then sketches in something of its history in relation to British cinema and previous cinematic representations of Scotland. The two films are then examined to demonstrate their different cominglings of social realism with melodrama. Whilst *Ae Fond Kiss* draws a subtle distinction between global and local identities, in *On a Clear Day* the question of a specific identity that can be described as global, local or even national recedes into the background as the film focuses on gendered identity in a post-industrial milieu. In *Ae Fond Kiss* Scotland plays an integral role as a location in which the action is set. In *On a Clear Day*, Scotland becomes a film set, a backdrop with resonances of industrial masculinity – long-established in previous cinematic representations of working-class life in Scotland's shipyards – against which to explore the future of post-industrial masculinity in the UK more generally.

Social Realism

French critic André Bazin is a key figure in early attempts to define cinematic realism. In *What is Cinema?* (1958) Bazin argues that cinema has the potential to produce a more objective image of the world than that of previous art forms because of the seemingly neutral agency of the technology of the camera. For Bazin, the camera's apparent innocent presence in the recording process sets cinema apart from other art forms, such as painting or sculpting, because the role of the individual artist in constructing an image of reality is less intrusive in filmmaking.[1] Bazin develops his argument by analysing certain films from the post-war Italian neo-realist movement, championing Vittorio De Sica's *Bicycle Thieves* (1948) for its use of the long take and depth of field. As opposed to editing, Bazin feels that these qualities of the cinematography of neorealism enable a far greater sense of realism thanks to their ability to capture events as they happen in real time – and in a single, unified space – as opposed to creating the illusion of a coherent, unified space through continuity editing. For Bazin, this form of realism is innovative in that, rather than constructing an artificial reality, it has the potential to reveal reality.

Since then critics and theoretical movements have developed and challenged Bazin's position, often pointing out the ideological ends to which cinema portrays, or constructs, a cinematic reality. In contrast to Bazin, critics nowadays will usually acknowledge the importance of the -ism in realism, such that realism is considered another aesthetic to be examined, perhaps in a similar manner to Expressionism or Surrealism. Yet the traits of realism that Bazin examines in Italian neo-realism – such as naturalistic acting (often by non-professionals), location shooting, a focus on the working or underclasses, minimal use of *mise-en-scène*, unobtrusive cinematography, the long take favoured over editing – remain the grounding principles on which many still view a film as realist, and, indeed, social realist. This is the case even though few would consider a camera's role to be particularly innocent, neutral or objective.

Building on these formal characteristics, contemporary definitions of social realism often stress the role of location in defining identity. For instance, in *Realism and Popular Cinema* (2000), Julia Hallam and Margaret Marshment define social realism thus,

> Social realism is a discursive term used by film critics and reviewers to describe films that aim to show the effects of environmental factors on the development of character through depictions that emphasise the relationship between location and identity. Traditionally associated in Britain with a reformist or occasionally revolutionary politics that deemed adverse social circumstances could be changed by the introduction of more enlightened social policies or structural changes in society, social realism tends to be associated with an observational style of camerawork that emphasises situations and events, and an episodic narrative structure, creating 'kitchen sink' dramas and 'gritty' character studies of the underbelly of urban life.[2]

This description encapsulates the essence of the social realist film as it appears on screen, and the reason why many people would label a certain type of film social realist. To briefly fill in some of the background that Hallam and Marshment are condensing it is worth considering John Hill's now seminal *Sex, Class and Realism* (1986), in which Hill noted that many British realist films of the 1950s and 1960s, whilst lauded for their aesthetic difference from more mainstream cinema, were equally problematic in their depiction of gender, sexuality and class as the popular genre films against which they positioned themselves as 'realist'.[3] Put another way, portraying events in a realist manner does not necessarily make a film progressive, there is still the matter of the ideological stance of the film and the way it represents different types of identities.

In Hill's position is an acknowledgement that too unthinking a valorisation of social realism for its aesthetic properties can tend towards an elitist championing of social realist cinemas in opposition to mainstream popular genre films when both types of film should be examined to uncover their respective constructions of identity in its many facets (national, diasporic, sexual, gendered, economic, class-based etc.). Hill demonstrates how many British realist films of the period (for example, *Room at the Top* (1959), *Saturday Night and Sunday Morning* (1960), *A Taste of Honey* (1961)) drew on mainstream narrative conventions familiar to cinema audiences. Drawing a parallel between *The Sound of Music* (1965) and *Saturday Night and Sunday Morning*, Hill concludes that 'for all their novelty (particularly of subject-matter), the social problem film and those of the "new wave" still remained attached to the basic conventions of "realism", the "habitual" versions of "dramatic reality", made familiar by the mainstream fiction film'.[4] Indeed, this ghostly presence of the popular and the mainstream within social realism can be traced back further than British cinema of the 1950s and 1960s. For instance, Hallam and Marshment note that Italian neorealism, although championed by Bazin at the time for its ability to reveal reality, was often a blend of realism and generic elements. They state,

> By the mid-1940s, neorealism was a vacant signifier available for adoption; foreign critics start using it as a way of describing the blend of traditional Italian melodrama and new style acting and filming that was first perceived in *Open City* (*Roma, città aperta*, Rossellini, 1945).[5]

As this chapter will discuss, this commingling of social realism with generic elements – especially those drawn from the melodrama – is evident in certain films shot in Scotland in the 1990s and 2000s, which use this blend to explore identity in different ways.

Social Realism in Scotland

Scotland cannot lay claim to an indigenous tradition of social realist cinema in the same way that British cinema can. Yet, although it is the cinema of the British New Wave that is most often associated with social realism in a British context, many discussions of this cinematic tradition acknowledge the role of the Scottish documentary maker John Grierson in its establishment. In *Screening Scotland* (2000), Duncan Petrie outlines in detail the impact of Grierson's Scottish educational background and his belief in the need to maintain a Scottish identity within the union of England and Scotland on his development of the British documentary in the 1930s.[6] For Petrie, Grierson's works at the Empire Marketing Board and then the General Post Office in the 1930s are not those of a Scot selling out his heritage whilst working in London but those of a Scot who believed in serving both the British state and the Scottish people. Petrie dedicates a chapter to the impact of the British documentary movement on Scottish film culture in the twentieth century, arguing that although many of the documentaries that Grierson set in Scotland, including *The Drifters* (1929), were actually intended to be representative of Britain and a resurgence of British rather than Scottish identity, Grierson's influence was key in facilitating the production of indigenous Scottish documentaries from the 1930s onwards. One of the most characteristic images associated with Scotland, that of the heavy shipbuilding industry on the River Clyde, comes directly from this tradition. The most high profile of the documentaries to establish this tradition internationally, *Seawards the Great Ships* (1960) – which won an Oscar – was a project developed from a treatment by Grierson.[7]

Yet, whilst Petrie hints in passing that certain feature films made in Scotland could be considered a part of the social realist, or documentary realist, tradition (including *Floodtide* (1949), *The Gorbals Story* (1950) and the Grierson produced Group 3 feature *The Brave Don't Cry* (1952)),[8] the cinematic legacy of Grierson on social realism is most evident in British, rather than Scottish cinema. As Samantha Lay argues in *British Social Realism* (2002), the British Free Cinema and more particularly the New Wave movement of the 1950s and 1960s can be seen in many ways as influenced by, and reacting against, the documentary realism of Grierson and the British Documentary Movement of the 1930s and 1940s.[9] As Andrew Higson, Hill and Lay all variously note, the filmmakers of the British New Wave embraced the social concern of the documentary, and the emphasis on the working classes, but shifted away from Grierson's mode of authoritarian documentary towards the poetic realism of documentary filmmakers like Humphrey Jennings.[10] This emphasis on the poetic transformation of reality was crucial to the New Wave directors, and was part of the individual filmmaker's desire to be independent, free of the constraints of mainstream filmmaking, such as an interfering producer or studio executive. It also, for Hill, ensures that the guiding hand of the director becomes more apparent in the New Wave films, their stylistic, poetic transformations of reality marking them out as works of auteurs, rather than as attempts at documenting reality in the raw. As he puts it, 'the look of the camera is . . . "authored"', ensuring that the often gritty narrative world is represented as though from a point of view from the '"outside"' that is 'rendered "visible"' by the obtrusiveness of the poetic form.[11] Indeed, for Higson, this view from the outside, which 'can only finally be contained by a naïve auteurism', reveals the bourgeois origin of the gaze of both camera and spectator.[12] Although realist, then, British social realism is a form of poetic realism that foregrounds the artistic hand of its director, potentially problematising the film's focus on the working classes by indirectly revealing the bourgeois position of the author/viewer created by the aesthetic.

To bring this discussion up to date (and to return it to Scotland), some years later, in *British Cinema in the 1980s* (1999), Hill discusses the manner in which the connection of social realism with the auteurism associated internationally with the art film 'gathered momentum'[13] when – in the search for international markets in which to recoup costs – British cinema emphasised the role of the individual filmmaker as auteur in line with critical and consumption trends in the international marketplace for European art cinema. Here again social realism is considered in combination with the notion of the director as auteur, one whose 'realism' demonstrates their ability to portray reality in a unique manner. Citing examples like Mike Leigh and Ken Loach (in addition to the more distinctive, not to mention more well recognised 'art cinema' auteurs like Derek Jarman and Peter Greenaway), Hill draws on the work of Christopher Williams to discuss how a 'British "social art" cinema'[14] emerged at that time. In particular, this was because of the availability of Channel 4 funds for British film production, and its

> joint commitment to the support of a 'national cinema' (which would win prestige internationally by circulating as 'art') and to the fulfilment of a public-service remit (which favoured a degree of engagement by cinema with matters of contemporary social concern).[15]

Thus, whilst there were no major Scottish filmmakers or films based in Scotland in the British New Wave, coinciding with the emergence of New Scottish Cinema in the 1990s (and drawing on the devolved lottery funding suddenly available in Scotland), the English social realist filmmaker Ken Loach made four films in Scotland in the 1990s and 2000s. Loach, who began his career in television in the 1960s, became a key figure in discussions of the British social realist tradition in cinema. Of his four recent Scotland-based films, *Carla's Song* I discussed in Chapter 2. In this chapter I focus on *Ae Fond Kiss*, the third of his 'Scottish Trilogy' (or sometimes, 'Glasgow Trilogy'), which also includes *My Name is Joe* (1998) and *Sweet Sixteen* (2002). In these films the British social realist tradition appears in Scottish cinema, associating Glasgow with heavy industry – particularly with shipbuilding on the Clyde, seen in documentaries like *Seawards the Great Ships*, and, indeed, popular genre films like *Floodtide* – and, in *My Name is Joe* and *Sweet Sixteen*, examining the impact of the decline of industrial manufacturing on Scotland's disenfranchised working classes in the later decades of the twentieth century. With Loach's appearance in Scotland (or, more accurately, Glasgow), again because of his collaborative partnership with Scottish scriptwriter Paul Laverty, the British social realist tradition (with its authorial view of the working classes) intermingles with Glasgow's central presence as an industrial city in the, often Grierson-inflected, British documentary tradition.

Loachian Melodrama

Ken Loach's social realist aesthetic is distinctive in its combination of social realist themes with aspects of the melodrama. In *The Cinema of Ken Loach* (2002) Jacob Leigh discusses this hybrid strategy, emphasising how key scenes are shot in a melodramatic mode that encourages an emotional attachment to the characters as they encounter difficult social circumstances. Developing previous analyses of the melodrama, Leigh argues that Loach's films are 'melodramas of protest' that invite viewers to experience, through their engagement with characters, impossibly difficult situations and events in order to 'rouse the audience, to activate a sense of outrage at the injustices or atrocities of the authorities against an innocent protagonist'.[16] Thus, Loach, who has argued that his films are about the state of Britain after the disenfranchising of the working classes in the 1980s under the Conservative rule of Margaret Thatcher,[17] uses conventional, mainstream melodramatic techniques – such as character identification with victims of circumstance – to engage as broad an audience as possible with otherwise difficult subject matter.

However, not everyone considers Loach's social realist melodrama the most pertinent style of filmmaking with which to address this subject in Scotland. Scottish director Peter Mullan, for instance, who starred in *My Name is Joe*, and won Best Actor at Cannes for his performance as Joe, has been highly critical of Loach. Mullan argues that

> the problem with the social realists is that they want to have their cake and eat it. They maintain that their films are in a social realist style and therefore credible, but they're not. Almost all social realist films revert to melodrama if and when it suits them. Take, *My Name is Joe*, a young lad throws himself out of a window with a rope around his neck, thus all sins are absolved and Joe might get together with the

woman. Absurd, it's absurd. It achieves nothing except moving an audience to tears. It gives us no insight into other options he might have taken.[18]

For Mullan, the intermingling of social realism with melodrama is a problem in that it appeals to audience emotions without addressing any 'real' solutions to bleak social circumstances. Mullan's directorial debut feature *Orphans* (1997) – which he was discussing in the interview quoted above – mingles social realism with surrealism, black comedy and expressionism to reexamine the way in which Scotland has previously been depicted in British cinema.[19] Here Mullan publicly differentiates his own experimentations with social realism and other forms of cinematic expression in *Orphans* from that of Loach at the point of his breakthrough into the film industry. Ironically, his next feature, *The Magdalene Sisters* (2002) was in precisely the same mould as Loach's social realist melodramas. Yet Mullan's point is interesting in the two different stances it evokes towards the role of social realist cinema. Mullan's disagreement with Loach lies in his desire to move an audience emotionally. Seemingly in response to this criticism, Mullan's *Orphans* offers a more contemplative form of filmmaking that avoids emotional engagement, its distinctly unemotional ending stressing instead the need for considered, cognitive reimaginings of community in contemporary Scotland at the turn of the twenty-first century. Yet Loach's appeal to audience emotions is not necessarily a 'negative' attribute. The section that follows examines how Loach's *Ae Fond Kiss* uses its 'emotional' engagement with a social realist story to examine precisely the 'other options' available to his characters as they negotiate their shifting identities in a global/local, as opposed to a distinctly national, Glasgow.

Ae Fond Kiss (2004)

Ae Fond Kiss was made on a budget of £3m, 40% of which came from the UK tax scheme, via Azure Films, and the remainder from various sources including pre-sale agreements and grants from Scottish Screen and the Glasgow Film Office.[20] Like the previous Glasgow–based Loach films, *Ae Fond Kiss* was based on a screenplay by Paul Laverty. Loach's first 'happy ending' film set in Glasgow, *Ae Fond Kiss*, centres on a quasi-Romeo and Juliet romance between a Muslim, Scottish-Pakistani entrepreneur, Casim (Atta Yaqub), and an Irish Catholic schoolteacher, Roisin (Eva Birthistle). It is 'quasi-Romeo and Juliet' in that, whilst the young multicultural romance impacts severely upon the integrity of Casim's family, Roisin's family is absent from the film (presumably in Ireland), and it is her professional life that suffers instead. Casim and Roisin meet when Casim's younger sister Tahara (Shabana Akhtar Bakhsh) has an altercation with some of the boys at the Catholic school where she is a pupil and Roisin is the music teacher. Their passion grows quickly, but, when on a short break in Spain, Casim admits to being engaged (an arranged marriage organised by his family), their future becomes uncertain. Casim breaks off his engagement and, despite the cost to his family's honour, is eventually reconciled with Roisin. Roisin, for her part, loses her job because of the strictness of the governing authorities at her Catholic school. In the end the two stay together, and are last seen happily kissing in their spacious flat in Glasgow's west end.

This plot, however, does not mean that *Ae Fond Kiss* is a 'romance' in the generic sense. Rather, it is a social realist melodrama about young middle-class people, including a well off diasporic suburban family and a trendy young urban couple. *Ae Fond Kiss* goes out of its way to represent post-industrial Glasgow as a city of ethnic and cultural diversity, despite the problematic relations that can arise when immigrant traditions meet Western modernity. As in *Danny the Dog*, here Glasgow functions as a space where various identities meet and mingle, be they Pakistani, Irish, Scottish, Muslim, Protestant or Catholic, and all the hybrids that exist between. Glasgow is shown to be connected to the global flows of people and trade that mingle in its urban spaces, both in the varied origins of the different characters and in the ease with which Casim and Roisin disappear to Spain for a weekend break.

Further placing the story in a global context, both Loach and Laverty have stated on numerous occasions that *Ae Fond Kiss* was intended to explore a multicultural area of Britain in the post-9/11 context to illustrate that various immigrants from different contexts are open to the same forms of prejudice and racism as Muslims faced in Britain after 9/11.[21] In this process, Loach argues, his focus on family is key: 'The film is about the family and about our common humanity, really, and that all families are the same once the surface differences are changed.'[22] It is this stress on the family that enables the film to explore hybrid identities amongst Glasgow's diasporic populations in a melodramatic manner, the family being a staple of the melodrama since silent cinema.[23] In this sense, *Ae Fond Kiss* is a social realist melodrama, its 'melodrama of protest' focusing on the way in which its characters, especially Casim's family, are affected by the mingling of hybrid identities in the contested but nonetheless multicultural middle-class spaces of Glasgow. Thus its social realist focus on the role of location in informing identity is joined by an emotional engagement with the characters typical of the melodrama. To understand how this process works in *Ae Fond Kiss*, it is necessary to return briefly to Hill.

For Hill, their use of documentary realist cinematography allows Loach's films to retain a degree of distanced objectivity, and because they remain committed to examining the role of location in the lives of the people they depict: 'What separates Loach's work from conventional melodrama . . . is not only the way that it discourages too strong an emotional identification with characters but its insistence upon the economic and social underpinnings of their actions.'[24]

Although Leigh has argued that Loach does, in fact, use cinematography to enable emotional engagement with characters in a manner that I will elaborate upon momentarily, Hill's point that Loach's film are melodramas of social, rather than personal circumstances is useful for *Ae Fond Kiss*. From this perspective, Hill's interpretation of the ending of *My Name is Joe* is more forgiving of Loach than Mullan's as he describes Liam's (David McKay) melodramatic suicide as a legitimate resolution that exposes the impasse to which he has been brought by the weight of his 'socio-economic situation'.[25] What is interesting about *Ae Fond Kiss*, then, is that it takes a bourgeois Scottish-Pakistani family from Glasgow and subjects the personal life of Casim to an examination of the confusion wrought on his personal circumstances by his social context. The film thus questions what 'other options' are available to him under these conditions, pitting bourgeois individualism against religious tradition, schooling and the family. In this way, in *Ae Fond Kiss*, middle-class minorities in Glasgow – the second-generation Scottish-Pakistani immigrant entrepreneur, the Irish Catholic schoolteacher – are given the treatment usually reserved for the working classes.

Spaces and Identities

The film's examination of this mingling of identities within both a family and a contested city space begins shortly after the opening. Tahara is pictured giving a presentation in front of her assembled classmates. As part of a speech about terrorism and the stereotyping of Muslims in the West she refers to the different types of identities that exist in her family:

> Take my family. My sister considers herself as a Muslim first. And, because she has a political streak, calls herself Black. My Dad's been in the country for over forty years, and is one hundred percent Pakistani, or so he thinks . . . I reject the West's definition of terrorism . . . I reject the West's simplification of a Muslim. I am a Glaswegian, Pakistani, teenager, woman of Muslim descent, who supports Glasgow Rangers in a Catholic school. I'm a dazzling mixture and I'm proud of it.

Tahara's conception of her hybrid identity chimes with research carried out into 'post-British' identities amongst Scottish-Pakistani teenagers in Glasgow by Amir Saeed, Neil Blain and Douglas Forbes in the late 1990s. Drawing on empirical research, and in line with the findings of theorists like Paul Gilroy, Homi Bhabha, Philip Schlesinger and Stuart Hall, they argue that the Pakistani community (the largest ethnic minority in Scotland) increasingly considers itself in 'bi-cultural' terms that emphasise the specificity of its location, as Scottish-Pakistani, or Scottish Muslim, as opposed to 'Black-British'.[26] Yet in *Ae Fond Kiss*, in many ways akin to the portrayals of Scots-Italians in Peter Capaldi's films (Chapter 2) or *American Cousins* (Chapter 6), Loach depicts this hyphenated Scottish-Pakistani identity as a global/local, as opposed to a national, phenomenon. It is in this respect that the film is as much about a post-9/11 as it is a post-British world. This is why the role of the diasporic middle-class family is so important in the film, with its various generational identities as outlined by Tahara, and, indeed, its existence in a space, an informing location, that is represented by Loach as global/local, rather than Scottish, or 'Scottish-'.

The film opens in a large modern nightclub that does not initially appear to be in Scotland. The music playing is not recognisably Western, the DJ appears to be from (or descended from immigrants from) somewhere on the Indian subcontinent and a Bollywood film is playing on a big screen. There are people of different ethnic backgrounds dancing in the crowd and the Bollywood film is subtitled in English, but these clues only place the film in an unspecified diasporic setting that could be in a number of countries, including the UK, USA, Canada, Australia and New Zealand. It is only after the titles appear that the image is 'translated' into Scotland for the viewer. An establishing shot of the city of Glasgow follows immediately afterwards, over which the music from the nightclub scene continues to play. This blending of city space and music suggests that the city's identity is like that of the nightclub, a diasporic mixture of peoples existing in an environment pervaded by international cultures in the same way that the music pervades the air of the city. A similar effect was created by the Korma Radio announcements used in *Nina's Heavenly Delights* (2006) to suggest a non-resident Indian diasporic identity to Glasgow. In this instance, however, we are seeing a defamiliarised view of Glasgow as a multicultural, global/local space, created using a typical device of social realism – to return to the quotation from Hallam and Marshment – the exploration of 'the effects of environmental factors on the development of character through depictions that emphasise the relationship between location and identity'.

In this multicultural Glasgow, Casim and Roisin play out the debate between tradition and modernity, 'original' and diasporic identities against backdrops which render their identities global/local, as opposed to national. The clearest example of this use of location to explore identity occurs when Casim and his friend Hamid (Shy Ramsan) discuss his dilemma of choosing between his love for Roisin and his family's honour. They stand on the balcony of Hamid's flat, and their conversation is rendered using a traditional-shot/reverse-shot pattern that encourages the kind of (emotional) engagement with character analysed by Leigh in relation to *Carla's Song*.[27] What is interesting, however, is the way the locations that appear in the background resonate with their differing points of view. With a mosque shrouded in trees in shot behind him, Hamid cautions Casim against breaking off his engagement:

> Don't fuck up your whole family, and her family back home. You've got a family to think about, you've got your religion to think about, you've got that [*he indicates the mosque*] to think about. How are you gonna walk in there?

Hamid puts forward a 'traditional' point of view on the situation, taking the same position as Casim's parents, a perspective that is global in its evocation of both the Muslim faith and the impact of Casim's actions in Pakistan. Casim, by contrast, as he tries to think through his 'other options', is framed in the reverse shot by famous local landmarks of Glasgow, namely, the distinctive façade of the Templeton Carpet Factory Building (originally modelled on the Doge's Palace, Venice) and the Winter Gardens on Glasgow Green (a vast Victorian greenhouse attached to Glasgow's popular local museum, the People's Palace). Glasgow Green is in the oldest part of the city, its local history recorded in the museum in the People's Palace. These contrasting locations, then, are seen to be in debate, taking sides with Casim (Glasgow Green and the specific local history of Glasgow) and Hamid (the mosque, representing the international dimension of the Muslim faith and the links between Pakistan and Scotland that both characters experience in their everyday lives). Whatever hybrid identity is formed as Casim struggles to reconcile his personal desires with the constraints of his Pakistani/Muslim background it is not a national identity but a global/local hybrid; whether it is Scottish-Pakistani, Scottish Muslim, or rather, Glaswegian-Pakistani, or Glaswegian Muslim it has rarely if ever been seen in cinema from Scotland before.

Ae Fond Kiss depicts the location of Glasgow as integral to the shaping of the hybrid identities of its inhabitants. This is a film set in Glasgow, as opposed to one using Glasgow as an anonymous film set. Instead, it is during the brief trip to Spain, where Casim and Roisin discuss the affinities between their Christian and Islamic beliefs, that location becomes simply an 'anywhere' (an anonymous beach resort) in which to discuss the similarities that exist between these two different Scottish minorities. This neutral space enables a discussion of the international similarities that the two religions offer these characters, similarities that are only contested by the diasporic history of Casim's family and the institutions they encounter when in Scotland. For example, there are several mentions of the racist abuse Casim's father suffered from the time of his arrival in Scotland; his family's desire to uphold Pakistani tradition is integral to the narrative's development; and organised religion shapes the lives of both the main characters. In this respect, Spain functions in *Ae Fond Kiss* much as it does in *Morvern Callar* (see Chapter 2) as a space in which to explore having no national identity (Scottish, Pakistani, Irish), even if only for a brief spell. This location acts precisely as a film set, enabling the social realist narrative to depart momentarily from its emphasis on the interconnectedness of location and identity before reverting to it as the characters return home to face the realities of location in their otherwise very similar lives.

In Glasgow, both Casim and Roisin suffer from the clash between their personal desires and the institutions they encounter. Roisin in particular has a trademark 'melodrama of protest' encounter with an extremely bigoted Catholic priest, Father David (Father David Wallace), who ensures she is removed from her post in the Catholic school because of her choice of a Muslim lover. This paralleling of Roisin's experiences with those of Casim was perhaps a necessary move by Loach and Laverty, as a story solely about the suffering of Casim without any correlative on the part of Roisin could have been misinterpreted as a Western-centric view of Scottish-Pakistani families and the traditions they attempt to uphold in a 'modern' European context. This could be argued, for instance, of previous British films like *East is East* (1999), which seems to pit a repressive immigrant tradition against an apparently more 'progressive', or, at least, permissive, Western context. On the other hand, for Roisin's story the location of Glasgow is actually also equally crucial to the film's exploration of Irish Catholic immigrants. Although the international strength of Catholic dogma, as interpreted by Father David at least, is too much for the local school authorities to counter (Roisin is only dismissed against the wishes of her supportive headmaster), Catholicism is rendered as informing of identity in a very specific way in this particular local context. At the start of the film, Tahara's male classmates insult her and her brother outside the school with racist abuse, but the most vehement reaction to her speech is as much the result of her stripping off her school shirt to reveal a

Glasgow Rangers top (traditionally a Protestant football club) as it is to her assertion of her Muslim descent and faith. In a Catholic school, where the majority of pupils are likely to support Glasgow Celtic Football Club, it is the sectarian division within the city that sparks off the racism as much as Tahara's status as member of a religious minority within the school. Thus, in the treatment of Tahara, *Ae Fond Kiss* creates an interesting reversal of the usual minority status of Catholics in the Christian community in Glasgow, where Protestantism is dominant. In Roisin's dismissal, however, it illustrates Loach and Laverty's contention that all immigrants face the same level of prejudice as Muslims in Britain in the wake of 9/11.

What is most noticeable about *Ae Fond Kiss* in relation to Loach's *ouevre* is that he departs from his usual pessimism over the fate of the working classes in Scotland (as seen in *My Name is Joe* and *Sweet Sixteen*) and posits an upbeat ending to this story of multicultural desire for these representatives of different diasporic minorities amongst Glasgow's middle classes. In this instance, the location of Glasgow is as crucial as it ever is in social realism, even though it is rendered as a middle-class city of 'trendy bars, clubs and IKEA furnished flats'.[28] *Ae Fond Kiss*, then, perhaps more accurately belongs to a 'Glasgow Trilogy' than a 'Scottish Trilogy'.

Yet, the shift in emphasis towards a positive resolution in *Ae Fond Kiss* is not solely a matter of the shift of focus to the middle classes, it also prefigures Loach's utopian conclusion to the 'Scottish' episode of *Tickets* (discussed in Chapter 2), that the working classes are now a global underclass but if they stick together they will ultimately be victorious. Loach has long been concerned to emphasise the similarities that link people from different backgrounds and contexts. Before he drew parallels between the working classes in Scotland and immigrants in Fortress Europe in *Tickets*, *Carla's Song* explored the affinities between a Scottish bus driver and the Sandanistas in Nicaragua. *Ae Fond Kiss*, then, is a continuation of this theme, although in this instance it is the younger generation of middle-class people in Glasgow (including its Muslim and Catholic minorities) who are shown to be equally one people, regardless of their respective international and cultural backgrounds. In *On a Clear Day*, by contrast, a film that appeared one year later, things are very different.

On a Clear Day (2005)

On a Clear Day was made by Icon Entertainment International on a budget of £4million, including funding from MEDIA, Glasgow Film Office and Scottish Screen. It was mostly shot in Glasgow, but several scenes, particularly of the outdoor swimming, were shot on location at

Loch Lomond, Dover and the Isle of Man. Of the two producers, Sarah Curtis had previously worked on the Scottish-set costume dramas *Mrs Brown* (1997) and *The Governess* (1998) and Dorothy Berwin, on the US indie film *Walking and Talking* (1996), which I briefly examine in the next chapter. Another social realist melodrama, *On a Clear Day* is a family story that focuses on Frank (Peter Mullan), a shipbuilder on Clydeside for over thirty years whose life is haunted by the drowning of one of his sons as a boy. The film commences with Frank being made redundant and examines his attempts to find a meaningful role in society. Unable to secure employment in an apparently female-dominated post-industrial workplace he decides instead to swim the English Channel to France. This unlikely endeavour brings together his motley crew of unemployed male friends in a common purpose and reunites Frank with his estranged son Rob (Jamie Sives). Analysing *On a Clear Day* after *Ae Fond Kiss* a shift in emphasis is visible from Scotland as an informing location in which the film is set (*Ae Fond Kiss*) to the use of Scotland as a film set (*On a Clear Day*)

Remasculinising Scotland

Any number of reviewers noted the similarities between *On a Clear Day* and the social realist tradition. Geoffrey Macnab observed that it was 'a Loach-style study of post-industrial society and a rousing family drama . . . [that] turns into a triumphalist wish-fulfilment fantasy'.[29] Similarly, much of the promotion attempted to link it to the same tradition. In an interview for *Empire*, Mullan says, 'It's an old-fashioned film in the tradition of the Ealing comedy, early Bill Forsyth or Ken Loach . . . This is like a Ken Loach film that your youngest daughter and oldest auntie can watch.'[30] In the film's Production Notes Mullan goes even further, comparing it to *Saturday Night and Sunday Morning*, *The Loneliness of the Long Distance Runner* and *Billy Liar*.[31] Numerous comparisons were also made to previous British films to mingle social realism with aspects of the comedy in their explorations of post-industrial British masculinity, such as *Brassed Off* (1996), *The Full Monty* (1997) and *Billy Elliott* (2000).[32] Yet, *On a Clear Day* is neither an 'old-fashioned' comedy or a social realist film, but a social realist melodrama that begins in a specific location (Clydeside), only to gradually divorce itself from it to explore post-industrial masculinity in a universally appealing, triumphal manner.

On a Clear Day was originally intended to be shot and set in Newcastle, England, with an English actor in the lead. According to Mullan, director Gaby Dellal moved the shoot to Glasgow to ensure he played Frank.[33]

Although the presence of the Glasgow shipyards is a coincidence, then, as this story could have been set in any post-industrial northern British city, its opening nonetheless resonates with previous cinematic depictions of industrial and post-industrial Clydeside. *On a Clear Day* begins with the launch of a massive ship into the Clyde as Frank packs his things to leave his workplace for the last time. As in documentaries like *Seawards the Great Ships*, which begins with an extended montage of ships launching and ends with a launching ceremony akin to that of *On a Clear Day*, the cranes of the shipyard and the residential buildings of the area are dwarfed by the ship. Its bulky presence defamiliarises our usual perception of size in urban spaces as it moves impressively to fill the frame, suddenly rendering tall buildings minuscule by comparison. In *On a Clear Day* the launch was a real event that the film crew were able to attend, with the crowd scene created later and intercut to create the illusion of their presence at the event.[34] Thus there is a documentary feel to the film at the opening as the launch seems to be taking place simultaneously with Frank leaving his office. Yet a rather interesting effect is created by this mixture of reality and fiction that has a bearing on the rendering of Scottish masculinity in the remainder of the film. As discussed in relation to *Dog Soldiers* in Chapter 5, an enduring feature of many of the cinematic myths of Scotland that replay Scottish history in an elegiac mode is the backward look of a male protagonist as he leaves behind the life that he has previously known.[35] It is noticeable that although the opening of *On a Clear Day* is about the decline of the shipyards and ripe for a Clydesideist backward look, Mullan's Frank, after briefly staring at the ship in dry dock, does not allow his sight to linger on the launch of the ship, even though the rest of his family have attended the event. Instead, he simply packs and leaves whilst the huge imposing image of the ship, moving off for the first time, dominates the shot. Admittedly, it may have been the pressures of shooting these scenes so as to create the illusion of their contemporaneity with the launch that resulted in Frank deliberately 'ignoring' the event itself. After all, none of the characters appear in the same shot as the ship as they were simply not there. However, in the context of the film's later depiction of Frank's transformation, the scene is almost a literal rendering of the film's decision to 'walk away' from Clydesideism (like Frank, without looking back, in anger or otherwise) and to emphasise instead a post-industrial masculinity in a new Scottish-anywhereland rather than mourn its loss.

After his retirement, Frank attends the Job Centre to register and begin to seek new employment. On arrival he is interviewed by his daughter-in-law, Angela (Jodhi May). As he flees the building after a brief panic attack

Frank is confronted by the sight of this wife Joan (Brenda Blethyn) learning to drive a bus. Thus, like predecessors *Brassed Off* and *The Full Monty*, *On a Clear Day* examines the crisis of post-industrial masculinity as the UK shifts away from manufacturing towards a 'feminised' services economy. Also like its predecessors it charts the rejuvenation of a homosocial group of loveable male misfits as they resurrect their sense of self and regain their pride with a venture that could loosely be considered a part of this new economy, although, much as was the case with one-off stripping in *The Full Monty*, Frank's triumphant swim is not really of any lasting economic benefit to anyone.

This process of remasculinisation explains why there are so many shots of men getting into and out of swimming pools and open water, their immersion in a womb-like environment metaphorically demonstrating their attempts to be born again as new men. Frank's final crisis at sea is perhaps the clearest example of this as he lies still in the water half-way across the channel and bellows like a newborn baby when he finally confronts his previous failure to save his drowning son all those years ago. After this he is at last reconciled with his remaining son, Rob. Yet, unlike *Ae Fond Kiss*, this is not an exploration of shifting identities in a specific part of Scotland *per se*. Writing in 2001, Andrew Spicer argues that late twentieth-century Britain's social and familial disintegration, along with the decline of the manufacturing base on which traditional masculinity was founded, has ensured that 'the figure of the damaged man is so frequent in recent British cinema that it could be said he has become its most representative image'.[36] Frank's masculine rebirth, then, like that of the characters in *The Full Monty* and other British films of the 1990s, is intended to represent British masculinity in general. Indeed, by the end of the film the homosocial male group has grown to include Mad Bob (Paul Ritter), an Englishman from Dover, and the English official there to oversee the legitimacy of the swim. This is a representatively British, as opposed to Scottish grouping, then (before we even consider the fact that the film concludes in France), as is the changing masculinity the film explores.

Doing and Talking

On a Clear Day explores masculine identity in a Clydeside film set, through its depiction of men both doing and talking. Here the focus is on Rob, Frank's son, who is a house-husband whilst Angela works. He is a proud, caring, but slightly over-protective father to his two sons because of the loss of his brother as a child. Rob holds the key to the film's view of how Frank should be remasculinised into a more caring, post-industrial new man. This is amply demonstrated through his association with shopping. Early on in the film, Rob is struggling home from the supermarket with his boys, laden with shopping, causing the passing Danny (Billy Boyd) to jibe good-naturedly, 'I'll leave you to it. Rather you than me.' This line is delivered over a close-up of a bag of shopping that has dropped to the ground as Rob tends to one of his twin boys who has skinned a knee playing football. Later in the film, however, Rob confronts Frank, accusing him of never caring enough for him as a child, giving as damning evidence the fact that Frank never went shopping to buy him a birthday present. This confrontational scene is played out in a curious manner, as Rob, angry with Frank, jumps into the swimming pool fully clothed as he shouts his feelings of fatherly pride at his role in bringing up his twin sons, declaring, 'I'm not ashamed like you think I should be.' Here Rob shows the redundant older generation of men how to be a new man, by both doing and talking. This forces the previously inarticulate Frank to respond with both action (holding Rob under the water until he is silent) and then a strangled verbal retort, through clenched teeth, that he worked twelve-hour shifts, five days a week for thirty years and never had the time for shopping.

In cinema, doing and talking are traditionally polarised as masculine and feminine activities respectively, with certain genres epitomising these gendered representations, such as the western as men doing and the melodrama as women talking. However, as Julian Stringer has shown of Hong Kong action movies of the 1980s, genre hybrids that incorporate melodramatic aspects can offer the possibility for male characters to inhabit both roles simultaneously.[37] In *On a Clear Day*, Rob is the character capable of inhabiting both male and female roles, the new man who can therefore exist in a post-industrial environment. He is both active (jumping into the pool) and talkative (confronting his father verbally), both house-husband out shopping (doing of a different sort) and loving father figure (able to talk about his emotions with his family). From Rob, Frank learns these new skills, combining shopping for his grandchildren for the first time ever – which he does immediately after his confrontation with Rob in the pool – and talking with them privately about his hopes for swimming the channel (the new man persona), and, indeed, the doing of the act itself (the 'hard' masculinity of the long distance swimmer). Similarly his gang of friends are able to find a voice through being a part of the 'active' project of the Channel swim, whether it be asking out the girl they fancy, quitting their menial job, standing up for themselves in the workplace, or overcoming seasickness. It is for this reason, then, that so many of the scenes in

Figure 8.1 No Looking Back Now: The post-industrial remasculinisation of the 'hard man' in *On a Clear Day* (2005)

water involve both swimming and unemployed men chatting, as the process of rebirth requires both skills to be honed before re-emergence into the outside world.

From the opening scenes in the shipyards, *On a Clear Day* slowly moves away from Clydeside (and, indeed, Clydesideism), eventually abandoning the River Clyde and even the city of Glasgow, and completing the rebirth of the male characters on an anonymous beach in France where Frank and Rob are reconciled. As in *Morvern Callar* and *Ae Fond Kiss*, the identity they find in this liminal space abroad is not Scottish but, in this case, a universalised post-industrial masculinity that functions through doing and talking. Like the ship launching into the Clyde on his final day at work, Frank begins his journey away from the hard man representations of Scottish masculinity of Clydesideism. As his swim carefully navigates the Channel the busy shipping lanes are shown. The massive ferries whose routes Frank is traversing carry his family to meet him, suggesting that he is negotiating a way through the treacherous legacy of previous representations of Scotland, seen in films like *Seawards the Great Ships*, towards a new identity. In the process, the social realist emphasis on the informing nature of place on identity is greatly reduced in significance, as Scotland becomes a film set of anonymous 'anywhere' places (living rooms, kitchens, job centres, bus depots, pubs, swimming pools, lakes, the sea) as opposed to the distinctive dockyards so resonant with the cinematic legacy of Clydesideism. It is in this use of Scotland as a set in which to explore gendered (rather than national, or even, global/ local) identities that *On a Clear Day* shifts much further from the class commentary of social realism, towards the typical focus of the melodrama on the family. Thus, whilst it is like *The Full Monty* in its rejuvenation of a masculine grouping, *On a Clear Day* is equally concerned with rejuvenating the family. The final scene on the beach in France combines the two (the doing of the male group with the talking of the family) with Frank purposefully choosing to invalidate his swim by illegally grasping his son's hand rather than affirming the previous work of his friends on his behalf by picking up a stone unaided and returning to the boat. Instead, as Rob and Frank support each other out of the sea, the angry confrontation in the pool is resolved in the uniting of the two male generations and their return to the family. In this respect, in spite of its social realist aspects, *On a Clear Day* is closer to the melodrama of the women's films discussed in the next chapter than it is to *Ae Fond Kiss*.

Notes

1. André Bazin, *What is Cinema? Part 1* (Berkeley: University of California Press, [1958] 1967), p. 13.
2. Julia Hallam with Margaret Marshment, *Realism and Popular Cinema* (Manchester: Manchester University Press, 2000), p. 184.
3. John Hill, *Sex, Class and Realism* (London: BFI, 1986), pp. 1–3.
4. Ibid., p. 60.
5. Hallam with Marshment, *Realism and Popular Cinema*, p. 40.
6. Duncan Petrie, *Screening Scotland* (London: BFI, 2000), pp. 20–4.
7. Ibid., p. 111.
8. Ibid., pp. 79–91.
9. Samantha Lay, *British Social Realism* (London: Wallflower, 2002), pp. 39–53.
10. Hill, *Sex, Class and Realism*, pp. 127–43; Andrew Higson, 'Space, Place and Spectacle', in, Andrew Higson, ed., *Dissolving Views* (London: Cassell, 1996), pp. 133–56, p. 138; Lay, *British Social Realism*, pp. 55–76.
11. Hill, *Sex, Class and Realism*, p. 134.
12. Higson, 'Space, Place and Spectacle', pp. 150–2.
13. John Hill, *British Cinema in the 1980s* (Oxford: Clarendon Press, 1999), p. 67.
14. Ibid., p. 66.
15. Ibid., p. 67.
16. Jacob Leigh, *The Cinema of Ken Loach* (London: Wallflower, 2002), p. 22.

17. Graham Fuller, (ed.), *Loach on Loach* (London: Faber & Faber, 1998), p. 111.
18. Liese Spencer, 'Tearing the Roof Off', *Sight and Sound*, 9: 4 (1999), pp. 13–14, p. 14.
19. David Martin-Jones, '*Orphans*, A Work of Minor Cinema from Post-Devolutionary Scotland', *Journal of British Cinema and Television* 1: 2 (2004), pp. 226–41.
20. Adam Minns, 'Loach Secures Azure Tax Funding', *Screen International*, 1411 (2003), p. 5.
21. See: Jen Foley, 'Ken Loach and Paul Laverty Interviewed', BBC Films website:http://www.bbc.co.uk/films/2004/09/10/ken_loach_paul_laverty_ae_fond_kiss_interview.shtml (19/05/08); Geoffrey Macnab, 'Under the Microscope', *Screen International*, 1471 (2004), p. 24; James Mottram, 'In the Mood for Love', *Sight and Sound*, 14: 3 (2004), pp. 22–3, p. 23.
22. Foley, 'Ken Loach and Paul Laverty Interviewed'.
23. John Mercer and Martin Shingler, *Melodrama* (London: Wallflower, 2004), p. 12.
24. John Hill, 'Failure and Utopianism', in Robert Murphy (ed.), *British Cinema of the 90s* (London: BFI, 2000), pp. 178–90, p. 180.
25. Ibid., p. 182.
26. Amir Saeed, Neil Blain and Douglas Forbes, 'New Ethnic and National Questions in Scotland', *Ethnic and Racial Social Studies*, 22: 5 (1999), pp. 821–44, p. 827 and p. 840.
27. Leigh, *The Cinema of Ken Loach*, p. 10.
28. Steve Blandford, *Film, Drama and the Break-Up of Britain* (Bristol: Intellect, 2007), p. 76.
29. Geoffrey Macnab, 'On a Clear Day', *Sight and Sound*, 15: 9 (2005), pp. 73–4, p. 74.
30. Steve O'Hagan, 'Swimming with Scots', *Empire*, 196 (October 2005), pp. 78–9, p. 79.
31. Anon., *On a Clear Day Production Notes* (Icon Entertainment, 2004), p. 14.
32. Geoffrey Macnab, 'On a Clear Day', *Sight and Sound*, 15: 9 (2005), pp. 73–4, p. 74;
33. O'Hagan, 'Swimming with Scots', p. 79.
34. Anon., *On a Clear Day Production Notes* (Icon Entertainment, 2004), p. 10.
35. John Caughie, 'Representing Scotland: New Questions for Scottish Cinema', Eddie Dick (ed.), *From Limelight to Satellite* (London: BFI/SFC, 1990), pp. 13–30, p. 24.
36. Andrew Spicer, *Typical Men* (London: I. B. Tauris, 2001), p. 195.
37. Julian Stringer, '"Your Tender Smiles Give Me Strength"', *Screen* 38: 1 (1997), pp. 25–41.

CHAPTER 9

Female Friendship/US Indie:
Women Talking

This chapter explores the confluence of the US independent (indie) model of filmmaking – previously seen in *Shallow Grave* (1994) and *Trainspotting* (1996) – with two films made and set in Scotland with female protagonists: *Women Talking Dirty* (1999) and *Beautiful Creatures* (2000). The chapter begins with introductions to films previously made in Scotland that feature female protagonists (of which there has been a flurry in the 1990s/ 2000s) and the influence of the US indie tradition on contemporary Scottish cinema. The two films are then examined to illustrate the convergence of these two styles. Both are typical of the female friendship film in their exploration of the possibilities female friendship offers in a constructed space that intersects with but also enables the exploration and challenge of the norms and conventions of patriarchy. In both instances, the manner in which Scotland is deployed as a film set (albeit slightly differently in each case), is integral to the construction of this 'unconventional' space in which to explore female friendship and changing female identities.

The Woman's Film in Scotland

There were isolated examples of cinematic explorations of female identity in Scotland before the 1990s, many of which can be considered to be a 'woman's film'. We might be tempted to cite films as diverse as Powell and Pressburger's *I Know Where I'm Going!* (1945),[1] Laura Mulvey and Peter Wollen's adaptation of Emma Tennant's *The Bad Sister* (1983) for Channel 4 television,[2] Michael Radford's adaptation of Jessie Kesson's *Another Time, Another Place* (1983) and possibly even Bill Forsyth's adaptation of Marilynne Robinson's *Housekeeping* (1987) – which, although undoubtedly a US film in practically every possible sense, provides an example of a Scottish director examining changing female identities – as precursors to the increased production of films about women of the 1990s and 2000s.

Since the 1990s these isolated examples have been joined by a growing body of films focused on women and made in Scotland, in some cases by women. Many of these films explore women's identities and women's desires, including: *Blue Black Permanent* (Margaret Tait, 1992), *Breaking the Waves* (1996), *Stella Does Tricks* (Coky Giedroyc, 1996), *Mary Reilly* (1996), *The Winter Guest* (1997), *Mrs Brown* (1997), *The Governess* (Sandra Goldbacher, 1998), *Women Talking Dirty* (Giedroyc), *Urban Ghost Story* (Geneviève Jolliffe, 1998), *Beautiful Creatures, Aberdeen* (2000), *One Life Stand* (May Miles Thomas, 2000), *Morvern Callar* (Lynne Ramsay, 2002), *Dear Frankie* (Shona Auerbach, 2004), *The Rocket Post* (2004), *Frozen* (Juliet McKoen, 2005), *The Descent* (2005), *Nina's Heavenly Delights* (Pratibha Parmar, 2006) and *Red Road* (Andrea Arnold, 2006). We might also add a film which, although set in Ireland, was filmed in Scotland, *The Magdalene Sisters* (2002). Viewing these recent woman's films as a loose grouping enables a manoeuvre similar to that of Carol Anderson's work on Scottish literature. In 'Listening to the Women Talk' (1993), Anderson charts an alternative, oft-neglected tradition of women writers in Scotland whose works share common concerns surrounding gender issues, especially female subjectivity and the challenges women encounter in society.[3] The correlation between this chapter and Anderson's work becomes clearer when you consider that, along with *The Bad Sister, Another Time, Another Place* and *Housekeeping* (all film adaptations from original novels by women writers), a number of these recent Scottish woman's films draw on literary sources. *The Winter Guest* was based on a play by Sharman Macdonald (who also wrote the screenplay) and both of Coky Giedroyc's films were scripted by women writers, *Stella Does Tricks* by A. L. Kennedy and *Women Talking Dirty* from a screenplay by Isla Dewar, based on her novel of the same name. As the presence of these films in other chapters suggests, many are also identifiable as costume dramas, art films, road movies, horror films (and so on), and therefore are not solely melodramas as one might expect from some definitions of the woman's film. However, their focus on female protagonists, albeit in conjunction with other generic styles or cinematic modes, still enables an exploration of female identities in which the location of Scotland plays a distinctive role.

It is not a straightforward matter to define what is meant by the term 'woman's film'. It has been discussed at length in film studies, particularly amongst feminist scholars. The term usually describes films about women made for women audiences (which may include films made by women), with a range of approaches exploring the role of representations of women in the lives of women in different parts of the world at different points in history. To even begin to do justice to the existing body of work on the woman's film requires more space than is available here. Rather, in the context of the sudden outpouring of films about women from Scotland in the 1990s and 2000s, I will examine two examples of a sub-genre of the woman's film, the female friendship film.

In *In the Company of Women* (1998), Karen Hollinger identifies the female friendship film as a subgenre of the woman's film that, in the last few decades, has included well-known mainstream Hollywood movies like *Desperately Seeking Susan* (1985), *Beaches* (1988), *Thelma and Louise* (1991), *A League of Their Own* (1992), *Boys on the Side* (1995) and *Bound* (1996). In the 2000s several British female friendship films also appeared, including *High Heels and Low Lifes* (2001), *My Summer of Love* (2004) and *The Edge of Love* (2008). For Hollinger, female friendship films have their roots in the woman's film (in 1950s melodramas, for example) but came into their own with the growth of the women's movement in the 1970s. Independent women and female friendships, then, exist in these films in an ambivalent, and at times oppositional, relationship with patriarchal societal norms.[4] Female friendship films 'attempt to assimilate into mainstream cultural representations ideas from the women's movement such as female autonomy and sisterhood'[5] to offer an alternative space in which to examine and explore women's identities in contemporary society. Unlike many films focused around male characters, female friendship films explore 'alternatives to women's complete dependence on men and family for self-affirmation'.[6] They offer different visions of 'female relationships and their impacts on women's personal lives',[7] as opposed to a direct, or oppositional political engagement with patriarchy. The question that is of most significance for this chapter, then, is how this 'alternative' space to patriarchy is created in *Women Talking Dirty* and *Beautiful Creatures* using an indie film style (post-*Trainspotting*) in Scottish locations that resonate with previously established meanings usually associated with issues of masculinity and/or the nation?

Scholars have already begun to explore the numerous female-focused films to emerge from Scotland in the 1990s and 2000s.[8] In an article on *Blue Black Permanent* and *Stella Does Tricks* Ian Goode argues that these films are able to express character interiority, a characteristic of much contemporary Scottish fiction that – in these films in particular – enables a break with previous cinematic constructions of the Scottish national past in an elegiac or nostalgic mode. Goode argues that 'the act of summoning the past in both films is expressive and affirmative rather than mournful and elegiac', concluding that they 'challenge the overtly masculine focus of many Scottish films'.[9] Indeed, as Jane Sillars and Myra Macdonald note in their contribution to *The Media in Scotland* (2008), in films such as *Breaking the Waves*, *Morvern Callar* and *Red Road*, 'gendered representations play a highly symbolic role as bearers of moments of transition', and through the cinematic 'imagining of space', enable an exploration of the nation as a psychic, as well as a physical, space.[10] Similarly, *Women Talking Dirty* and *Beautiful Creatures* depart from traditional (masculine oriented) views of Scotland and Scottishness, such as the hard-man myth of Clydesideism, whilst using the resonances of these myths as a backdrop against which to play out (or in many instances, talk through) the changing face of post-industrial female identities. Thus, although my argument follows these initial mappings of this territory, what is slightly different about *Women Talking Dirty* and *Beautiful Creatures* is that Scotland becomes a backdrop against which the expressions of interiority, or 'psychic spaces' of female identities are explored. Against this backdrop, their deployment of female desire is akin to that of both *Nina's Heavenly Delights* and *The Governess* (discussed in Chapters 3 and 6 respectively), only here it is not alternative or fantasy diasporic Scotlands that are created but alternative (fantasy), post-industrial female Scotlands.

The US Indie Tradition in Scotland

Before moving on to examine the films it is first necessary to see how they stand out from the others listed above because of their engagement with the US indie model of filmmaking. Various academics have noted the adoption in the 1990s of aesthetic techniques derived from the US indie cinema model. Jonathan Murray, for example, notes that this trend was most clearly set by *Shallow Grave*, which 'adapted narrative and aesthetic strategies associated with late 1980s and early 1990s American independent cinema'.[11] This strategy was adopted to enable a small emergent national cinema to make low-budget films with a chance of reaching audiences beyond its national borders. The films usually discussed in this context are *Shallow Grave* (1994), *Trainspotting* (1996), *Small Faces* (1996), *Late Night Shopping* (2001) and *16 Years of Alcohol* (2003), in which the influence of US indie and slacker film directors like Martin Scorsese and Kevin Smith are apparent. In his monograph on *Trainspotting*, Murray Smith notes its similarities to the US cinema tradition that includes such recognised indie auteurs as Scorsese and Quentin Tarantino.[12] The film's opening provides the clearest example of this, the freeze frames as each character is introduced (along with the appearance of their name on the screen), being a direct homage to Scorsese's *Mean Streets* (1973). Thus, the indie characteristics of these films allow them to be grouped together, characteristics that include their emphasis on shooting in interiors (the use of sets helping to minimise budget by reducing the unpredictability of location shooting), their focus on character development (often through conversation and/or voiceover), their episodic and at times jumbled narrative temporality and their foregrounded manipulation of aspects of the cinematic form such as cinematography, *mise-en-scène* and editing. In other words, as opposed to the narrative realism of Hollywood cinema, which rarely allows the constructed nature of the fiction to be revealed, these films include a foregrounded appreciation of film form as part of the viewing experience.

The ubiquity of critical enquiry that *Trainspotting* has received is at least partly a result of its distinctive indie style, and partly, of its controversial subject matter (heroin addiction and petty crime). However, it is also famous because of its phenomenal financial success. *Trainspotting* made around $72 million from an initial budget of less than $3.5 million or £1.7 million, primarily from Channel Four Films. This is a feat rarely matched before or since, although it is worth mentioning that PolyGram spent £850,000 marketing the film, which puts its success in perspective in relation to the fate of most similar low-budget British films.[13] In any case, it was no wonder, given such a phenomenal turnover, that so many films would attempt to follow in a similar mould, blending the gritty depiction of life in the UK typical of the British social realist tradition with a youth-oriented story (and perhaps an element of drugs and crime), all packaged within a US indie inflected style. Yet, beyond the shared textual characteristics listed above, what links together the films which dominate discussion of the influence of the US indie film on Scottish cinema is their focus on masculinity (in many cases in relation to homosocial groupings, youth and crime) and changing male identities in contemporary post-industrial society. The discussion can be broadened, however, if we include these two female friendship films.

Beautiful Creatures evidently fits into this discussion, being clearly indebted to the international success of Tarantino's *Pulp Fiction* (1994) and *Trainspotting*. Like Tarantino's film it is a tongue-in-cheek tale of gangsters and their molls, complete with grotesque ultra-violence, that mingles contemporary life with characters who have stepped out of 1950s pulp noir fiction. It is heavily stylised, not just in its use of period locations and costumes, but also its aesthetic. The stand-out moment in this respect is a sequence shot from the point of view of an attendant in a service station, who imagines a woman he sees chained to a metal ring to be writhing provocatively in the style of a pornographic film whereas in reality she is in apparent distress and exclaiming, 'shit, shit, oh shit'. These similarities led Allan Hunter to refer to *Beautiful Creatures* as 'tepid tartan Tarantini'.[14] As in *Trainspotting*, it is the blending of these US indie stylistics with a story of heroin users in a gritty UK setting (in this case, Glasgow high-rise flats) that marks out the film's approach to selling itself abroad. Just as Smith argues of the film's predecessor, *Trainspotting*, *Beautiful Creatures* interacts with and transforms cultural influences from the USA in order to sell them back to US audiences.[15] The major difference, however, is the central presence of two female characters in the narrative. The indie packaging is clearly evident, but the emphasis on masculinity seen in the previous films is replaced by female friendship.

Women Talking Dirty also draws on the same indie tradition, which is most immediately apparent because its Director of Photography, Brian Tufano, also worked on *Shallow Grave*, *Trainspotting* and *Late Night Shopping*. It is no surprise, then, that in early scenes directly reminiscent of *Trainspotting*, two characters in *Women Talking Dirty* take drugs, go shoplifting and are pictured running through the streets and alleys of Edinburgh to a techno musical accompaniment. Moreover, the film commences with a brief glimpse of an event that recurs halfway through the narrative, a device also used in *Trainspotting* and drawn from US predecessors *Goodfellas* (1990) and *Pulp Fiction*. However, *Women Talking Dirty* is also influenced by a very different strand of US indie cinema, the female-centred movies of US indie directors like Woody Allen (*Hannah and Her Sisters*, 1986), John Sayles (*Lianna*, 1983) and Nicole Holofcener (*Walking and Talking*, 1996). These are films in which a great deal of time is spent watching women talking, and consequently, as Geoff King notes in *American Independent Cinema* (2005), a slow paced narrative is created as a result of the emphasis on the 'close texture of [female] relationships'.[16] Like *Walking and Talking*, *Women Talking Dirty* repeatedly cuts back and forth between the parallel lives of its two female protagonists and their various romantic relationships, as they periodically intersect and pull apart again. Thus, the only constant relationship throughout the film is that of the female friendship. In this respect it is a little like a conventional rom-com such as *You've Got Mail* (1998), in which the narrative cuts back and forth between its male and female leads; observing the similar structure of *Walking and Talking*, Celestino Deleyto comment that it 'reverses the conventions of the [rom-com] genre and presents various heterosexual relationships as the obstacles to the survival of the friendship between its two female protagonists'.[17] This observation can equally be applied to *Women Talking Dirty*, a female friendship film that uses aspects of the US indie film tradition to package explorations of female identity. In it the role played by Scotland as a film set becomes integral to the construction of new possibilities for female friendship.

Women Talking Dirty (1999)

Women Talking Dirty was the second feature by director Coky Giedroyc, whose first, Stella Does Tricks, examined the traumatic life of young Glaswegian prostitute Stella (Kelly Macdonald) and her abusive relationships with her father, pimp and drug addict boyfriend. Women Talking Dirty is a more mainstream, upbeat story that focuses on the friendship between two women in Edinburgh, Ellen (Gina McKee), an introverted graphic artist (author of the 'Gangster Women' comic strip), and Cora (Helena Bonham Carter), a somewhat batty young mother of two. The characters are introduced separately, Ellen through her romance and subsequent marriage to gambling womaniser Daniel (James Purefoy) and Cora through her tumultuous but doomed love affair with fellow university student Claude (Julien Lambroschini), who rapidly departs for his homeland of France once Cora becomes pregnant. The action takes place over the course of several years, during which time Daniel misleads Cora as to his identity, sleeps with her and fathers her second child (a secret which they keep from Ellen) before leaving for London because of his gambling debts, breaking Ellen's heart in the process. When he returns, Daniel is greeted by a stronger Ellen, her friendship with Cora having seen both of them through the years without romance, and although Ellen and Cora eventually do fall out over the revelation that Daniel is the father of Cora's second son, they are reunited and are ultimately the best of friends. They are helped through this process by the community of friends they have cultivated from in and around Ellen's exclusive neighbourhood. The film concludes with Ellen finding Daniel's hidden stash of money in her sofa; she shares it with Cora, and Daniel is locked out of their lives for good.

Gilda Williams describes Women Talking Dirty as a 'women's buddy film set in Cool Britannia', noting that the '"Love Will Prevail" idiom which drives recent Hollywood-friendly British film (Notting Hill, Bridget Jones's Diary) applies to the unbreakable bond between the two central women'.[18] In fact, Women Talking Dirty creates a different potential space that is seemingly parallel with, and at times intersects, whilst simultaneously remaining 'outside' or 'alternative' to heterosexual norms. Thus, whilst Ellen is married to Daniel, and Cora is a mother, neither manages to build a successful relationship with a male counterpart, their female friendship being stronger and more permanent than any heterosexual romance. Moreover, neither character is cut out for their roles as wife and career woman (Ellen), or housewife and mother (Cora). Instead, after meeting in a pub to the ironic accompaniment of Dolly Parton's

'Joleen', Cora and Ellen become the odd couple, experiencing childbirth together and attempting to build interlocking lives as friends, independent of their partners and parents. The film foregrounds their friendship's existence within an 'alternative' community that consists of ageing matriarch Emily (Eileen Atkins), the gay couple Ronald (Richard Wilson) and George (Kenneth Cranham) and the sensitive new man, Stanley (James Nesbitt). This non-normative community is united in its opposition to the manipulative chancer, Daniel, the workshy gambler and irresponsible father. Thus, although structured like a rom-com in its narrative's constant cutting back and forth between the parallel lives of Ellen and Cora, *Women Talking Dirty* does not explore how to construct a normative heterosexual relationship but, rather, the life strategies of artist and businesswoman, Ellen, and single-mother, Cora, as they define themselves in an alternative manner to that of the normative positions of married woman, housewife, or mother within a successful (that is, male and female, father and mother) family unit.

Noticeably, when Isla Dewar wrote the screenplay perhaps the most significant changes she made to her novel were her transformation of the somewhat aloof graphic artist, Stanley, into a likeable new man and her reduction of the part of Daniel to a more two-dimensional negative foil against which to measure the friendship of the female leads. In the novel, Daniel has more psychological depth. An entire chapter is dedicated to his childhood backstory, and he is not such a villainous, caddish character as his screen counterpart. The male roles, then, are refashioned to enable the film to posit an alternative to the normative heterosexual boundaries of patriarchy, a space in which to explore the limits of being 'moody' (Ellen) or 'mad' (Cora). In this process of exploration their female friendship is central. The two characters function as each other's inverse mirror, and in their lengthy, extended conversations they critique each other's personalities – Ellen pointing out Cora's scattiness, just as Cora counters by emphasising Ellen's sulkiness and introversion – and develop their lives together through friendship.

In the film's construction of an alternative space of friendship outside societal norms Edinburgh plays a crucial role. Of the film's selective depiction of Edinburgh Williams observes, 'Its portrayal of contemporary Britain is unrecognisable. The adorable courtyard flat unemployed Cora shares with her two children in central Edinburgh is a far cry from *Trainspotting*'s concrete council hell.'[19] This criticism seems strange, however, as, although *Women Talking Dirty* does produce a pleasant, touristic Edinburgh through its choice of locations on and around the Royal Mile, it is equally as stylised a representation of a certain part of the Old

Town as *Trainspotting* is of places like Leith. Indeed, neither of these films can claim to be the definitive word on 'contemporary Britain', despite the assumption on the part of the reviewer that *Trainspotting*'s focus on its male junky underclass at the city's periphery is somehow more 'real' than *Women Talking Dirty*'s tale of quirky thirty-something women in the pica-resque Old Town. Bizarrely, considering the mannered indie stylings of *Trainspotting* (its 'black magic realism' to quote Murray Smith),[20] Williams seems to consider it more 'realist' than *Women Talking Dirty* and to valor-ise it accordingly. Instead, I would argue that the touristic beauty of the area of Edinburgh that functions as a backdrop in *Women Talking Dirty* – its winding, cobbled streets free of traffic or pollution, the ubiquitous sightings of the castle in the background, scenic views of the city and the Firth of Forth from Carlton Hill, courtyards brimming with flower baskets, beautiful old stone buildings, spacious converted loft apartments and brightly coloured cafes and shops – renders the film's 'alternative' space an aspirational fantasy or a holiday type of space.

By setting *Women Talking Dirty* in the Old Town, the novel's more up-and-coming urban environment (which, ironically, is the Leith of Irvine Welsh's *Trainspotting*) is transformed into a more touristic locale, the pleasant space which Ellen and Cora inhabit providing the possibility of an alternative identity in much the same way as one might try out a new persona on holiday. Despite the increased popularity with visitors to Edinburgh of Leith's newly rejuvenated yuppie flats and trendy dockside restaurants, the Old Town spaces in which the narrative unfolds are still those most likely to be experienced by a tourist in Edinburgh. They even include carnivalesque moments when circus performers and mime artists cross the path of Cora and Ellen, recreating the colourful atmosphere of the annual Edinburgh Festival. There is thus no chance of a stray camera angle revealing the somewhat grim tenements that still exist in Leith, directly abutting the gentrified waterfront, peering out from in between buildings as a reminder of the area's past as an industrial port very much off the tourist trail. Edinburgh in *Women Talking Dirty*, then, functions as a space in which an alternative lifestyle can be explored by the viewer as though on holiday; indeed, the very idea of an alternative space to societal norms is figured as a 'holiday from normality'. In this the film joins the Edinburgh-set predecessors discussed in Chapter 1, the comedies that revolve around sexual relations, or the topic of sex, from *The Battle of the Sexes* (1959) and *The Prime of Miss Jean Brodie* (1969) to *Festival* (2005). Like *Festival* especially, *Women Talking Dirty* depicts a tourist Edinburgh in which everyday life can be momentarily suspended to be replaced by an alternative lifestyle that also sells Edinburgh to the tourist gaze.

The opening of the film is the opposite of the young heterosexual couple kissing energetically that opens *The Battle of the Sexes*, as Cora and Ellen briefly flirt with the idea of lesbian desire, discussing masturbation whilst scantily clad in the bathroom before swiftly rejecting the notion that they might kiss. Here sexual desire (be it hetero- or homosexual) is replaced by an 'almost homosocial', or, perhaps, 'almost matriarchal' space, free of the complications of heterosexual romance, in which female friendship can flourish. Moreover, by making Daniel the father of Cora's second child (which is not the case in the novel), *Women Talking Dirty* is able to pit Cora and Ellen's female friendship against the normative focus on heterosexual resolution of much mainstream cinema. As Yvonne Tasker observes in her discussion of female friendship films in *Working Girls* (1998), 'across a range of genres, the cost of heterosexuality . . . is the death of female friendship.'[21] In *Women Talking Dirty*, by contrast, the narrative resolves the binary of 'heterosexuality versus female friendship' not with the familiar heterosexual pairing conventional in rom-coms (as, for example, in *You've Got Mail*), but by closing its parallel story with Ellen and Cora reunited in locking the irresponsible Daniel out of their friendship. Thus, whilst a heterosexual coupling is desired by both women it is ultimately unsatisfactory in comparison with the more constant support of a female friend. Here, again, comparisons with *Walking and Talking* are evident, as they are with Holofcener's more famous ouput as one of the original directors of the internationally famous US television series about female friendship, *Sex and the City* (1998–2004).

In a certain sense, the tourist Edinburgh of *Women Talking Dirty* functions much as the rural backdrops do in earlier woman's films' set in Scotland. As Duncan Petrie notes of the woman's films *Another Time, Another Place* and *Breaking the Waves*, harsh, rural, claustrophobic landscapes are used as backgrounds that facilitate their respective attempts to 'penetrate and convey the psychological and emotional states of the characters'.[22] Both 'emotional and physical landscapes',[23] these locations enable an exploration of female interiority as (to paraphrase Sillars and Macdonald) both psychical and physical spaces that emphasise the harsh, isolated, repressed emotional lives of the women involved. The Edinburgh of *Women Talking Dirty*, by contrast, provides numerous attractive locations (pubs, cafes, flats) in which conversations between Ellen, Cora and the other 'acceptable' non-heterosexual male characters enable an exploration of female interiority in a fantasy space in which anything (or at any rate, anything other than heterosexual romance at the cost of female friendship) might be possible. These conversations about womanhood and life choices are ubiquitous in the film and include such topics as female masturbation, child maintenance, breast size, pregnancy, the right choice in men, marriage, having children, screwing around, Dolly Parton, child birth, coping with a young child, abortion, divorce, career versus family, true love, being faithful, letting go and, above all, female friendship. Admittedly there is nothing like the same level of introspection as in the even more 'talky' *Walking and Talking*, which is often compared with Woody Allen films for its verbosity. Rather, and more conventionally, *Women Talking Dirty* maintains its lighthearted narrative's momentum in the movements of Ellen and Cora through the streets of Edinburgh (and occasionally into the countryside or to the beach) and in montage sequences that speed the story onwards. Nevertheless, in *Women Talking Dirty* it is through talking (dirty or otherwise) that female friendship develops, providing an alternative to patriarchal, heterosexual norms. The film's stance is neatly summarised during one representative conversation between Cora and matriarch Emily about Cora's relationship with Ellen. Cora describes Ellen as the best friend she has ever had, for whom she feels something more than love. Emily replies that 'if you have real friendship with a woman, then you have something rare and wonderful.'

Beautiful Creatures (2000)

Directed by Bill Eagles (who like Giedroyc managed two feature films before returning to work in television), *Beautiful Creatures* focuses on the friendship of Dorothy (Susan Lynch) and Petula (Rachel Weisz), two young women in Glasgow. Both have verbally and physically abusive boyfriends, and their stories intertwine one night when Dorothy saves Petula from a beating administered by her gangster lover, Brian McMinn (Tom Mannion). After inadvertently killing Brian the two women hide his corpse in Dorothy's high-rise flat, fake his kidnapping and blackmail his elder brother, local crime boss Ronnie McMinn (Maurice Roëves), to the tune of £1 million. They are caught, however, between three men: the suspicious Ronnie, corrupt cop Detective Inspector Hepburn (Alex Norton), who deviously raises the sum to £2 million, and Dorothy's violent, drug-pushing boyfriend, Tony (Iain Glen). The two friends support each other throughout their various perils and ordeals, and, in the final showdown, after Tony kills Hepburn and Ronnie kills Tony, Petula returns Dorothy's favour from the start of the film and saves her life by killing Ronnie. The conclusion sees the two friends departing from Glasgow together with the money.

Beautiful Creatures was made by DNA Films with funding from the Arts Council of England. DNA Films, a small British studio subsidised by £29 million of lottery funding, was founded in 1997 by Duncan Kenworthy (producer of *Four Weddings and a Funeral* (1994)) and Andrew Macdonald (producer of *Trainspotting* (1996)). In September 2003 DNA announced its imminent partnership with Fox Searchlight (Fox's independent film production and distribution arm, which had previously distributed British films such as *Bend it Like Beckham* (2002)) in order to maximise its ability to recoup costs through worldwide distribution.[24] Although DNA has since been responsible for several high profile British films – including *The Last King of Scotland* (2006), for which Forest Whitaker won the Oscar for best actor, and two films by *Shallow Grave* and *Trainspotting* director, Danny Boyle, *28 Days Later* (2002) and *Sunshine* (2007) – the five films made up to the time of the partnership had been rather financially hit and miss. They included *Strictly Sinatra* (2001) (discussed in Chapters 2 and 7) and *Beautiful Creatures*. From an initial budget of £4 million (around half of which came from Lottery money provided by the Arts Council of England, the rest as an advance from pre-sales by Universal Pictures International), *Beautiful Creatures* only made a little over £200,000 at the UK box office. Although this was around ten times the £21,000 made by *Women Talking Dirty* from its original £3 million budget, *Beautiful Creatures* was also a box office flop. Writer/producer Simon Donald had already written and directed another Lottery funded flop, the gangster film *The Life of Stuff* (1997) on a £1 million lottery grant.[25] As Julian Petley has shown, despite the flaws in *Beautiful Creatures* the film was the victim of a critical savaging in the British press that began months prior to its release and was as much due to the media's imposition of its (entirely unrealistic) anti-public subsidy agenda onto this particular Lottery funded film as it was to inherent failures in the film itself.[26] Yet what is important for this discussion is not whether it is a 'good' or 'bad' film, or, indeed, whether its use of Scotland as a film set is 'positive' or 'negative', but, rather, how it uses Glasgow as a backdrop that adds an additional resonance to its story of female friendship.

In contrast to the alternative space to patriarchy constructed by *Women Talking Dirty* amidst the touristic areas of Edinburgh *Beautiful Creatures* creates an anti-patriarchal space of combative defiance towards normative heterosexual society. In this its indie styled self-consciousness is an evident feature. The film begins with a series of foregrounded intertextual references to other films about women in combative relationships with patriarchal society, including *Fatal Attraction* (1987) and *Thelma and Louise* (1991). At the start of the film Dorothy returns home to her flat to gather her things and escape from Tony. There she finds her dog strung up on the porch, and her bra deep-frying in the kitchen. This latter is a Glasgow-inflected reference to the boiling bunny in *Fatal Attraction*, Glasgow being famous for its deep-fried delicacies, including fish and chips and Mars bars. This time, however, the roles are reversed and it is the woman who is threatened by her unhinged male lover not the misogynistically portrayed bunny boiling, obsessive 'woman scorned' of the Hollywood film. Shortly afterwards, Petula's boyfriend, Brian, is murdered when, while he is beating her repeatedly on the bonnet of his car, Dorothy approaches him from behind and hits him across the head with a large piece of steel scaffolding. Here, it is the catalyst to the narrative of *Thelma and Louise* – the shooting of a male rapist against a car – that is referenced, the two events together positioning the women as victims of male violence who fight back in self-defence. From this point onwards they become proactive in their pursuit of financial reward, their friendship empowering them to take on the violent male figures in their lives, destroy them and create an alternative future for themselves. Thus, although critics were not positive about the film – for instance, Allan Hunter argues that 'a lurid, Tarantino-style romp of murder, greed and sweet liberation, *Beautiful Creatures* does not have the substance or skill to live up to its pre-screening reputation as a British *Thelma and Louise*'[27] – the indie stylings of the film, in particular its intertextual references, engage with a tradition of films about violent women who will not accept a marginalised position within patriarchal society (*Fatal Attraction*), or who choose to opt out of this society because of the strength they derive from their female friendship (*Thelma and Louise*). Thus, in a contrasting environment to the alternative, touristic space for female friendship of *Women Talking Dirty*, within the indie styled, Tarantino-esque, noirish fantasy of *Beautiful Creatures'* dark, seedy, criminal Glasgow, female friendship is explored in an oppositional form to (violent) patriarchy.

The comments of reviewers are again helpful in understanding this process. Claire Monk notes the correlations with *Thelma and Louise* but criticises *Beautiful Creatures* for lacking a clear purpose and for appearing to have been made more for its 'marketability' than its substance.[28] Observing both that the script is 'highly verbal' (suggesting the woman's film) and the manner in which the film encourages the audience to both empathise with and objectify Weisz's 'dumb-blonde', Petula, Monk argues that

> *Beautiful Creatures'* contradictions suggest an attempt to multiply its potential audiences – feminists, fashionistas, 18 to 24 year-old *Loaded* readers – but at the inevitable expense of coherence or substance. To this list . . . should be added 20th-century design enthusiasts. Petula inhabits a fabulous modern-movement villa;

Ronnie's wood-panelled office is the height of current retro fashion. Yet here too
chic wins out over credibility: the credits boast of location shooting in Scotland, but
the interiors seem straight out of Shoreditch.

Initially the confluence of the indie style, the 'tepid tartan Tarantini'
aspect of the film, with the female friendship film is viewed as something
of a disaster in that the film loses any meaning. However, Monk's critique
of the way locations were selectively chosen from around Glasgow to
create a 'chic' setting (leaving aside Monk's mistaken assumption that
Glasgow does not contain areas as exclusive as London's affluent neighbourhood of Shoreditch) is suggestive of the fantasy life that is created for
the female friends to inhabit against this urban backdrop. The apparent
clash of expensive interiors with the gritty streets and bleak high-rise flats
illustrates that the lives of the two women are taking place in a setting
that strives not for 'credibility' (an authentic Scottishness) but to create
an 'anywhereland' equally accessible to Glaswegians as to viewers in
Shoreditch in which to explore the friends' defiance of the constraining
forces of patriarchy. Although *Beautiful Creatures* is clearly shot in
Glasgow (the closing credits even declaring as much) it is a Glasgow of
anonymous flats in anonymous estates; the focus is on non-specific interiors in the indie manner of both *Trainspotting* and *Shallow Grave* rather
than on the city's more recognisable vistas which would establish the location. Thus, although Monk's criticism chimes with concerns raised at the
time of DNA's partnership with Fox Searchlight – that DNA might
henceforth solely produce films designed for international consumption
rather than using its lottery funding to engage with issues of interest to
UK audiences – this female friendship film focuses beyond the national to
appeal internationally to a variety of audiences, not least of whom are
women.

Gangster Women

As a location, *Beautiful Creatures*'s post-industrial Glasgow evokes the
hard men of Clydesidism through the gangster brothers Brian and Ronnie
McMinn, the corrupt cop Hepburn and bra-frying boyfriend Tony.
However, these hard cases are all ultimately destroyed through the intervention of Dorothy and Petula in their previously male dominated world.
It is no coincidence that Dorothy has a strong Irish accent (and, when
fleeing the city, attempts to catch a bus to London) whereas Petula has an
English accent. As in *Morven Callar* (2002) (Chapter 2), these female pro-
tagonists are not Scottish characters, even though the society in which

they move is, with Tony, Hepburn and the McMinns all speaking with strong Scottish accents. Here, then, Scotland is an alternative space that the women can use as a backdrop against which to build their friendship, only this time it is a violent gangland fantasy (Glasgow), rather than a beautiful touristic destination (Edinburgh). To emphasise the sense of this location as a fantasy space, the film begins and ends with close-ups of railway tracks, as Dorothy is transported into Glasgow for the duration of the film (her land of Oz) and, at the close, as Dorothy and Petula are carried out of town once more. For a brief while, Dorothy and Petula, along with the viewer, inhabit a dangerous world of petty criminals, corrupt cops and organised mobsters. These overblown, violent representatives of masculine authority are set up to be destroyed by the power of their female friendship. Thus, in *Beautiful Creatures* Glasgow functions as a location that makes the violence they encounter more credible, because of the association of the city with the hard-man tradition of Clydesideism and the recent representations of the Lowland Scottish cities of Edinburgh and Glasgow as dangerous centres of post-industrial, male underclass violence (*Small Faces, Trainspotting, 16 Years of Alcohol* etc). This is clear both in the noir lighting evocative of *Shallow Grave*, and in the obligatory, post-*Trainspotting*, sequence of heroin use. In this fantasy space, battling violent male gangsters and corrupt cops who are far more overblown and pulpy than the small-time grifter Daniel in *Women Talking Dirty*, the ever practical Dorothy joins Petula. Petula is a gangster's moll and pornographic actress who could easily have stepped out of US indies like *Pulp Fiction, Bound* or *Lost Highway* (1997), and whose presence furthers the film's indie self-consciousness as it establishes a space in which to explore female friendship.

Finally, the most recognisable of Scottish elements in the film, Tony's much sought after golf clubs (which function rather like the sofa full of money in *Women Talking Dirty* as an illicit secret kept by the man within the domestic space) turn out to contain drugs and guns. This association of the most internationally recognisably Scottish of pastimes with Tony's violent lifestyle firmly establishes the post-industrial Glasgow into which the viewer is transported as a dangerous space within which Dorothy and Petula will explore their (anti-patriarchal) fantasy identities without men.

As in *Women Talking Dirty*, in *Beautiful Creatures* conversation is again central in exploring female identities, topics this time including the male use of violent language against women; Petula's desire to visit her mother overseas when Brian has her passport; hairstyles; the legal right to self-defence against domestic violence; the logistics of moving a body; love at first sight; using ransom money to escape together; having sex in the workplace (twice) and so on. Yet, as the somewhat varied topics suggest, this is not as straightforward a 'woman-centric' conversational film as *Women Talking Dirty*. Rather, its generic form as a crime thriller (more usually a genre featuring male characters 'doing' rather than women 'talking') ensures both that the conversations include rather grisly subjects and also that Dorothy and Petula's talking is joined by a lot more doing than in the previous film. Instead, in a way that is a little similar to the construction of masculinity in *On a Clear Day* (discussed in chapter eight), post-industrial femininity in *Beautiful Creatures* requires both talking and doing. In many instances this means trying on new roles, or new identities, including those of men.

Not only do Dorothy and Petula dream up their kidnapping scheme together (performing the roles of kidnappers), they are also active in creating the impression that it is a male kidnapping. Parodying stereotypical masculine behaviour they make a mess in Brian's boat to create the impression that he has been held captive there. They make the mess look 'male' by spraying beer around the room, putting pornography into the video, and liberally spreading around dirty underwear and take-away food. Moreover, Dorothy tries on the role of 'boyfriend' to Petula, soothing her to sleep over the phone with the children's rhyme, 'night night, sleep tight, don't let the bugs bite'. This was a saying that (we later discover through subtle inference) was prominent in her previous, heterosexual relationship with Tony as he nursed her through the cold turkey he had inflicted upon her along with heroin addiction. Petula, for her part, attempting to drive the now deceased Brian's car, speaks his (abusive) words of tutelage verbatim to master the controls. Finally, in order to release their new identities physically, Dorothy cuts Petula's hair and Petula presents Dorothy with a new wardrobe. This experimenting with identities, then, enables Dorothy and Petula to act together as friends when hiding the body of Brian, setting up the fake kidnapping and freeing each other from the men who are about to kill them. Ultimately this process of identity transformation, and the bond it develops between them, is the catalyst which facilitates their escape in the film's conclusion.

Talking More Than Doing

Despite the active roles demanded of the women in *Beautiful Creatures* by the genre in which they find themselves in both films it is primarily through talking that an exploration of femininity, and female friendship, occurs. In *Women Talking Dirty* this extended conversation about what it means to be a woman without a man is played out against the backdrop of tourist Edinburgh, a fantasy space in which to imagine an alternative to societal norms. In *Beautiful Creatures*, both actions and conversations take place against a grim portrait of Glasgow's high-rise projects resonant with the hard-man mythology of Clydesideism. This provides a location against which to explore – in this instance both verbally and, in some instances, physically – a new, post-industrial femininity that stands in (if necessary, violent) opposition to traditional notions of aggressive masculinity.

As Hollinger argues, female friendship films 'offer their female audience the pleasure of identifying with positive female characters as well as with a narrative resolution that constitutes a female victory'.[29] In the specific case of *Women Talking Dirty* the female friendship is created by women in the roles of writer, director and actresses, ensuring that, 'spaces can be found in certain female-oriented film genres where dominant ideas are challenged and shifts in representations of women do occur'.[30] In fact, in both films the alternative spaces that are created in which to explore female friendship function as they do because they are – in different ways – recognisably 'Scottish', whether due to their association with previous Edinburgh-set comedies like *The Battle of the Sexes* or the decrepit post-industrial Scotland of *Trainspotting*. Thus, although neither film should be considered a 'Scottish' production (in spite of the fact that *Women Talking Dirty* had its origins in Dewar's novel and screenplay it is ultimately a Rocket Pictures (London) production, with much of its press coverage stressing English pop star Elton John's role as founder of the company) this does not mean that Scotland does not feature in the two films. Scotland is used as a film set, but this is a set which provides an additional dimension to their respective explorations of female friendship.

Writing on Michael Radford's *Another Time, Another Place* in *Cencrastus* in 1985, Connie Balides notes that, although a film set in Scotland with a female protagonist, *Another Time, Another Place* was guilty of dealing 'with the issue of Scotland at the expense of the woman'.[31] By the turn of the millenium, in both *Women Talking Dirty* and *Beautiful Creatures*, this process has come full circle, with the focus now on female friendship at the 'expense' of any engagement with issues surrounding Scotland or Scottish identity, and with the two cities functioning as backdrops, or sets, integral to this process. Crucially, however, these are recognisably Scottish sets with particular touristic and cinematic resonances that inform their fantasy examinations of female friendship in post-industrial society.

Notes

1. Pam Cook, *I Know Where I'm Going!* (London: BFI, 2002), pp. 25–9.
2. Lucy Fischer, *Shot/Countershot* (London: BFI/Macmillan, 1989), pp. 194–205.
3. Carol Anderson, 'Listening to the Women Talk', in Gavin Wallace and Randall Stevenson (eds), *The Scottish Novel Since the Seventies* (Edinburgh: Edinburgh University Press, 1993), pp. 170–86, pp. 170–2.
4. Karen Hollinger, *In the Company of Women* (Minneapolis, MN: University of Minnesota Press, 1998), pp. 2–3.
5. Ibid., p. 6.
6. Ibid., pp. 236–7.
7. Ibid., p. 240.
8. See also Sarah Neely, 'Contemporary Scottish Cinema', in Neil Blain and David Hutchinson (eds), *The Media in Scotland* (Edinburgh: Edinburgh University Press, 2008), pp. 151–65.
9. Ian Goode, 'Scottish Cinema and Scottish Imaginings', *Screen*, 46: 2 (2005), pp. 235–9, p. 239.
10. Jane Sillars and Myra Macdonald, 'Gender, Spaces, Changes', in Neil Blain and David Hutchinson (eds), *The Media in Scotland* (Edinburgh: Edinburgh University Press, 2008), pp. 183–98, pp. 183–4.
11. Jonathan Murray, 'Kids in America?' *Screen*, 46: 2 (2005), pp. 217–25, p. 218.
12. Murray Smith, *Trainspotting* (London: BFI, 2000), p. 9.
13. Mike Wayne, *The Politics of Contemporary European Cinema* (Bristol: Intellect, 2002), p. 43.
14. Allan Hunter, 'Tepid Tartan Tarantini', *Screen International*, 1292 (2001), p. 35.
15. Smith, *Trainspotting*, p. 87.
16. Geoff King, *American Independent Cinema* (London: I. B. Tauris, 2005), p. 226.
17. Celestino Deleyto, 'Between Friends: Love and Friendship in Contemporary Hollywood Romantic Comedy', *Screen*, 44: 2 (2003), pp. 167–82, p. 177.
18. Gilda Williams, 'Women Talking Dirty', *Sight and Sound*, 11: 10 (2001), p 60.
19. Ibid.
20. Smith, *Trainspotting*, p. 75.
21. Yvonne Tasker, *Working Girls* (London: Routledge, 1998), p. 140.
22. Duncan Petrie, *Screening Scotland* (London: British Film Institute, 2000), p. 162.
23. Ibid.
24. Geoffrey Macnab, 'Choose Cash', *The Guardian*, 13 November 2003. http://arts.guardian.co.uk/features/story/0,,1083690,00.html (04/06/08).
25. Jonathan Murray, 'Sundance in Scotland?' *Vertigo*, 2: 2 (2002), pp. 10–11.

26. Julian Petley, 'From Brit-flicks to Shit-flicks', *Journal of Popular British Cinema*, 5 (2002), pp. 37–52, pp. 48–9.
27. Hunter, 'Tepid Tartan Tarantini', p. 35.
28. Claire Monk, 'Beautiful Creatures', *Sight and Sound*, 11: 2 (2001), p. 35.
29. Hollinger, *In the Company of Women*, p. 4.
30. Ibid.
31. Connie Balides, '*Another Time, Another Place* . . . Another Male View?' *Cencrastus*, 16 (1984), pp. 37–41, p. 41.

CHAPTER 10

Art Cinema: The Global Limits of Cinematic Scotland

The final chapter begins with the development of art cinema in Scotland, from the painstaking first shoots of creativity in the works of home-grown director Bill Douglas in the 1970s through the flourishing of internationally recognised auteurs like Peter Mullan, Lynne Ramsay and David Mackenzie in the 1990s to the establishment of the Advance Party Initiative, a coproduction agreement between Scotland and Denmark that led to the Cannes Grand Jury Prize winning *Red Road* (2006). Understanding this history entails a discussion of exactly what art cinema is, which involves understanding both the art film's aesthetic characteristics and its relationship to the global marketplace. *Young Adam* (2003) is then examined to explore the strategies for international success on the film festival circuit and the independent cinema networks currently pursued by Scottish filmmakers like David Mackenzie. As in previous chapters, this entails a consideration of the extent to which films like *Young Adam* self-exoticise their Scottishness for international consumption. In conclusion I consider the differences between *Young Adam* and *Red Road* and suggest reasons why the latter was a greater success internationally, and the impact this is likely to have on the Scottish art film in the future.

Art Cinema in Scotland

Although it is still a young national cinema, when originators of Scottish cinema are sought three names are most often mentioned: John Grierson, Bill Forsyth and Bill Douglas. These figures suggest three possible origins and three possible histories of cinema in Scotland. As I discussed in Chapter 1, Bill Forsyth's name is synonymous with what many consider Scotland's first ever indigenous feature film productions, whose status as comedies are often downplayed by critics in search of a 'serious' auteur figure on whom to pin the identity of Scotland's emergent national cinema. John Grierson, as I discussed in Chapter 8, is a Scot often considered the father of the documentary, whose influence on British social realist cinema is still evident in films like *On a Clear Day* (2005). Bill

Douglas, however, is the least well known, partly because his initial films were not feature length and partly because of their 'artistic' aesthetic, which latter perhaps explains their lack of widespread availability in relation to the more popular comedies of Bill Forsyth.

Douglas's films are visually striking. The first two parts of his *Childhood Trilogy*, *My Childhood* (1972) and *My Ain Folk* (1973) (the third part is *My Way Home* (1978)), are incredibly bleak reimagined portrayals of Douglas's upbringing in the impoverished Scottish mining town of Newcraighall, near Edinburgh. The black–and–white images (the first film was shot in colour but printed in black and white),[1] coupled with the stark poverty of the surroundings, Douglas's creation of numerous still, silent images and acting that is at times so mannered as to give an almost theatrical feel ensure that Douglas's *Childhood Trilogy* has been compared with silent cinema or described as poetic realism.[2] Memorable images include exterior shots in which black–clad figures contrast starkly with rural settings (as, for instance, in the sight of a black, horse-drawn hearse crossing the exposed countryside in *My Ain Folk*), at times creating an almost surreal quality akin to films by Ingmar Bergman (Sweden), Federico Fellini (Italy) and Aleksandr Dozhenko (Russia).

The extent to which Douglas's films are indigenously 'Scottish' is hard to pinpoint precisely. The *Childhood Trilogy* films were funded by Mamoun Hassan, then head of the British Film Institute, on extremely small budgets (£3,000, £12,000 and £33,000 respectively), and much of the crew was English.[3] Douglas was refused funding closer to home by the Films of Scotland Committee (1937-8, and 1954-82) – who had previously funded *Seawards the Great Ships* (1966) – because he did not intend a 'forward-looking' image of Scotland that gelled with the committee's remit.[4] To be fair to the committee, there was very little funding, so projects that did receive money had to be commercially viable, which Douglas's may not have appeared to be.[5] Indeed, the *Childhood Trilogy* was unlikely to have satisfied the agendas of certain members of the committee, such as those representing industry and the tourist trade, who may have preferred the more celebratory tone of films like *Seawards the Great Ships*.[6] Even so, prior to the emergence of Forsyth in the 1980s Douglas was as close to a home-grown artistic filmmaker as it was possible to find in Scotland.

Academic study of Bill Douglas's films, in particular his *Childhood Trilogy*, began around the time of his death in 1991. Andrew Noble's enthused contribution to *From Limelight to Satellite* (1990) critiques what was then the only text on Scottish cinema, *Scotch Reels* (1982), for failing to provide an engaged discussion with Douglas's work. Noble argues that for the contributors to *Scotch Reels* to have done so would have seriously undermined the anthology's thesis, that cinematic images of Scotland were, in general, uncritical reassertions of stereotypes like Tartanry and the Kailyard.[7] In Douglas, then, an auteur was found (Douglas was both writer and director of the *Childhood Trilogy* and his only other feature *Comrades* (1986)) on whose work to build an alternative history of Scottish (art) cinema that could move the field beyond *Scotch Reels'* negative take on externally produced popular representations of Scotland. Noble's piece was followed by a collection dedicated to Douglas, *Bill Douglas: A Lanternist's Account* (1993). This contained a fuller exploration of Douglas' oeuvre, including an interesting piece by John Caughie calling for a more engaged discussion of Douglas's works, which he describes as pointing the way towards the 'sustained, hard-edged and diverse *European* tradition of art cinema'.[8]

In *Screening Scotland* (2000) Duncan Petrie outlined in more detail the narrative of development of a Scottish art cinema previously suggested by Caughie. This illustrated not only the impact of Douglas on subsequent Scottish art films but also the different context that had emerged for aspiring filmmakers in Scotland. In a different way to the Scottish art films made in the 1980s and early 1990s that can be said to follow in the footsteps of Douglas – *Another Time Another Place* (1983), *Venus Peter* (1989), *Prague* (1992) (the latter two directed by Iain Sellar, who had previously worked with Douglas), *Play Me Something* (1989), *Silent Scream* (1990), *Blue Black Permanent* (1992) and the Scottish-Gaelic television feature *As An Eilean* (1993) – many films of the 1990s and early 2000s seem to expand this tradition. These include Gillies Mackinnon's *Small Faces* (1996) and *Regeneration* (1997), *Stella Does Tricks* (1996), *The Winter Guest* (1997), Ken Loach's *Carla's Song* (1996), *My Name is Joe* (1998), *Sweet Sixteen* (2002) and *Ae Fond Kiss* (2004), Peter Mullan's *Orphans* (1997) and *The Magdalene Sisters* (2002), Lynne Ramsay's *Ratcatcher* (1999) and *Morvern Callar* (2002), David Mackenzie's *Young Adam*, *Asylum* (2005) and *Hallam Foe* (2007), Richard Jobson's *16 Years of Alcohol* (2003) and *A Woman in Winter* (2005) and the Scottish-Gaelic feature *Seachd: The Inaccessible Pinnacle* (2007). All are the product of a very different institutional and industrial context.

The Scottish art films of the mid-1990s onwards emerged after the success of *Shallow Grave* (1994) and *Trainspotting* (1996) drew international attention to filmmaking in Scotland. They also owe much to the devolution of National Lottery funding to Scotland in 1995 and reaped the dividends of the growth of the Scottish Film Production Fund (SFPF) in the 1980s (and ultimately the establishment of Scottish Screen in 1997), the development of the Glasgow Film Fund and the increased revenue for filmmaking forthcoming from television companies such as Channel 4 (like SFPF already a major investor in the films of the 1980s and 1990s), BBC Scotland and the Scottish-Gaelic television committee now known as MG ALBA (the operating name of Serbheis Nam Meadhanan Gàidhlig/Gaelic Media Services (GMS)).[9] The majority, if not all, of these films were made with funding and production assistance from one or more of these organisations. Thus, the major difference between the two moments is that, rather than competing for film funding with filmmakers from all over Britain (a process that typically enabled only a handful of Scottish films to be made during the 1980s), an institutional context had emerged by the mid-to-late 1990s that was, as Petrie notes, dedicated to the 'nurturing of Scottish feature film production'.[10] In this context, with the more modest budgets (around £1–3m) typical of the European art film, Scottish art cinema thrived. Fittingly, perhaps, this movement was contemporaneous with increasing political debate within Scotland, especially in relation to devolution, as to whether the nation's identity was best conceived in relation to England (as part of the state of Britain) or in a broader, European context.

In terms of contemporary Scottish cinema the influence of Douglas is now increasingly apparent, and has been noted by several commentators. Along with Petrie's exploration of the influence of Douglas on Scottish art cinema in *Screening Scotland*, which was reaffirmed by Tony McKibbin in *Cencrastus*, Hannah McGill succinctly labelled this tradition, or history, in her *Sight and Sound* article on *Red Road*, as 'an oft-maligned tradition of slum-bound Scottish miserablism that stretches from Bill Douglas to Lynne Ramsay and David Mackenzie'.[11] Yet, although there is a history of the Scottish art film – albeit what some might somewhat reductively consider a miserablist one – that stretches from Douglas to the present, there is a noticeable difference between 'then' (Douglas) and 'now' (Mullan, Ramsay, Mackenzie). This contrast is a product of the changed institutional and funding context. Whilst Douglas's films were autobiographical labours of love, made almost in spite of the Scottish film industry at that time (witness the refusal of funding for *My Childhood* by Films of Scotland), the recent development of conditions in Scotland conducive to the creation of art cinema have led to a more astute creation of films deliberately conceived with an eye to making an impact internationally on the festival circuit. The most apparent of these manoeuvres is that of the Advance Party Initiative, and the first of its three projects, *Red Road*. Before I move on to examine this new phenomenon in Scottish filmmaking, however, it is necessary to briefly clear up one small matter. Just what exactly is art cinema?

What is Art Cinema . . . and Where is it . . .

One of the major difficulties in defining art cinema is that it means different things to different people. In many parts of the world this is because
experiencing art cinema means watching films from other countries,
perhaps films in foreign languages, in independent cinemas or from DVD
distributors like Tartan or Artificial Eye who specialise in bringing 'world
cinema' to international audiences. These films, often heterogeneous in
style (and sometimes including popular genre films), are thus consumed as
'art cinema' by virtue of their cultural and national difference (at times
evoking a certain degree of exoticism) and, indeed, the homogenising suggestion of their having been collected under the all-encompassing banner
heading of 'world cinema'. Just a quick glance at the varied range of films
listed above as Scottish art films (some of which I have discussed in other
chapters as genre films) bears out this point.

One way to provide further clarity is to understand the different, over-
lapping textual and contextual factors that determine which films become
known as art cinema. Firstly, there is the aesthetic level. In 1979, David
Bordwell defined art cinema in terms of its aesthetic. Positioning art films
of directors from Europe in opposition to classic Hollywood cinema,
Bordwell's approach (whilst potentially liable to homogenise very different films) points to the niche market in international cinema that is carved
out by art cinema – what Catherine Fowler tellingly describes as 'a *bona
fide* European genre'[12] – in relation to the global dominance of Hollywood.
Tracing the history of the art film back to European cinematic movements
of the 1920s and 1930s, Bordwell focuses on the resurgence of art cinema
after World War II, from Italian neo-realism through the New Waves to
the mature auteurs of international art cinema in the 1960s and 1970s
(Fellini, Resnais, Bergman, Pasolini etc). In contrast to the causality of the
classical Hollywood narrative and its goal-oriented characters racing to
meet deadlines, art films are characterised by characters who 'lack defined
desires and goals'.[13] Accordingly the narrative has a 'drifting episodic
quality' as 'psychologically complex characters . . . slide passively from
one situation to another'.[14] Moreover, as part of an in-depth exploration of
character psychology, autobiographical events such as memories of childhood, along with a character's fantasies or dreams, become informative of
the viewer's understanding of character psychology, albeit to the detri-
ment of narrative linearity. For this reason, whilst often striving towards a
documentary realism in their cinematography, many art films explore the
relationship between reality and illusion in a self-conscious manner.
Finally, for Bordwell, the art film is characterised by the aesthetically or

thematically foregrounded presence of the auteur as a creative individual whose preoccupations can be seen at work most clearly when several of their films are examined together, as though each were 'a chapter in an *ouvre*'.[15]

This aesthetic definition of art cinema illustrates how well Bill Douglas's works – especially the *Childhood Trilogy* – conform to the model of the European art film with their autobiographical focus, their realist portrayal of an impoverished context and their pronounced poetic aesthetic that reveals the guiding hand of the auteur. It also enables us to consider more clearly, as I have discussed in Chapter 2, whether a film like Bill Forsyth's *Gregory's Two Girls* (1999) is an art film about loneliness and isolation or, whether, as I contend, an 'edgy' comedy that explores serious issues in a comedic mode. Bordwell's focus on the aesthetic also complicates the way we conceive of Ken Loach's films, which are at once auteur films and would be seen by many as art films (especially as they circulate through the festival and independent cinema networks) but are considered by many to be social realist films, albeit with a melodramatic component, and – as I demonstrated in Chapter 2 – can at times also be considered road movies. Moreover, this aesthetic definition provides an opportunity to separate films like *Shallow Grave*, *Trainspotting*, *Late Night Shopping* (2001) and *16 Years of Alcohol* from the rest of the films listed above as they have an aesthetic closer to that of US independent cinema than European art cinema (see Chapter 9). Even so, thanks to the cross-fertilising of both the British social realist tradition and US independent cinema with the European art film, both of these examples are open to debate. What we can say for sure, however, is that the aesthetic model of the European art film established by Bordwell describes much indigenous Scottish cinematic output of the 1980s and 1990s.

Shortly after Bordwell's article in *Film Criticism*, Steve Neale added another dimension to the debate in 'Art Cinema as Institution' in *Screen* (1981). Neale noted that art cinema not only developed in order to take advantage of a niche in a global marketplace otherwise dominated by Hollywood but was also used 'to foster a film industry and a film culture' within specific nations.[16] As he argues, the art film is 'the space in which an indigenous cinema can develop and make its critical and economic mark'.[17] Neale then goes on to discuss the development of art cinemas in France, Germany and Italy, illustrating the 'differences and specificities'[18] that grew up when indigenous art cinemas from different nations took advantage of their informing cultural and institutional contexts. Neale's work enables us to view the flourishing of art cinema in Scotland since the 1990s as an attempt to 'foster a film industry and film culture' in Scotland that is both a part of the heritage started by Douglas and a product of the specificities of the revamped institutional context in which – amongst other factors – growing but still limited funding opportunities favoured the creation of relatively low-budget art films. In particular, Neale's argument is illuminating for this period in the development of the Scottish art film because its conclusion points towards the 'political' role that art cinema performs in an international context and stresses the 'balance' that art films attempt to strike between national and international aspects, to ensure that the films are both economic and critical successes at home and abroad.[19] This is a balancing act between being successful internationally whilst simultaneously being recognised as 'national', as a product of Scotland. Yet, because of the politics of the international film festival circuit, this balancing act is no simple matter.

. . . and Who Decides . . .?

For many small national cinemas it can be unclear whether films that are successful on the festival circuit present a 'national' viewpoint and can even be seen as representative of a country like Scotland, or whether they are appreciated internationally because they conform to preconceived notions of how 'Scotland' should appear in cinema. As Thomas Elsaesser notes in his work on European film festivals, this distribution network has now become so important for films hoping to compete in the global marketplace that some films are constructed specifically for the festival circuit, as though (auto–exotically) 'made to measure' or 'made to order'[20] for the expectations of this forum. Accordingly, there is a danger that this process creates a degree of 'self–othering' on the part of filmmakers from small national cinemas.[21] It is at this point that the issue of how Scotland is represented in cinema stretches back in a bungee-like manner to the *Scotch Reels* debate of the early 1980s (are these representations 'positive' or 'negative', and who decides this?) before catapulting us back to the present to explore the different context into which Scottish art cinema emerged in the 1990s. In spite of arguments stressing the role of the auteur in the creation of art cinema, then, the art cinema balancing act inevitably impacts upon the types of films that are made as a small nation attempts to establish its cinema in the global marketplace.

In terms of the impact of the global marketplace for art cinema on recent Scottish art films it is worth further interrogating the status of the auteur. It is sometimes a surprise to people to discover that a filmmaker from their nation, whose work may not be considered popular in their own country, is venerated internationally as its global representative. In the

British context the clearest example is the puzzlement expressed by Brits at the international popularity of Ken Loach, a director whose work only occasionally crosses over into the mainstream (*The Wind that Shakes the Barley* (2006), for instance) to compete with popular films like *The Full Monty* (1997), *Notting Hill* (1999), *Billy Elliott* (2000), *Bridget Jones's Diary* (2001), *Shaun of the Dead* (2004), *Love Actually* (2003), *Hot Fuzz* (2007) and the James Bond and Harry Potter franchises. To a large extent this is because, as critics have shown (from Neale to Timothy Corrigan to Catherine Grant), whether it is always deserved or not the name of the auteur – both on the international festival circuit and in some cases in the Anglophone mainstream (for example, Steven Spielberg, Francis Ford Coppola, Quentin Tarantino) – has become a 'brand name'.[22] On the festival circuit this brand not only sells a film in the same way that a star's name does in Hollywood it may also become synonymous with the national cinema itself, even if the director's work is not representative of the films that the majority of people in the nation watch. As I discussed in Chapter 1, this can explain why a director like Bill Forsyth is discussed as a 'serious' filmmaker by film critics and academics as they attempt to elevate his work to the status of national representative on the international map of world cinema. It also explains why certain publicly funded institutions, like Scottish Screen, promote directors of art films internationally. After all, success in a major festival can propel not only the director but also the national (read, art) cinema into the international limelight.

It is equally possible for an international film festival to make a point of praising directors from certain nations, to use the global visibility, hype and publicity that surrounds festival awards to make a political statement. At the broadest level this is often done to align certain filmmakers from 'other' countries with the European art cinema model, acknowledging a similarity of purpose that enables filmmakers like Hsiao-hsien Hou from Taiwan, Satyajit Ray from India, Wong Kar Wai from Hong Kong and Takeshi Kitano from Japan to be listed alongside European auteurs, even though their films are very different to those of the mainstream film industries of these nations. At a purely aesthetic level this can be seen as the expansion of the European niche product around the world and as a means of increasing its market share in relation to Hollywood. Yet, with this practice, there is always the danger of cultural elitism as certain directors (and, by extension, nations) are allowed into the elite club and others are not. Here the European mode of art cinema becomes a standard against which other cinemas are judged, the reception of films from many countries being tainted with a certain type of Eurocentrism as critics and festival juries assess films on the strength of an aesthetic model which may not apply to filmmakers drawing upon their indigenous aesthetic and filmmaking traditions and practices.

Furthermore, when economically 'smaller' countries are invited into the elite international club the award of a prize on the festival circuit can also appear problematic or contentious for political reasons. Iranian art films, for example, are very different from popular films screened in Iran. Many of the Iranian films to receive international acclaim from European festivals can be said to conform to Western views of Iran as a country where life is extremely hard for the population under Islamic rule. This is especially so of films depicting women in contemporary Iran, such as *Roozi ke zan shodam/ The Day I Became a Woman* (2000) and *Dayereh/ The Circle* (2000). There is, thus, always a balancing act to be assessed between the positive merits of exploring such issues in the international arena and the politics of the way such films are received, 'judged' and distributed. A similar danger faces contemporary Scottish directors, especially considering the bleakness of the 'miserablist' art cinema tradition handed down from Douglas (with its emphasis on childhood and poverty), and their potential for fuelling existing stereotypes of Scotland, like Clydesideism, that present a problematically dire picture of post-industrial Scotland.

Finally, as it is extremely difficult for small national cinemas to recoup the costs of filmmaking within the nation, many art films from small nations are designed to have transnational appeal. Art cinema is often inextricably linked to distribution realities as low-budget films attempt to compete internationally in the niche networks and circuits (film festivals, independent cinema chains) that exist outside the Hollywood-dominated multiplex mainstream. In the case of at least two Scottish directors of the 1990s/2000s, the development of their oeuvres has illustrated a tendency to erase national concerns in order to be more internationally acceptable. Whilst Peter Mullan's debut art film, *Orphans*, was, as I have shown elsewhere, directly engaged with representing Scotland,[23] his follow-up, the even more successful *The Magdalene Sisters* (which won several awards, including the Golden Lion at Venice), whilst shot in Scotland was set in Ireland and had a universal appeal because of its focus on young women struggling to overcome physical and mental adversity in the harsh confines of a Magdalene laundry. Similarly, Lynne Ramsay's *Ratcatcher*, the Scottish film most indebted to Douglas's *Childhood Trilogy*, deliberately engaged with Scotland and the question of how best to represent it. *Morvern Callar*, however, as I discussed in Chapter 2, with its lengthy sequences in Spain, provoked concern over whether or not it was engaged with Scottish identity or was simply 'taking a break' from all such considerations in sunny Spain. In terms of transnational distribution, then, Scottish art cinema treads a wary path between establishing a unique national identity and simultaneously erasing anything too off-puttingly Scottish. As I will show momentarily, something similar can be said of David Mackenzie.

In the case of art cinema from Scotland the picture is further complicated by the unusual dynamics that exist between Scottish filmmakers and the rest of the British film industry. Although the situation that developed in Scotland in the 1990s favoured the growth of indigenous production several films made since then have received funding from British sources. For certain filmmakers the situation may not always have appeared so different from that of the 1980s, when Scottish filmmakers had to compete with everyone else in Britain for funding. *Orphans*, for instance, was largely funded by Channel 4, but they were not interested in distributing the finished film. Only after it won awards at the Venice Film Festival did it receive distribution, a fact that illustrates the power of the international arena to establish a director as representative of their own nation.[24] This is not an occurrence solely applicable to Scotland by any means, but it illustrates the additional difficulties Scottish filmmakers face having almost to overcome their position within the British state to gain international recognition beyond it. The absolutely disgraceful, and still unexplained decision by BAFTA not to nominate either the Welsh film *Calon Gaeth* (2006) or the Scottish-Gaelic *Seachd* for a Foreign Language Oscar in 2007, but instead to send in no film at all, is another case in point. This international arena, then, fraught as it is with deceptive political undercurrents, has been the testing ground for contemporary Scottish art cinema and has had a marked impact on the types of art films produced in Scotland.

The international success of a Scottish art film, therefore, does not necessarily provide a clear-cut answer to whether or not the filmmakers (and their financial backers and promoters) have managed to create the perfect balance between national and international faces of the art film. The difficulty of determining whether an art film is an international success on its own merits or is simply conforming to type for international eyes is akin to the difficulties critics have encountered since *Scotch Reels* over whether cinematic depictions of Scotland are 'positive' or 'negative', when in actual fact they may be equally productively considered as being both at the same time, depending on your (national or international) standpoint. With this exploration of the politics of the international arena in mind an analysis of the ways in which Scottish art cinema is developing to target this market can now be undertaken.

Sigma Films, Advance Party, *Red Road*

Young Adam is the second feature by Scottish director David Mackenzie. Along with producer Gillian Berrie and his actor brother, Alastair, Mackenzie was one of the original founders of the independent production company Sigma Films, Glasgow, in 1996.[25] Sigma produced Mackenzie's first feature, starring his brother Alastair, *The Last Great Wilderness* (2002). This low-budget film was shot digitally, received seventy-five per cent of its budget from Lottery funding,[26] and was coproduced with Zentropa, the Danish production company founded in 1992 by director Lars von Trier and producer Peter Aalbæk Jensen. Zentropa had previously filmed *Breaking the Waves* (1996) in Scotland. Sigma went on to act as the UK coproducer on other Zentropa projects, such as the comedy set in Scotland, *Wilbur Wants to Kill Himself* (2002).

Following on from *Wilbur Wants to Kill Himself*, in 2002 – in collaboration with Zentropa and with the support of the Glasgow Film Office, Scottish Screen and the UK Film Council – Sigma established the Advance Party Initiative. A three-film project, the Sigma website describes it thus:

> The project was initiated by Lars von Trier along with Gillian Berrie and Sisse Graum Jorgensen. 'Advance Party' has been specifically designed to encourage collaboration and will be director led. Lone Scherfig and Anders Thomas Jensen have created characters which will appear in all three films played by the same actors. Each film will be shot in Scotland and will be directed by feature film debutants Andrea Arnold (who recently won the Oscar for her short film 'Wasp'), BAFTA winner Morag Mckinnon and Danish director Mikkel Norgaard.[27]

A set of pre-established rules for minimal filmmaking designed by Thomas Anders Jensen and Lone Scherfig was issued for the three films, a little like those stated in von Trier's now famous 'Vow of Chastity' in his Dogme95 Manifesto, but with significantly more room for expression on the part of the filmmaker.[28] Each of the Advance Party films must be shot digitally within Glasgow. Shooting must complete within six weeks, budgets must not exceed £1.2 million and, whilst each film must be independent of the others, they must use the same characters and actors. The first of the three films, *Red Road*, was a huge success internationally, winning the Jury Prize at Cannes. The second feature, *Rounding Up Donkeys*, directed by Morag McKinnon, is in production as I write, and future plans are in place for *Advance Part II* (eight films to be developed in partnership between Sigma, Zentropa and Ireland's Subotica).

Despite being released three years after *Young Adam*, *Red Road* has already received far more critical attention than its predecessor. Several pieces already exist dedicated to *Red Road*, including Jonathan Murray's discussion in *The Cinema of Small Nations* (2007) and chapters by Jane Sillars and Myra Macdonald, Mette Hjort, and Lynne Hibberd are forthcoming at time of writing.[29] With its Dogme-like rules constraining the production of the film (not to mention the media interest that they bring to the productions), its low budget and the initiative's director-led approach *Red Road* is perhaps the clearest example so far of a Scottish art film being deliberately manufactured for the international film festival circuit. This has not gone unnoticed by critics.

Addressing the issue of Scottish cinema's development in relation to its international aims during the 1990s and 2000s, Jonathan Murray's survey of the ten years that followed *Trainspotting* argues that the Scottish film industry has, even during such a limited time span, seen a rise and fall in its fortunes. In his usual sophisticated and well-informed manner, Murray argues that this has been effected by a shift in budgetary emphasis from projects of under £2 million (like *Trainspotting*) that were commercial and critical successes to more ambitious, £3 million to £5 million projects – often with Lottery and/or Channel 4 funding – aimed at the 'international Anglophone mainstream' (like *Regeneration* and *The Winter Guest*) which did not fare particularly well critically or at the box office.[30] In financial terms the return to smaller budgets that follows the relative failures of these more ambitious films of the late 1990s has favoured the art film. As Murray notes, by the mid-2000s many Scottish art films, including *Young Adam* and *Red Road*, were European coproductions aiming at the film festival circuit. Murray concludes by discussing *Red Road* and the Advance Party Initiative, stressing the factors that mark out its '"European-ness"',[31] including its budget, coproduction status, avoidance of a specific 'grand, totalising statement about present-day urban Scotland' as presented by a film like *Orphans*[32] and (aesthetically) its lack of extensive dialogue, subjugation of 'narrative coherence . . . to a psychological exploration of female interiority',[33] and foregrounded exploration of grief and loss. All these factors are, as I demonstrated above, characteristics of the art film.

As this existing literature on *Red Road* emphasises how, from its artificially constructed Dogme-like constraints, it creates an end product that conforms to the European art cinema aesthetic I will not examine *Red Road* in any depth. Rather, I will focus on how the fate of *Young Adam* (a precursor to *Red Road* in its deliberate attempts to reach a European audience) can illuminate some of the limitations of autoethnographic self-othering when it comes to gaining acceptance in the international art cinema arena and I will conclude by briefly considering why *Red Road* is the success story and not *Young Adam*.

Young Adam (2003)

Young Adam was a Recorded Picture Company production with development input from Sigma Films, who are also credited as Associate Producers. The total budget was £4.5 million, with investment from a range of sources including Scottish Screen and the UK Film Council Premiere Fund. It was distribution in the UK by Warner Brothers and pre-sold internationally to several foreign territories by HanWay Films.[34]

Young Adam is set during the 1950s and follows Joe (Ewan McGregor), a young man from Glasgow who is a mate on a barge that takes cargo between Glasgow and Edinburgh. The barge belongs to Ella (Tilda Swinton) and is crewed by Les (Peter Mullan) and Joe. One morning, Joe and Les pull the corpse of a pregnant young woman from the river and report their finding to the authorities. Joe embarks on a torrid affair with Ella. Les, discovering the affair, leaves the barge. Joe soon departs as well, returning to Glasgow to follow the trial of a man accused of murdering the young woman whose corpse he pulled from the Clyde. Through a series of jumbled, non-chronological flashbacks Joe's backstory is gradually filled in. We discover that the drowned woman, Cathie (Emily Mortimer), and Joe were previously a couple, and she had been supporting him as he attempted to become a writer. After they broke up a chance encounter brought them together for one last tryst, following which she informed him that she was pregnant; she then accidentally drowned. The film concludes with an innocent man condemned for her murder and the existentialist Joe (we are never sure if he feels guilt over Cathie's death, or indeed, feels anything at all) wandering away from the river.

It is not difficult to find characteristics of the art film in *Young Adam*. Set mostly on a canal barge it has an almost literal 'drifting episodic quality', and Joe is precisely the psychologically complex character, sliding passively from situation to situation, observed by Bordwell. Joe's flashbacks disrupt the narrative's drive in the present but also serve to unlock his psychology, demonstrating the connection between his past and the present moment of his story. Indeed, whilst the period setting attempts a type of documentary realism in its gritty portrayal of life on the barge, the repeated, mannered use of close-ups on body parts and the stark blue filters used to shoot several scenes foreground the formal expressivity of the guiding hand of auteur (director/writer) Mackenzie, precisely in the European art cinema tradition.

Young Adam also demonstrates the balancing act noted by Neale, between national and international aspects, typical of the art film. On the one hand, it is clearly set in Scotland, and to a certain extent is engaged

with the issue of how Scotland is represented in cinema. The barge has
'GLASGOW' emblazoned across its stern, Les is forever reading the
Glasgow Telegraph newspaper and Ella discusses her fantasy of retirement
in one of the quieter suburbs of Edinburgh. The industrial milieu through
which the barge travels and the period setting of the 1950s evoke the
Clydeside view of Scotland seen in films like *Floodtide* (1949) and discussed by McArthur in *Scotch Reels*. Moreover, the pulling of the body
from an industrial dockyard on the banks of the Clyde at the start of the
film is finally matched by the deliberate blurring of focus on the back of
the departing Joe at the end as he leaves the river behind. In this way a
sense of mourning is created for a 'lost' industrial life on the Clyde that is
now past and forgotten.

Thus, the film's social realist emphasis on dirt and grime and recreating
authentic working and living conditions is blended with a poetic formal
expressivity that precisely evokes the works of Douglas and his miserablist
tradition. The presence of dressed-down Hollywood heartthrob McGregor
alongside two of Scotland's most well-known character actors, Swinton
and Mullan, also ensures its 'Scottish' credentials. The source material,
Alexander Trocchi's book of 1954, provides a Scottish origin and enables
Sight and Sound reviewer Ryan Gilbey to discuss Trocchi's artistic talent
in the same breath as Mackenzie's filmmaking genius as Scottish auteur.[35]
Even so, however, *Young Adam* does not fall into the trap of being so
specific to Scotland that it will not also appeal to international audiences.

Young Adam, whilst labelling itself Scottish, also attempts to position
itself as a European film within the international art cinema canon. Most
noticeably, the dialogue is extremely sparse. There would be no confusion
caused by a strong Glaswegian accent for the international viewer as there
might be with films like *Trainspotting* and *Orphans*. Instead, the story is
told visually in a manner that erects very few language barriers. The film
is reminiscent of numerous European predecessors, most especially Jean
Vigo's work of French poetic realism, *L'Atalante* (1934), which also concerns the inhabitants of a barge, two men, one woman and one young boy.
Indeed, Mullan's character Les specifically evokes Michel Simon's character, Père Jules in Vigo's film, with his sailor's songs and his tattooed
back.

Furthermore, *Young Adam*'s use of an invasive flashback structure
ensures comparison with various films by famous art cinema auteurs like
Fellini from Italy or Alain Resnais from France. Whilst evocative of
Clydesideism, the film's grim setting is also familiar to international audiences as recognisably 'British' because of Ken Loach's social realist view
of Scotland in films like *My Name is Joe* and *Sweet Sixteen*. The presence

of Swinton and Mullan is telling (in comparison, say, to other internationally well-known Scottish actors like Robert Carlyle or Ewan Bremner) as
they are perhaps the two most well-known Scottish actors (and Mullan
also as auteur) on the international art cinema circuit. Whilst the film is
adapted from a novel by the Scottish 'Beat' writer Alexander Trocchi,
Young Adam was first published, albeit in a more pornographic format, by
a French publisher. The period setting (which avoids any recognisable
Glasgow locations apart from the briefest glimpse of Glasgow University
from Kelvingrove Park) is more evocative of a period (the 1950s) than a
particular place (Glasgow). It is possible for international audiences to
enjoy the film because of its evocation of nostalgia for a certain time of
post-war austerity that was experienced across Europe, rather than a
specific place. In this sense, *Young Adam*'s Scotland could be almost anywhere in 1950s Europe.

This balancing act between the national and the international ensures
that *Young Adam* displays a self-consciousness about its Scottish cinematic
heritage as it attempts both to label its story as an authentically 'Scottish'
tale and yet to ensure that it engages with the broader, European tradition
of art cinema. In this sense, the film seems to be deliberately creating a
European art cinema with a Scottish flavour.

Finally, *Young Adam* used the international platform provided by the
festival circuit to promote the creation of a European-styled art cinema in
Scotland. Both McGregor and Swinton were openly critical of the UK
Film Council for not funding the film when private backer Baker Street
pulled out, even though the Council did provide £500,000 at the last
minute to enable completion. At the Cannes Film Festival McGregor
argued, 'Had I gone to them with a romantic comedy there would have
been no problem.'[36] Swinton was also adamant that because the majority
of the funding for the film was from Scottish sources (with Lottery
funding from Scottish Screen in particular) it should not be called a
British film.[37] There was an ensuing media row, in which the Film Council
reputedly dubbed McGregor and Swinton 'spoiled brats' for their comments.[38] What is most interesting about this exchange is the manner in
which McGregor used the context of the festival circuit to argue for additional backing for an art film as opposed to a popular genre movie. His
comments could be seen as an attempt to position *Young Adam* as a belea-
guered production that had to struggle to get made without the support of
the British state. Coupled to Swinton's emphasis on the film's Scottish
backing there is a sense that the film is being used as an illustration of the
type of Scottish art cinema that is possible, and perhaps even the type of
national Scottish (again, read art) cinema that could appear on the festival

circuit. This is the case even if the UK Film Council may generally favour financially securer investment in genre films, in particular now that the dominant, primarily London-based art cinema auteurs of the 1980s and 1990s, Derek Jarman, Sally Potter and Peter Greenaway, are no longer in the international spotlight.

Scotland in Europe, Scotland in the World

In all these ways *Young Adam* demonstrates the manner in which a Scottish art film can be self-consciously constructed with an eye to success on the art cinema festival circuit. The mystery that surrounds *Young Adam*, then, which screened in Un Certain Regard at Cannes, is why such a carefully constructed work did not succeed internationally as films like *The Magdalene Sisters* (Venice) did before, or *Red Road* (Cannes), afterwards? It is tempting to follow the line of trade press periodical *Screen International*, that the film lacked sufficient support from the UK Film Council, and had it been selected to play in competition at Cannes during an uninspiring year it would undoubtedly have received awards.[39] However, it is equally instructive to consider the changing international arena into which it emerged.

After the end of the Cold War the international festival circuit is consolidating its global presence to such a degree that, although in many ways still European in its focus, it has become a global arena. *Young Adam*, then, is a 'made to order' film that missed its pitch in the marketplace. The success of *Red Road* suggests that *Young Adam*'s major failing was that it did not take its self-othering far enough and retained too much that was recognisably Scottish. Whilst *Young Adam* displayed a sense of Scottish character and heritage in its period-set narrative *Red Road* deliberately avoids such recognisable markers of Scotland or Scottishness in its fantasy Scotland. *Young Adam*, then, is a film from another era, of the international dominance of the European art cinema model. In the new, global arena of world cinema, by contrast, it is not self-othering that is needed so much as a greater eradication of the self/nation, a process which creates films that literally anyone anywhere can engage with, like *Red Road*. This may explain why Mackenzie's two films after *Young Adam*, *Asylum* (2005) and *Hallam Foe* (2007), whilst they may have deployed recognisable Scottish locations as, effectively, film sets, avoided setting their narratives so firmly in Scotland.

As Lynne Hibberd argues, *Red Road*, though briefly establishing its 'Scottish' location, deliberately avoids any foregrounding of the setting as specific to Glasgow. The loss of identity examined in the film's narrative is, to some degree, reflected in its use of Scotland as both setting and film set and is a result of the transforming global marketplace for art cinema.[40] Accompanying this shift in emphasis towards the international marketplace enabled by the changing institutional conditions in Scotland in the 1990s and 2000s the international marketplace itself has changed in consistency. The greater success of a film like *Red Road*, then, may well be to do with its global appeal both within and beyond Europe. Whilst *Young Adam* was self-consciously 'European' in aesthetic and content *Red Road* drew on the broader international reputation of the Dogme brand, which reaches well beyond Europe with certificates being awarded to films from a diversity of countries, such as the USA, Argentina, Chile, Mexico, Canada, Turkey, South Africa, and Australia. Thus *Young Adam*, with its nostalgia for 1950s Europe, appears a rather belated, even formulaic, homage to the New Waves of Western European countries at precisely the time when the market was expanding globally. It would seem that in the international arena, the art film's peculiar balancing act between the national and the international is currently tipping away from the nationally specific, and even the European, and towards the universally understood and globally applicable, towards the further use of Scotland as a (gritty, miserablist) film set. With the Advance Party Initiative, Scotland's art cinema is following suit.

Notes

1. Andrew Noble, 'The Making of the *Trilogy*', in Eddie Dick, Andrew Noble and Duncan Petrie (eds), *Bill Douglas* (London: BFI/SFC, 1993), pp. 117–72, p. 127.
2. Ibid., p. 136.
3. Ibid., p. 118.
4. Ibid., p. 126; and Andrew Noble, 'Bill Douglas's *Trilogy*', in Eddie Dick (ed.), *From Limelight to Satellite* (London: BFI/SFC, 1990), pp. 133–250, p. 148.
5. Forsyth Hardy, 'An Interview with Forsyth Hardy', in Colin McArthur (ed.), *Scotch Reels* (London: BFI, 1980), pp. 73–92, p. 88.
6. Forsyth Hardy, *Scotland in Film* (Edinburgh: Edinburgh University Press, 1990), pp. 104, 109 and 120–1.
7. Noble, 'Bill Douglas's *Trilogy*', p. 149.
8. John Caughie, 'Don't Mourn – Analyse', in Dick, Noble and Petrie (eds), *Bill Douglas*, pp. 197–204, p. 197.
9. Duncan Petrie, *Screening Scotland* (London: BFI, 2000), pp. 172–90 and pp. 191–221; and Duncan Petrie, 'The New Scottish Cinema', in Mette Hjort and Scott Mackenzie (eds), *Cinema & Nation* (London: Routledge, 2000), pp. 153–69.

10. Petrie, 'The New Scottish Cinema', p. 158.
11. Petrie, *Screening Scotland*, pp. 158–68; Tony McKibbin, 'Singular Visions and Studio Possibilities', *Cencrastus*, 71 (2002), pp. 32–4, p. 32; Hannah McGill, 'Mean Streets', *Sight and Sound*, 16: 11 (2006), pp. 26–8, p. 28.
12. Catherine Fowler, 'Introduction to Part Three', in Catherine Fowler, ed., *The European Cinema Reader* (London: Routledge, 2002), pp. 87–93, p. 87.
13. David Bordwell, 'Art Cinema as Mode of Film Practice', in Fowler (ed.), *The European Cinema Reader*, pp. 94–102, p. 96.
14. Ibid.
15. Ibid., p. 97.
16. Steve Neale, 'Art Cinema as Institution', in Fowler (ed.), *The European Cinema Reader*, pp. 103–20, p. 103.
17. Ibid., p. 104.
18. Ibid., p. 105.
19. Ibid., p. 117.
20. Thomas Elsaesser, *European Cinema* (Amsterdam: University of Amsterdam Press, 2005), p. 88.
21. Ibid., p. 508.
22. Neale, 'Art Cinema as Institution', p. 119; Timothy Corrigan, *A Cinema without Walls: Movies and Culture After Vietnam* (New Brunswick, NJ: Rutgers University Press, 1991), pp. 101–36; Catherine Grant, 'www.auteur.com?', *Screen*, 41: 1 (2000), pp. 101–8.
23. David Martin-Jones, '*Orphans*: A Work of Minor Cinema from Post-Devolutionary Scotland', *Journal of British Cinema and Television*, 1: 2 (2004): 226–41.
24. Ibid., p. 227.
25. Sigma Films website: http://www.sigmafilms.com/index.php (11/04/08).
26. Nick Hunt, 'Case Study: *The Last Great Wilderness*', *Screen International*, no. 1367 (09/08/02), p. 14.
27. Sigma Films website.
28. Dogme 95 website, 'Vow of Chastity' webpage: http://www.dogme95.dk/menu/menuset.htm (11/04/08).
29. Jane Sillars and Myra Macdonald, 'Gender, Spaces, Changes: Emergent Identities in a Scotland in Transition', in Neil Blain and David Hutchison (eds), *The Media in Scotland* (Edinburgh: Edinburgh University Press, 2008), pp. 183–98; Mette Hjort, 'Affinitive and Milieu-Building Transnationalism', in Dina Iordanova, David Martin-Jones and Belén Vidal (eds), 'Cinema at the Periphery' (Detroit: Wayne State University Press, forthcoming); and Lynne Hibberd, '"Scottish" Screen? Exploring the Role of National Identity in Scotland's Screen Agency', in Ruby Cheung with David Fleming (eds), *Cinema, Identities and Beyond* (Newcastle: Cambridge Scholars Press, 2009), pp. 144–55.
30. Jonathan Murray, 'Scotland', in Mette Hjort and Duncan Petrie (eds), *The*

Cinema of Small Nations (Edinburgh: Edinburgh University Press, 2007), pp. 76–92, p. 82.

31. Ibid., p. 86.
32. Ibid., p. 89.
33. Ibid., p. 86.
34. Email correspondence with *Young Adam* co-producer Alexandra Stone, Recorded Picture Company (26/04/08).
35. Ryan Gilbey, 'Written on the Body', *Sight and Sound*, 13: 9 (2003), pp. 16–19, p. 16.
36. Fiachra Gibbons, 'McGregor Rages at Film Fund's Agenda', *The Guardian* 19/05/03: http://www.guardian.co.uk/world/2003/may/19/cannes2003.cannesfilmfestival1 (12/04/08).
37. James Morrison, 'Film Chiefs Attack Britain's "Spoilt Stars"', *The Independent* 1/06/03 http://findarticles.com/p/articles/mi_qn4159/is_20030601/ai_n12740839 (12/04/08).
38. Ibid.
39. Adam Minns, 'A Very Public Affair', *Screen International*, 1415 (2003), pp. 16–17, p. 16; Allan Hunter. 'Could do Better', *Screen International*, 1406 (2003), pp. 102, p. 1; Allan Hunter, 'Cannes Post-mortem', *Screen International*, 1407 (2003), pp. 1–2, p. 2.
40. Hibberd, 'Scottish Screen?', p. 152.

Conclusion

I write these concluding words in late 2008. Most likely the book will appear on the shelves of libraries and bookstores in late 2009 or early 2010. It ends as the last twenty years of dramatic change, which have seen a marked increase in film production in Scotland (indigenous production, international coproductions and location shoots), draws to a close. A new era is hopefully beginning, which could well be defined by the changes to the industry wrought by the merging of Scottish Screen into Creative Scotland, just as the previous decade's local production was marked by the devolution of Lottery funding to Scotland. Although it is impossible to foresee the future, I am hopeful that this will not be a book that functions as a tombstone, marking the end of a brief flurry of activity in the sector, but, rather, as a further step along the route paved by previous works on Scotland and cinema since *Scotch Reels* in 1982, illustrating the continued cultural and economic importance of cinema in Scotland.

It would appear that indigenous film production is likely to continue to expand. Even if Scotland remains a small national cinema in global terms it is to be hoped that it will carry on making a big impact globally. Whether it does or not, however, it seems probable that international coproductions and location shooting will, because of the mutual benefit that Scotland's landscape brings to filmmakers from outside Scotland, the Scottish film industry, and related industries like the tourist trade. Therefore, as I have shown in this book, fantastic as they often are, there is as much to be gained by understanding the manner in which the variously constructed cinematic Scotlands function as there is in focusing exclusively on indigenous productions, even if the best of these are lauded by European film festivals like Venice and Cannes.

Even as I write, intriguing questions continue to arise, necessitating that Scotland be addressed in terms of both its art and genre films, and indeed, in its position as a 'Global Cinema'. For instance, how should we consider the works of one of Scotland's most talented directors, Kenny Glenaan, whose first two features were made and set in the north of England? The excellent art film *Summer* (2008), has just been awarded the BAFTA Scotland for best film from a line up that included the zombie film *Outpost* (Chapter 5), which was made in Scotland but set in Eastern Europe, but that omitted Neil Marshall's sci-fi-horror film – made and set in Scotland – *Doomsday*. The increasingly blurry boundaries surrounding the category of 'Scottish' cinema therefore require that we reconsider Scottish filmmaking and filmmaking in Scotland inclusively, both in terms of its artistic and popular merits and in relation to an increasingly global context of production and distribution. Scotland: Global Cinema.

Moreover, a brief survey of a few of the films I did not have room to discuss in the book illustrates the variety of fantasy Scotlands that continue to exist and that have been created by filmmakers within, and from outside, Scotland, and the exploration of identities they facilitate. These include the award winning porn film *Scottish Loveknot* (2003), which posits a series of fantasy porn-*Brigadoon* scenarios; the US independent film *The Jacket* (2005), which uses an anonymised Scotland as a location shoot that stands in for Vermont and a (fantasy? – we cannot be sure) exploration of a man's future; *Seachd: The Inaccessible Pinnacle* (2007), made by Young Films on Skye, a Scottish-Gaelic film about the role of fantasy and story-telling in maintaining an ancient oral tradition and culture in the Gàidhealtachd/Gaeldom; *Stardust* (2007), a big budget Hollywood fantasy extravaganza shot on location in Scotland about a magical world beyond our everyday life; *GamerZ* (2005), the low budget indigenous Scottish comedy (Pure Magic Films, Glasgow) about young Dungeons and Dragons role players and the fantasy worlds they create; *Made of Honor* (2008), a Hollywood rom-com in which characters travel to Scotland for a wedding and encounter a tourist's fantasy of baronial Scotland (complete with a stay at Eilean Donan Castle, whisky tasting, a Highland Games and a bagpipe-accompanied banquet of freshly killed venison); and (currently in production), *Valhalla Rising* (2009), a historical story of Vikings in Scotland coproduced by companies from Denmark, Scotland (La Belle Allee, Glasgow) and England. In all these instances, the Scotland we see is, as is very often the case in films made and set in Scotland, at once Scotland and not Scotland; at once true to life, and fantasy; at once an image of Scotland recognisable to foreign audiences (and therefore capable of selling Scotland abroad) even whilst it is both 'unrecognisable' and simultaneously understandable to local audiences as a celluloid reconstruction of the nation as seen by others; and at once national and variously global/local, diasporic etc.

Inevitably, the frameworks through which I have examined the films I chose for the previous ten chapters are not the only ones worth pursuing. For example, I was struck by the existence of several contemporary films set in Scotland that focus on children, above and beyond the art cinema examples noted by Petrie in *Contemporary Scottish Fictions*, and explored by Sarah Neely in relation to Scottish and Irish heritage cinema.[1] These family films, including *Greyfriar's Bobby* (2005), *Seachd* and *The Water Horse* (2007), provide a further rich terrain for future exploration. Thrillers have been another area of growth in the 2000s, with predecessors like Roaring Fire Films' *The Ticking Man* (2003) and *Retribution* (2005), and Eleanor Yule's *Blinded* (2004) (part of Scottish Screen's New Found Films project) now being joined by the likes of Richard Jobson's *New Town Killers* (2008), Plum Films' *Senseless* (2008), and projects in development including Crab Apple Film's *Clever*, Synchronicity Films's *Crying With Laughter* and Mandragora Productions' *Dark Nature*. There are doubtless other possible cinematic histories of Scotland, fantasies of Scotland and identities of Scotland to be uncovered by grouping the films discussed in this book (and many that are not) in different ways again. One noticeable omission from this discussion of the myriad identities available in cinematic Scotland is the Scottish-Gaelic film *Seachd*, which I have engaged with elsewhere.[2] Another displaced topic of study was the many regional identities explored in indigenous Scottish (not to mention British) films, another subject I have begun to examine elsewhere.[3] What I have tried to provide in this book, then, is a gesture towards the possible expansion of the field of study, pursuing a number of different directions in the hope of beginning the mapping of the unexplored fantasylands of cinema in Scotland, the myriad cinematic Scotlands (its numerous Brigadoons) and the various identities they enable.

Dundee/St Andrews – Pickering–London, 2006–9

Notes

1. Duncan Petrie, *Contemporary Scottish Fictions* (Edinburgh: Edinburgh University Press, 2004), pp. 164–73; Sarah Neely, 'The Conquering Heritage of British Cinema Studies and the "Celtic Fringe"', in John Hill and Kevin Rockett (eds), *Film History and National Cinema* (Dublin: Four Courts Press, 2005), pp. 47–56.
2. David Martin-Jones, 'Islands at the Edge of History', in Dina Iordanova, David Martin-Jones and Belén Vidal (eds), *Cinema at the Periphery* (Detroit: Wayne State University Press, forthcoming).
3. David Martin-Jones, 'Scotland's Other Kingdoms', in Jonathan Murray, Fidelma Farley and Rod Stoneman (eds), *Scottish Cinema Now* (Newcastle: Cambridge Scholars Press, 2009), pp. 105–121.

Select Bibliography

Books

Anderson, Benedict (1983), *Imagined Communities*, London: Verso.

Anderson, Lin (2005), *Braveheart*, Edinburgh: Luath Press Ltd.

Barr, Charles (ed.) (1986), *All Our Yesterdays*, London: BFI.

Bazin, André [1958] (1967), *What is Cinema? Part 1*, Berkeley, CA: University of California Press.

Bhabha, Homi (1994), *The Location of Culture*, London: Routledge.

Blain, Neil and David Hutchinson (eds) (2008), *The Media in Scotland*, Edinburgh: Edinburgh University Press.

Blandford, Steve (2007), *Film, Drama and the Break-Up of Britain*, Bristol: Intellect Books.

Bondanella, Peter (2004), *Hollywood Italians*, New York: Continuum.

Bruce, David (1996), *Scotland: The Movie*, Edinburgh: Polygon.

Bruzzi, Stella (1997), *Undressing Cinema*, London: Routledge.

Campbell, Steuart (2002), *The Loch Ness Monster*, Edinburgh: Birlinn.

Carroll, Nöel (1998), *Interpreting the Moving Image*, Cambridge: Cambridge University Press.

Chibnall Steve and Robert Murphy (eds) (1999), *British Crime Cinema*, London: Routledge.

Cohan, Steven and Ina Rae Hark (eds) (1997), *The Road Movie Book*, London: Routledge.

Cook, Pam (1996), *Fashioning the Nation*, London: BFI.

Cook, Pam (2002), *I Know Where I'm Going!* London: BFI.

Corrigan, Timothy (1991), *Cinema Without Walls*, New Brunswick, NJ: Rutgers University Press.

Craig, Cairns (1996), *Out of History*, Edinburgh: Polygon.

Creed, Barbara (1993), *The Monstrous Feminine*, London: Routledge.

Devine, T. M. (1999), *The Scottish Nation 1700–2000*, London: Allen Lane.

Devine, T. M. (2003), *Scotland's Empire 1600–1815*, London: Penguin.

Dewar, Isla (1996), *Women Talking Dirty*, London: Review.

Dick, Eddie (ed.) (1990), *From Limelight to Satellite*, London: BFI/SFC.

Dick, Eddie, Andrew Noble and Duncan Petrie (eds) (1993). *Bill Douglas*, London: BFI/SFC.

Drucker, Peter F. (1968), *The Age of Discontinuity*, London: Heinemann.

Dudrah, Rajinder Kumar (2006), *Bollywood*, New Delhi: Sage Publications.

Dwyer, Rachel (2000), *All You Want is Money, All You Need is Love*, London: Cassell.

Dyer, Richard and Ginette Vincendeau (eds) (1992), *Popular European Cinema*, London: Routledge.

Edensor, Tim (2002), *National Identity, Popular Culture and Everyday Life*, Oxford: Berg.

Eleftheriotis, Dimitris (2001), *Popular Cinemas of Europe*, London: Continuum.

Elsaesser, Thomas (2005), *European Cinema*, Amsterdam: Amsterdam University Press.

Fowler, Catherine (ed.) (2002), *The European Cinema Reader*, London: Routledge.

Friedman, Lester D. (ed.) (1993), *Fires Were Started*, London: UCL Press.

Fuller, Graham (ed.) (1998), *Loach on Loach*, London: Faber & Faber.

Galt, Rosalind (2006), *The New European Cinema* (New York: Columbia University Press).

Ganti, Tejaswini (2004), *Bollywood*, London: Routledge.

Gold, John R. and Margaret M. Gold (1995), *Imagining Scotland*, Aldershot: Scolar Press.

Gopinath, Gayatri (2005), *Impossible Desires*, Durham, NC, and London: Duke University Press.

Grant, Barry Keith (ed.) (1984), *Planks of Reason*, London: Scarecrow Press.

Grieveson, Lee, Esther Sonnet and Peter Stanfield (eds) (2005), *Mob Culture*, Oxford: Berg.

Hallam, Julia with Margaret Marshment (2000), *Realism and Popular Cinema*, Manchester: Manchester University Press.

Hardy, Forsyth (1990), *Scotland in Film*, Edinburgh: Edinburgh University Press.

Harper, Sue (1994), *Picturing the Past*, London: BFI.

Higson, Andrew (1995), *Waving the Flag*, Oxford: Clarendon Press.

Higson, Andrew (ed.) (1996), *Dissolving Views*, London: Cassell.

Higson, Andrew (2003), *English Heritage, English Cinema*, Oxford: Oxford University Press.

Hill, John (1986), *Sex, Class and Realism*, London: British Film Institute.

Hill, John (1999), *British Cinema in the 1980s*, Oxford: Clarendon Press.

Hjort, Mette (2005), *Small Nation, Global Cinema*, Minneapolis, MN: University of Minnesota Press.

Hjort, Mette and Scott Mackenzie (eds) (2000), *Cinema & Nation*, London: Routledge.

Hjort, Mette and Duncan Petrie (eds) (2007), *The Cinema of Small Nations*, Edinburgh: Edinburgh University Press.

Hollinger, Karen (1998), *In the Company of Women*, Minneapolis, MN: University of Minnesota Press.

Hutchings, Peter (1993), *Hammer and Beyond*, Manchester: Manchester University Press.

Iordanova, Dina, David Martin-Jones and Belén Vidal (eds) (forthcoming), *Cinema at the Periphery*, Detroit, MI: Wayne State University Press.

Jancovich, Mark (1996), *Rational Fears*, Manchester: Manchester University Press.

Kaur, Raminder and Ajay J. Sinha (eds) (2005), *Bollyworld*, New Delhi: Sage.

Keating, Michael (1996), *Nations Against the State*, London: Macmillan.

Kemp, Philip (1991), *Lethal Innocence*, London: Methuen.

King, Geoff (2002), *Film Comedy*, London: Wallflower.

King, Geoff (2005), *American Independent Cinema*, London: I. B. Tauris.

King-Smith, Dick [1990] (2008), *The Water Horse*, London: Puffin.

Kuhn, Michael (2002), *One Hundred Films and a Funeral*, London: Thorogood.

Laderman, David (2002), *Driving Visions*, Austin, TX: University of Texas Press.

Lay, Samantha (2002), *British Social Realism*, London: Wallflower.

Leach, Jim (2004), *British Film*, Cambridge: Cambridge University Press.

Leigh, Jacob (2002), *The Cinema of Ken Loach*, London: Wallflower.

Maan, Bashir (1992), *The New Scots*, Edinburgh: John Donald.

McArthur, Colin (1972), *Underworld USA*, London: Secker & Warburg.

McArthur, Colin (ed.) (1982), *Scotch Reels*, London: BFI.

McArthur, Colin (2003), *Whisky Galore! and The Maggie*, London: I. B. Tauris.

McArthur, Colin (2003), *Brigadoon, Braveheart and the Scots* London: I. B. Tauris.

McCrone, David (2001), *Understanding Scotland*, 2nd edn, London: Routledge

Marks, Laura U. (2000), *The Skin of the Film*, Durham, NC, and London: Duke University Press.

Martin-Jones, David (2006), *Deleuze, Cinema and National Identity*, Edinburgh: Edinburgh University Press.

Mather, Nigel (2006), *Tears of Laughter*, Manchester: Manchester University Press.

Mazierska, Ewa and Laura Rascaroli (2006), *Crossing New Europe*, London: Wallflower.

Mercer, John and Martin Shingler (2004), *Melodrama*, London: Wallflower.

Mishra, Vijay (2002), *Bollywood Cinema*, London: Routledge.

Monk, Claire and Amy Sargeant (eds) (2002), *British Historical Cinema*, London: Routledge.

Munby, Jonathan (1999), *Public Enemies, Public Heroes*, Chicago, IL: University of Chicago Press.

Murphy, Robert (ed.) (2000), *British Cinema of the 90s*, London: BFI.

Murphy, Robert (ed.) (2001), *The British Cinema Book*, 2nd edn, London: BFI.

Murray, Jonathan (2006), *That Thinking Feeling*, Glasgow: Scottish Screen/ Edinburgh College of Art.

Murray, Jonathan, Fidelma Farley and Rod Stoneman (eds) (2009), *Scottish Cinema Now*, Newcastle: Cambridge Scholars Press.

Murray, Jonathan, Lesley Stevenson, Stephen Harper and Benjamin Franks (eds) (2005), *Constructing the Wicker Man*, Glasgow: University of Glasgow, Crichton Publications.

Nairn, Tom (1977), *The Break Up of Britain*, London: Verso.

Nairn, Tom (2000), *After Britain*, London: Granta.

Nochimson, Martha P. (2007), *Dying to Belong*, Oxford: Blackwell.

Petrie, Duncan (2000), *Screening Scotland*, London: BFI.

Petrie, Duncan (2004), *Contemporary Scottish Fictions*, Edinburgh: Edinburgh University Press.

Pidduck, Julianne (2004), *Contemporary Costume Film*, London: BFI.

Pieri, Joe (2005), *The Scots-Italians*, Edinburgh: Mercat Press.

Pittock, Murray (1991), *The Invention of Scotland*, London: Routledge.

Pratt, Mary Louise (1992), *Imperial Eyes*, London: Routledge.

Sargeant, Jack and Stephanie Watson (eds) (1999), *Lost Highways*, Washington, DC: Creation Books.

Sassen, Saskia (1991), *The Global City*, Princeton, NJ: Princeton University Press.

Shadoian, Jack (2003), *Dreams and Dead Ends*, Oxford: Oxford University Press.

Showalter, Elaine (1990), *Sexual Anarchy*, London: Virago.

Smith, Murray (2002), *Trainspotting*, London: BFI.

Spicer, Andrew (2001), *Typical Men*, London: I. B. Tauris.

Street, Sarah Street (2002), *Transatlantic Crossings*, London: Continuum.

Tasker, Yvonne (1998), *Working Girls*, London: Routledge.

Trocchi, Alexander [1954] (2003), *Young Adam*, London: Calder.

Tudor, Andrew (1989), *Monsters and Mad Scientists*, Oxford: Blackwell.

Turner, Graeme (1994), *Making it National*, St Leonards, NSW: Allen & Unwin.

Wallace, Gavin and Randall Stevenson (eds) (1993), *The Scottish Novel Since the Seventies*, Edinburgh: Edinburgh University Press.

Warshow, Robert (2001), *The Immediate Experience*, Cambridge, MA: Harvard University Press.

Wayne, Mike (2002), *The Politics of Contemporary European Cinema*, Bristol: Intellect.

Williams, Linda Ruth (2005), *The Erotic Thriller in Contemporary Cinema*, Edinburgh: Edinburgh University Press.

Wood, Mary P. (2007), *Contemporary European Cinema*, London: Hodder Arnold.

Articles/Book Chapters

Adair, Gilbert (1981), 'One Elephant, Two Elephant', *Sight and Sound*, 50: 3, pp. 206–7.

Balides, Connie (1984), '*Another Time, Another Place* . . . Another Male View?' *Cencrastus*, 16, pp. 37–41.

Brown, John (1983), 'A Suitable Job for a Scot', *Sight and Sound*, 52: 3, pp. 157–62.

Caughie, John (1983), 'Support whose Local Hero?', *Cencrastus*, 14, pp. 44–6.

Caughie, John (2007), '*Morvern Callar*, Art Cinema and the "Monstrous Archive"', *Scottish Studies Review*, 8: 1, pp. 101–15.

Church Gibson, Pamela (2002), 'From Dancing Queen to Plaster Virgin', *Journal of Popular British Cinema*, 5, pp. 133–41.

Crawford, Robert (1997), 'Dedefining Scotland', in Susan Bassnet (ed.), *Studying British Cultures*, London: Routledge, pp. 83–96.

Deleyto, Celestino (2003), 'Between Friends', *Screen*, 44: 2, pp. 167–82.

Evans, Walter (1973), 'Monster Movies', *Journal of Popular Film*, 2: 4, pp. 353–65.

Felber, Lynette (2001), 'Capturing the Shadows of Ghosts', *Film Quarterly*, 54: 4, pp. 27–37.

Geetha, J. (2003), 'Bollywood Ending', *Sight and Sound*, 13: 6, pp. 31–2.

Girelli, Elisabetta (2005), 'Transnational Maleness', *Cinema Journal*, 44: 4, pp. 44–56.

Goode, Ian (2005), 'Scottish Cinema and Scottish Imaginings', *Screen*, 46: 2, pp. 235–9.

Goode, Ian (2007), 'Meditating the rural', in Robert Fish (ed.), *Cinematic Countrysides*, Manchester: Manchester University Press, pp. 109–16.

Grant, Catherine (2000), 'www.auteur.com?', *Screen*, 41: 1, pp. 101–8.

Harper, Sue (1987), 'Historical Pleasures', in Christine Gledhill (ed.), *Home is Where the Heart Is*, London: BFI, pp. 167–96.

Hibberd, Lynne (2009), 'Scottish Screen?', in Ruby Cheung with David Fleming (eds), *Cinema, Identities and Beyond*, Newcastle: Cambridge Scholars Press, pp. 144–55.

Hunter, Allan (2000), 'Scotland Takes the High Road', *Screen International*, 1281, p. 11.

Hunter, Allan (2002), 'Glasgow Smiles', *Screen International*, 1354, p. 10.

Hunter, Allan (2004), 'Scotland the Brave, *Screen International*, 1442, pp. 16–17.

Iwabuchi, Koichi (2002), 'Nostalgia for a (Different) Asian Modernity', *Positions*, 10: 3, pp. 547–73.

Jones, Alan (2002), 'The Bark and Bite of *Dog Soldiers*', *Fangoria* 212, pp. 40–4.

Kaur, Raminder (2005), 'Cruising on the *Vilayeti* Bandwagon', in Raminder Kaur and Ajay J. Sinha (eds) *Bollyworld*, New Delhi: Sage, pp. 309–29.

Kaur, Ravinder (2002), 'Viewing the West through Bollywood', *Contemporary South Asia*, 1: 2, pp. 199–209.

Kennedy, Harlan (1982), 'Things that go Howl in the Id', *Film Comment*, 18: 2, pp. 37–9

Klein, Christina (2004), '*Crouching Tiger Hidden Dragon.*' *Cinema Journal*, 43: 4, pp. 18–42.

Lovell, Alan (1972), 'The Unknown Cinema of Britain', *Cinema Journal*, 11: 2, pp. 1–8.

Lu, Sheldon H. (2005), 'Crouching Tiger, Hidden Dragon, Bouncing Angels', in Sheldon H. Lu and Emilie Yueh-yu Yeh (eds) *Chinese-Language Film*, Honolulu: University of Hawaii Press, pp. 220–33.

McArthur, Colin (1985), 'Scotland's Story', *Framework*, 26–7, pp. 64–74.

McArthur, Colin (1993), 'On the Trail of Two Scottish Road Movies', *Scottish Film and Visual Arts*, 4: 2, pp. 7–8.

McIntyre, Steve (1993), 'Inventing the Future', *Scottish Film and Visual Arts*, 5, pp. 17–19

Martin-Jones, David (2004), '*Orphans*, A Work of Minor Cinema from Post-Devolutionary Scotland', *Journal of British Cinema and Television*, 1: 2, pp. 226–41.

Martin-Jones, David (2005), 'Sexual Healing', *Screen*, 26: 2, pp. 227–33.

Martin-Jones, David (2006), 'Kabhi India, Kabhie Scotland', *South Asian Popular Culture*, 4: 1, pp. 49–60.

Martin-Jones, David (2008), 'National Symbols', *Symbolism: International Journal of Critical Aesthetics*, 7, pp. 169–200.

Murray, Jonathan (2002), 'Sundance in Scotland?' *Vertigo*, 2: 2, pp. 10–11.

Murray, Jonathan (2005), 'Kids in America?', *Screen*, 46: 2, pp. 217–25

Neale, Steve (1995), 'Questions of Genre', in Barry Keith Grant (ed.), *Film Genre Reader II*, Austin, TX: University of Texas Press, pp. 159–83.

Neely, Sarah (2005), 'Scotland, Heritage and Devolving British Cinema', *Screen*, 46: 2, pp. 241–5.

Neely, Sarah (2005), 'The Conquering Heritage of British Cinema Studies and the "Celtic Fringe"', in John Hill and Kevin Rockett (eds), *Film History and National Cinema*, Dublin: Four Courts Press, pp. 47–56.

Negra, Diane (2006), 'Romance and/as Tourism', in Elizabeth Ezra and Terry Rowden, *Transnational Cinema the Film Reader*, London: Routledge, pp. 169–180.

Petley, Julian (2002), 'From Brit-flicks to Shit-flicks', *Journal of Popular British Cinema*, 5, pp. 37–52.

Petrie, Duncan (1996), 'Peripheral Visions', in Wendy Everett (ed.), *European Identity in Cinema*, Exeter: Intellect, pp. 93–101.

Petrie, Duncan (2005), 'Scottish Cinema', *Screen*, 46: 2, pp. 213–16.

Romney, Jonathan (2005), 'Edinburgh Cringe', *Sight and Sound*, 15: 8, pp. 26–9.

Ryan, Susan and Richard Porton (1998), 'The Politics of Everyday Life', *Cineaste*, 24: 1, pp. 22–7.

Saeed, Amir, Neil Blain and Douglas Forbes (1999), 'New Ethnic and National Questions in Scotland', *Ethnic and Racial Social Studies*, 22: 5, pp. 821–44.

Scullion, Adrienne (1995), 'Feminine Pleasures and Masculine Indignities', in Christopher Whyte (ed.), *Gendering the Nation*, Edinburgh: Edinburgh University Press, pp. 169–204.

Sillars, Jane (1999), 'Drama, Devolution and Dominant Representations', in Jane Stokes and Anna Reading (eds), *The Media in Britain*, London: MacMillan, pp. 246–54.

Spencer, Liese (1999), 'Tearing the Roof Off', *Sight and Sound*, 9: 4, pp. 13–14

Stringer, Julian (1997), '"Your Tender Smiles Give Me Strength"', *Screen*, 38: 1, pp. 25–41.

Vidal, Belén (2005), 'Playing in a Minor Key', in Mireia Aragay (ed.), *Books in Motion*, Amsterdam/New York: Rodolphi, pp. 263–85.

Wayne, Mike (2001/2), 'The Re-invention of Tradition', *EnterText*, 2: 1, pp. 38–66

Wayne, Mike (2006), 'Working Title Mark II', *International Journal of Media and Cultural Politics*, 2: 1, pp. 5–73.

Williams, Tony (2000), 'Under "Western Eyes"', *Cinema Journal*, 40: 1, pp. 3–24.

Wills, Andrew (2003), 'Locating Bollywood', in Julian Stringer (ed.), *Movie Blockbusters*, London: Routledge, pp. 255–68

Select Filmography

Aberdeen (UK/Norway/Sweden, Hans Petter Moland, 2000)
Ae Fond Kiss (UK/Belgium/Germany/Italy/Spain, Ken Loach, 2004)
American Cousins (UK, Don Coutts, 2003)
Beautiful Creatures (UK, Bill Eagles, 2000)
Braveheart (US, Mel Gibson, 1995)
Brigadoon (US, Vincente Minnelli, 1954)
Carla's Song (UK/Spain/Germany, Ken Loach, 1996)
Danny the Dog (a.k.a *Unleashed*) (France/US/UK, Louis Leterrier, 2005)
Descent, The (UK, Neil Marshall, 2005)
Dog Soldiers (UK/Luxembourg, Neil Marshall, 2002)
Doomsday (UK/US/South Africa/Germany, 2008)
Festival (UK, Annie Griffin, 2005)
Gregory's Two Girls (UK/Germany, Bill Forsyth, 1999)
Governess, The (UK, Sandra Goldbacher, 1998)
Inheritance, The (UK, Charles Henri Belleville, 2007)
Kandukondain Kandukondain (India, Rajiv Menon, 2000)
Kuch Kuch Hota Hai (India, Karan Johar, 1998)
Last Great Wilderness, The (UK/Denmark, David Mackenzie, 2002)
Local Hero (UK, Bill Forsyth, 1983)
Loch Ness (UK/US, John Henderson, 1996)
Morvern Callar (UK, Lynne Ramsay, 2002)
Nina's Heavenly Delights (UK, Pratibha Parmar, 2006)
On a Clear Day (UK, Gaby Dellal, 2005)
Pyaar Ishq aur Mohabbat (India, Rajiv Rai, 2001)
Red Road (UK/Denmark, Andrea Arnold, 2006)
Rob Roy (US, Michael Caton-Jones, 1995)
Secret of the Loch, The (UK, Milton Rosmer, 1934)
Soft Top, Hard Shoulder (UK, Stefan Schwartz, 1993)
Tickets (Italy/UK, Ermanno Olmi, Abbas Kiarostami, Ken Loach, 2005)
Trainspotting (UK, Danny Boyle, 1996)
Walking and Talking (UK/US/Germany, Nicole Holofcener, 1996)

Water Horse, The (US/UK, Jay Russell, 2007)
Wicker Man, The (UK, Robin Hardy, 1973)
Wild Country (UK, Craig Strachan, 2005)
Women Talking Dirty (UK/US, Coky Giedroyc, 1999)
Work, Rest and Play (UK, Douglas Aubrey, 1994)
Young Adam (UK/France, David Mackenzie, 2003)

Throughout the book, dates cited refer to the year of film release, all of which are accurate to the information available on the Internet Movie Database (IMDB) at the time of publication.

Index